CO-AVZ-642

PITTSBURGH THEOLOGICAL MONOGRAPHS

New Series

Dikran Y. Hadidian

General Editor

The Catholic Theological Union LIBRARY Chicago, Ill. WITHDRAWN

4

FOR GOD AND CLARITY

New Essays in honor of Austin Farrer

THE REVEREND DR. AUSTIN MARSDEN FARRER

Seventh Warden of Keble

FOR GOD AND CLARITY

New Essays in Honor of Austin Farrer

Edited by

Jeffrey C. Eaton and Ann Loades

The Catholic
Theological Union
LIBRARY
Chicago, Ill.

PICKWICK PUBLICATIONS
Allison Park, Pennsylvania
1983

Copyright © 1983 by **Pickwick Publications**
4137 Timberlane Drive, Allison Park, PA 15101

All rights reserved.
Printed in the United States of America

Library of Congress Cataloging in Publication Data
Main entry under title:

For God and clarity.

(Pittsburgh theological monographs. New series ; 4)
Bibliography: p.
Contents: Austin Marsden Farrer (1904-1968)/Jeffrey C. Eaton and Ann
Loades—Austin Farrer as philosophical theologian/Julian Hartt—The agent's
world/Robert H. King—[etc.]
1. Theology—Addresses, essays, lectures. 2. Philosophical theology—Addresses,
essays, lectures. 3. Farrer, Austin Marsden—Addresses, essays, lectures. I. Farrer,
Austin Marsden. II. Eaton, Jeffrey C. III. Loades, Ann. IV. Series.
BR50.F564 1983   230′.3′0924   83-2451
ISBN 0-915138-52-2

CONTENTS

Preface and Acknowledgments: **Jeffrey C. Eaton** and **Ann Loades** vii

The Contributors ix

Austin Marsden Farrer (1904-1968): **Jeffrey C. Eaton** and **Ann Loades** xi

Note on Citations or Abbreviations xv

Austin Farrer as Philosophical Theologian: A Retrospective and Appreciation: **Julian Hartt** 1

The Agent's World: Farrer's Contribution to Cosmology: **Robert H. King** 23

Origen Redivivus: Farrer's Scriptural Divinity: **Charles C. Hefling, Jr.** 35

Austin Farrer and the Analogy of Other Minds: **Charles Conti** 51

Austin Farrer on <u>Love Almighty</u>: **Ann Loades** 93

'Apprehension' in <u>Finite and Infinite</u>: **Rodger Forsman** . . 111

Austin Farrer's Notion of "Conscience as an Appetite for Moral Truth": its Metaphysical Foundation and Importance To Contemporary Moral Philosophy: **John Underwood Lewis** 131

Three Necessary Conditions for Thinking Theistically: **Jeffrey C. Eaton** 151

The Experiential Verification of Religious Belief in the
        Theology of Austin Farrer: **Brian Hebblethwaite** . . . 163

Two Approaches to the Philosophy of Religion: **Basil
        Mitchell** 177

A Chronological List of Austin M. Farrer's Published
        Writings: 1933-1981: Compiled by **Charles
        Conti** 191

Books and Articles on Farrer 201

New and Forthcoming Publications 204

PREFACE AND ACKNOWLEDGMENTS

The essays in this volume were presented at a conference on the thought of Austin Farrer at Princeton Theological Seminary in January, 1981. They are as various in their subjects as was Farrer's work, which is to say, they run the gamut from issues surrounding the epistemology of theism to consideration of Farrer's startling proposals for the interpretation of Scripture. And in between there are studies in theological ethics, on the problem of evil, and on the topic of cosmology. Some of these essays are primarily analyses of Farrer's contributions and some are primarily efforts to draw out the implications of Farrer's work for the ongoing project of theological inquiry. Although there is no substitute for reading Farrer's writings themselves, these essays--each in their own way--reflect the riches in Farrer's work and the freshness of his theological vision. It is hoped that they will be of interest and use not only to those who know Farrer's writings well, but to those whose acquaintance with Farrer's work is more casual or who have perhaps not yet been introduced to it.

We gratefully acknowledge the special contribution of Charles Conti in proposing the title for this volume and compiling an up-to-date bibliography of Farrer's writings and a secondary source bibliography. We wish also to express our thanks to Dr. James I. McCord, President of Princeton Theological Seminary, for his and his institution's support for the Conference on Farrer's work. And finally, thanks are due to our own institutions, Hamilton College and Durham University for the valuable assistance they have given to this project.

We are grateful for the permission to quote material from the following sources:

Finite and Infinite: A Philosophical Essay by Austin Farrer. Copyright © 1979 by the Trustees of K. D. Farrer, deceased. Reprinted by permission of Seabury Press, Inc. and the Trustees of Mrs. Farrer.

The End of Man by Austin Farrer. Copyright © 1973 by the Trustees of K. D. Farrer. Reprinted by permission of SPCK.

Faith and Logic, edited by Basil Mitchell. Copyright ©
1957. Reprinted by permission of George Allen & Unwin
(Publishers) Ltd.

The Freedom of the Will by Austin Farrer. Copyright ©
1958. Reprinted by permission of the Trustees of K. D.
Farrer.

Reflective Faith by Austin Farrer. Copyright © 1974. Reprinted by permission of SPCK and Wm. B. Eerdmans Publishing Co.

Faith and Speculation by Austin Farrer. Copyright © 1967
by Austin Farrer. Reprinted by permission of New York
University Press.

Love Almighty and Ills Unlimited by Austin Farrer. Copyright © 1961 by Austin Farrer. Reprinted by permission
of Doubleday & Company, Inc.

Jeffrey C. Eaton
Ann Loades

CONTRIBUTORS

Charles C. Conti: Lecturer in the School of English and American Studies, University of Sussex, Brighton, England.

Jeffrey C. Eaton: Chaplain and Assistant Professor of Religion, Hamilton College, Clinton, New York.

Rodger Forsman: Professor, Department of Religious Studies, Acadia University, Wolfville, Nova Scotia, Canada.

Julian Hartt: Professor Emeritus, Department of Religious Studies, University of Virginia, Charlottesville, Virginia.

Brian Hebblethwaite: Dean of the Chapel, Queens College, Cambridge, and University Lecturer in Theology.

Charles C. Hefling, Jr.: Assistant Professor, Department of Theology, Boston College, Chestnut Hill, Massachusetts.

Robert H. King: Vice President and Dean, Millsaps College, Jackson, Mississippi.

John Underwood Lewis: Professor, Department of Philosophy, University of Windsor, Windsor, Ontario, Canada.

Ann Loades: Senior Lecturer, Department of Theology, Durham University, Durham, England.

Basil Mitchell: Nolloth Professor of the Philosophy of the Christian Religion, Oxford University, England.

AUSTIN MARSDEN FARRER
(1904-1968)

Every few years a group of scholars and clerics gather on this or that side of the Atlantic to reconsider the work of Austin Farrer and attempt to follow through some of the implications of his work for current theology and philosophy. The man who is the occasion for these gatherings has been dead for nearly fourteen years, and most of his books have been allowed to pass out of print. Yet the quality of Farrer's thought continues to inspire these (roughly) triennial conferences.

Austin Farrer is at first glance a donnishly ordinary figure. Born the son of a Baptist minister and his wife, he received a first-rate education, initially at St. Paul's and then at Balliol College, Oxford. He was ordained a priest of the Church of England, and after briefly serving a parish he returned to Oxford where he was to remain for the rest of his life; as chaplain and tutor at St. Edmund Hall until 1935, as fellow and chaplain at Trinity until 1960, and as Warden of Keble until his sudden and unexpected death in 1968. He was an Oxford man through and through.

But Farrer was no ordinary don. He had an extraordinarily penetrating and original mind, and, whether analyzing the argument of some philosopher or re-thinking the thoughts of the earliest Evangelist, he took his readers into regions of inquiry they would not have thought of entering on their own. That is, if they could keep up with him. His intellectual pace was for many simply too swift and his imaginative leaps too great. His writing is invariably elegant, but often the arguments expressed in his work are so compressed that the reader who is unfamiliar with the controversies to which Farrer was applying himself feels left behind. This characteristic is especially pronounced in the last of his books published during his lifetime, **Faith and Speculation,** in which the argument slips again and again into the form of a dialogue between Farrer and several interlocutors, and in which the allusions to the background and details of the debates being carried on are especially subtle. This subtlety is one significant factor in accounting for the limited appreciation of Farrer's writings.

Another factor is that Farrer did not limit his investigations to a single field of inquiry. As a glance at the bibliography of his works will show, he moved from philosophical themes to biblical studies to works of Christian apologetics to philosophical theology, thereby defying any easy classification of his place in the scholarly world. His willingness to trespass into several academic preserves seems to have been the result of his desire to explore territory on his own and in exploring to find out what is there to be known. He wrote not to establish his reputation but to inquire in a systematic way, to pursue alternatives that were going begging for reasons that seemed often to have more to do with scholarly fashion than available evidence. Wherever he found questionable assumptions, he questioned them, and sometimes he found them in fields not traditionally surveyed by philosophically-minded theologians. One thinks especially of his biblical studies which if not entirely convincing the professional exegetes, nevertheless exposed the conjectural nature of some of the suppositions which were the "experts" stock-in-trade. In any case, the variousness of his works made him a bit of an enigma to specialists used to thinking in terms of tidy self-contained disciplines.

However diverse his writings, there is one consideration which runs through them all and which gives unity to his work, and this is Farrer's desire to understand how God may be thought to work upon and in the world of creaturely existence. The pressure of the divine hand would have to be light indeed if creatures were to act autonomously, were to have lives of their own, and yet the dependence upon God would have to be real enough to warrant belief in One whose touch was so elusive. To carry out this inquiry Farrer had to examine the relation of finite and infinite in the realms of both nature and grace, in the world of physical fact and revealed mystery. These examinations were never simply the mannered speculations of an academic theologian. There was a practical urgency about them, the urgency of a man who was seeking to understand the faith he believed and to defend it against error and imposture.

Writing about John Keble, one of the luminaries of the Oxford Movement, Farrer said, "After all the detection of shams and the clarification of argument and the sifting of evidence-- after all criticism, all analysis--a man must make up his mind what there is most worthy of love, and most binding on conduct, in the world of real existence. It is this decision, or this discovery, that is the supreme exercise of the truth-seeking intelligence."* Farrer was a man possessed of such an intelligence. His works

* Austin Farrer, "Keble and His College," **The End of Man,** edited by Charles Conti (London: Hodder & Stoughton, 1975) 157.

exhibit a philosophical incisiveness and a breadth of imagination that are the equal of the most gifted thinkers of his generation. More than this, however, his writings reveal the commitments of a man who had made up his mind about what is worth loving.

It may well be that we understand Farrer best if we think of him as one whose primary vocation was that of a priest dedicated to the care of souls, whether through the preaching of the Christian faith, the administration of the sacraments, or the writing of books for learned specialists and interested laity. He humbly employed his considerable gifts toward the end of making the love of God explicit. The legacy of those labors are some splendid volumes which exhibit on nearly every page Farrer's passion for God and clarity.

Jeffrey C. Eaton
Ann Loades

NOTE ON CITATIONS

Many of the authors of papers in this volume employ abbreviations to indicate sources in Farrer's writings. The abbreviations and the works to which they refer are as follows.

FI	Finite and Infinite
GV	The Glass of Vision
RI	A Rebirth of Images
Study	A Study in St. Mark
CR	The Crown of the Year
SMSM	St. Matthew and St. Mark
FL	Faith and Logic (Basil Mitchell, ed.)
FW	The Freedom of the Will
LIB	Lord, I Believe
SS	Said or Sung (U.S.: FOO A Faith of our Own)
LA	Love Almighty and Ills Unlimited
RSJ	The Revelation of St. John the Divine
SB	Saving Belief
TV	The Triple Victory
SG	A Science of God?
FS	Faith and Speculation
CF	A Celebration of Faith (Leslie Houlden, ed.)
RF	Reflective Faith (Charles C. Conti, ed.)
EM	The End of Man (Charles C. Conti, ed.)
BM	The Brink of Mystery (Charles C. Conti, ed.)
IB	Interpretation and Belief (Charles C. Conti, ed.)

For a full citation of the above works see the bibliography of Farrer's writings at the end of this volume.

AUSTIN FARRER AS PHILOSOPHICAL THEOLOGIAN

A Retrospective and Appreciation

Julian Hartt

In the first part of this paper I sketch our situation in the decade of the Forties; that was the period in which we discovered Farrer. Then I venture an answer to the question, What did we hear? What did we discover? It will, I hope, strike you as plausible to go thence to the question, What did we make of what we heard? The final question may strike you as inevitable: What did we make of subsequent developments of Farrer's program as a philosophical theologian?

Questions antecedent to these programmatic ones will certainly have occurred to you. Whose situation? What happened to whom?, etc. By way of answering such preliminary questions I hasten to say that this paper is not a specimen of theology-as-autobiography or of autobiography-as-theology. The we-talk prodigally employed here refers to philosophical theologians in America who were up and about during the Forties, to start with. I shall use personal history somewhat as Descartes used it in **The Discourse:** to delineate significant features of a historical situation that seemed fraught with real peril and doubtful promise for theological reflection sensitive to developments in philosophy.

I

The situation was such that the reality and future of philosophical theology seemed highly problematical. It suffered from comparison with philosophy of religion, which could be done safely and with incontestable propriety within the philosophy department; one had only to be a believer in the high prerogatives and unsullied integrity of philosophical criticism. Philosophical

1

theology seemed less chaste than that; and it was rarely pursued with a clear mind and untroubled heart. Some of us were still using Tennant's classical text (**Philosophical Theology**, 1927-29) but with a strong sense that it wasn't really working. If you want a signal reason for that here is one: Tennant was pre-Ayer. Tennant could hardly have known in the Twenties that by the mid-Thirties metaphysics, both in pure state and in theological composts, would be banished to the Siberia of Nonsense.

But the confessional theologians were making trouble, too; their contribution was harder to endure. There was Barth's striking version of the ancient reproach, 'What has Jerusalem to do with Athens?' This attack came from a theologian who had proved in his Anselmbuch (1932) that he was philosophically sophisticated--no country preacher he inveighing against the vain deceits of philosophy! Moreover, the lineaments of Barth's "biblical positivism" were already evident, a view claiming the absolute priority of Revelation both in the order of being and of knowledge. (Cf. **Knowledge of God and Service of God**, 1949). For Christian faith "the strange new world of the bible" is absolutely real. It is in no way a philosophical construction: a <u>weltanschauung</u> or a metaphysical theory.

So it began to appear that there was something at once philosophically and Christianly dubious about dallying with the metaphysics of theism. But not simply because of its traditional Apologetical stance. There was also the inclination of philosophical theologians to give religious hostages to <u>atheos</u> (one of Tennant's contributions) rationality; and to appeal to generic features of experience rather than to the singularities of Christian experience.

Our situation was further complicated by the fact that the cause of Liberal Christianity, both as doctrine and as social strategy, was still largely bound up with Personalist metaphysics. (More so, I think than such a peer figure as Reinhold Niebuhr would have admitted. The way he went on about The Biblical View of Man persuaded a lot of people, beginning with himself, that he had somehow driven the mind-body problem completely off the theological court). But was it proper for theologians to make a heavy investment in <u>any</u> metaphysical system? We remembered Tennant's profound reluctance to do that, despite his indebtedness to his great teacher, James Ward. Perhaps there was a way of building on Kant, that exemplary taskmaster of metaphysics, that would insure the autonomy of theology, relative to metaphysical system, Idealist or otherwise.

I pause to remind you that the cloud of Transcendental Kantianism was no larger than a small hand on our horizon. We had heard of Père Marechal; some of us had actually read him. It would have required uncanny prophetic powers to foresee a time when Marechal would cross the Alps, ford the Rubicon after a diversion in Innsbruck, and advance irresistably upon Rome.

If Kant was a significant presence in our situation it was largely in Neo-Kantian permutations. Cassirer, for instance. His **Philosophy of Symbolic Forms** (German text, 1923; English 1955. By the decade of the 30's Wilbur M. Urban was making **Philosophy of Symbolic Forms** available to his graduate students at Yale.) was read as a magisterial vindication of the integrity of religious language; and of metaphysics. There was at least as significant a Neo-Kantian presence in the discovery that inter-pretation is the ordained--so to speak--medium of knowledge and truth, and of reality itself; thus, inevitably, of Revelation. So Kantian and Hegelian lines merged well short of infinity.

That convergence was most apparent in the interpretation of history. Here the influence of Collingwood was immense. His historiographical idealism did much to make historical relativ-ism all but inevitable for many theologians. Witness H. Richard Niebuhr. (Having alluded to him I want to file the opinion that his **Meaning of Revelation** is fundamentally an essay in philosophi-cal theology. His great objective in it is to provide a philosophical foundation and warrant for a confessionalist method in theology.)

Thus History stood in a fair way to supplant Nature in the affections of philosophical theology. This development can easily be related to movements on the scientific-cosmological front. Von Weizsächer, for instance, was saying that after all everything is historical, not least the development of the galaxies. (In **The History of Nature**, 1949). Moreover substance had long since been banished from physics (cf. Cassirer, **Substance and Function**, 1923); and was even then taking a solid thrashing in the social sciences. Remember, too, how early metaphysical appropriations of quantum theory construed the order of nature as brimming with flexibility, with chance as a positive quasi-causal factor, and with openness to genuine novelty: in one word, with all the rudiments of freedom. So where natural theology in its classical modes had held that the hierarchical structure of the created world required, or at least included, the ontological integrity of the physical realm, historicistic views installed spirit on every level; though it was sometimes called Creativity, Élan Vital, The Nisus, and other things redolent of Romantic verve.

There was, then, some optimism over the prospects of theological reflection so nicely attuned to contemporary sensi-bilities and so responsive to the latest news from the cosmological-scientific front.

But there were some wayward doubts and niggling anxi-eties. Was it really the case that the doctrine of Creation, for example, was properly treated in those up-to-date theologies? Was there no safe and fair country between archaic supernaturalism and liberal reduction of Creation to a poetic symbol of the ultimacy of Spirit both in Nature and History?

Beset by such questions some of us had turned for philosophical assurance to Neo-Thomism. Perhaps Analogia Entis was a mighty fortress. Perhaps Proper Proportionality was a providential oasis in a dry and thirsty land. Had not the philosophia perennis endured through all the seasons in which lesser creeds had flourished withered and died, Nominalisms, Materialisms old and new, Spiritualisms galore?

Such assurances came in at a fairly high price. Were we so sure that in the middle ages Aquinas was a philosophical winner rather than an ecclesiastical-theological one? Was it clear, for example, that Aquinas was superior to Scotus on the principle of individuation? Wasn't it possible that the philosophical integrity of the Five Proofs was inextricably bound up with a primitive logic? What kind of sense could be made of the Thomist view of God's unrelatedness to the world, not just metaphysical sense but practical religious sense? Is it possible to show that the doctrine of God as Pure Act can be rendered responsive to modern dynamical and energistic notions of being? Or congruent with modern sensibilities about the irreducible and ultimate reality of Time?

Then came **Finite and Infinite** (1943). Caught in the crossfire of positivists, logical and revelational; worried about the stunning successes of historical relativism; wary of the emerging syntheses of naturalism and idealism, ambiguously attracted to Neo-Thomism; we went out to hear a fresh voice in the wilderness of philosophical theology.

What did we hear? What did we see?

II

We saw Farrer step forth unblushingly clad in the garb of metaphysician. He had not come to do philosophy of religion; perhaps his dismissal of that enterprise was unnecessarily brusque but it was certainly entertaining. Nor did he launch into some sort of sociocultural analysis in the hope of finding there either the propaedeutic or the content of theology. He was not about to re-tell the Christian story. The philosophical theologian is not obliged to praise or condemn such endeavors, unless they are presented as ordained replacements for the metaphysical venture.

Farrer had already given some hints as to how he would treat Revelationist postures. In **Finite and Infinite** he took on the Logical Positivists. In this he followed his own excellent advice: the possibility of something follows excellently from its actuality, and hardly from anything else. Which is to say that the defense of metaphysics in the abstract doesn't come to much; probably to little more than attacks on the mere possibility of metaphysics as such--such as Ayer's early run at it, or Hume's remarkable discovery that "the strife of systems" had produced only sterile results. So Farrer set himself to the vindication of a particular metaphysical systematic: a doctrine of substance.

He began by showing that Logical Positivism had not after all cut the tap root of substance. We were puzzled by this approach. Why didn't he launch a full-scale dialectical barrage against Positivism? We could sense that he had the weapons. The Positivists were generously furnishing the vulnerability. Well, then, let them have it, cannister, grape, shrapnel, solid ball, give them the full treatment!--But he didn't. Instead he went about to build a positive case; he built it with care and subtlety.

I do not intend to go here into the details of that case, either to expound them or to appraise them. For this abstention I offer an historical explanation: we were interested in something else. That was how he construed the central nerves, so to speak, of substance as an ontological category.

For Farrer (in **Finite and Infinite**) the fundamental question about substance is what effects real unity (=practically efficacious) among multiple and diverse operations. This is not the same as asking what super-property unifies lesser ones and thus constitutes an entity. Farrer looks for concentration, the gathering-up into ontological coherence, the orchestration of effects of which only transcendental efficacy (=agency) is capable. So the Positivists were right in stressing persistence of phenomenal effect--look, that patch is still (not that Hume could handle that) and really blue!--and an environment committed, miraculously, to generating phenomenal regularities in us. But their failure to come to terms with experienced efficacy, with real agency, is complete.

Where then is real agency, causal efficacy, experienced/ known as and for what it is? Here Farrer made a decision warrantably identified as metaphysical: he asserts the ontological-- not merely psychological--priority of interiority. Substantial entities have insides and outsides, surfaces and springs of originating action. It is not entirely clear in **Finite and Infinite** whether something lies behind that decision, namely that activity, prima facie distinguishable from passivity or inertness, is per se a function of interiority. Be that as it may, Farrer makes the human self the paradigm for the distinction between interiority and exteriority. It is also the paradigm of real agency. (Please note that I do not use paradigm with any intention of detonating Kuhnish theories).

Tracking along the interior way Farrer uncovers the cosmological relation. This is a primitive metaphysical fact. As intuitively certain as the sense of self-as-finite there is the sense of being-related to the infinite. I have put this awkwardly. There are not two such senses; there are these distinguishable elements of one intuition, one act of unitary and unitive apprehension in which self and God are both given.

We heard in this something familiar and something novel. The familiar element was a suggestion of an epistemological realism similar to what we had learned from Douglas Clyde Macintosh: Critical Monistic Realism. This theory asserts a significant measure of identity between what is in the mind and independently existing objects; so that epistemological objects are also in some measure or manner ontological entities. It is the job of critical intelligence to make out that measure of identity. (In firm disagreement with Santayana, Macintosh claimed that this faculty, critical intelligence, could make reality-appraisals that were not arbitrary, thus were more than proddings of "animal faith").

Later on Farrer backed off a ways from the front established in **Finite and Infinite** for apprehension. (As for instance in the second edition of **Finite and Infinite,** 1959). I do not here go into the question whether that was in effect a dilution of his epistemological realism. Rather I want to mention something that struck us as novel. That was his claim that the R in the cosmological situation is essentially a relating rather than a relation; and it is a relating done from the other side; done not only from the objective pole of experience, as Dorothy Emmet was then calling it (**The Nature of Metaphysical Thinking,** 1953), but from/by the transcendent Object. Thus the primordial experience of being-contingent is actually awareness of being-created; that is, of being constituted in coming-to-be. So did Descartes really mean that the existence/reality of the infinite was an inference from the self's awareness of its own ontological fragility and derivativeness? Could he really have meant that any proposition, or set of propositions, expressing the essential limitations of the self implied a proposition, or set of propositions, about God? If he did he was wrong. Ontological fragility does not entail the existence of a being free of that defect and at the same time responsible for the occurrence of that defect in other beings. Moreover derivativeness does not necessarily mean being-created. Spinoza's finite modes are derivative but they are not created.

On the other hand being-created does not necessarily mean being-derived. In a rich and confusing variety of religious metaphor the self is said to have come from God. In the cool sober world of philosophical theology that metaphor expresses the sense of being-constituted, of being wholly engaged as coming-to-be in relation to One who wholly and perfectly is.

I little doubt that I have just given a grossly inadequate account of what struck us as novel in Farrer's starting (in **Finite and Infinite**) with that primordial intuition in which self and God are both given. In another run at it I shall contrast what we perceived Farrer to be doing with our understanding of Schleiermacher and of Whitehead.

What we capitalized in Schleiermacher were his claims for and about the sense of absolute dependence. These claims had been a powerful influence in the formation of the Liberal consensus on Creation. In that consensus Creation does not mean the inexpressibly great and perfectly singular act by which God made a world to be where nothing was. Not origination but constitutive relationship, there's the heart of the matter. A residue of ancient doctrine persists in the view that creating is going on all the while. So new life and new values are always emerging in the incessant reshuffling of the cosmical elements and the restructuring of the vitalities of history. Thus the once-for-all character which the classical tradition imputed to God's act as Creator was generalized by the Liberal consensus, and emerges as a generic characteristic of reality in all its parts and permutations. Thus whatever really exists is as truly engaged in the creating business as God; not as fully, of course, surely not as enduringly, but nonetheless as truly. Primus inter pares . . .

I hope this suggests to you how naturally and insensibly we brought Whitehead into the theological weave. Some of us boggled a bit over making God an exemplification of the categories. But that did not seem an unreasonably high price to pay for great gains in metaphysical wisdom and religious relevance. One of the greatest of those gains was a full allowance for a partnership of God and man in the creation and enhancement of value. Not much lower in our esteem was Whitehead's eloquent celebration of God's rule as moral suasion. As Liberals we had long ago banished predestinarian doctrines to an exile from which we designed they were never to return. For their great flaming and incurable defect was that they installed a rigid determinism of efficient causality at the heart of the Christian faith. Their archaic views of time and eternity were not so appallingly wrong; they were simply irrelevant to modern sensibilities, they were "out of sync" with modern experience. That Grace should be efficacious was something we could live with. That Grace should be irresistible, never! Irresistible grace was a cosmological causality principle masquerading as a Christian truth. That grace should be prevenient, well, that was hardly more than an awkward way of saying that God as God enjoys an indefeasible priority of being and an unexceptionable perfection of goodness.

So into Whitehead's lofty principle of moral suasion as the power by which God rules the world (what other power does Whitehead's God have?) we sought gracefully to insinuate a Kantian doctrine of the Realm of Ends and Kant's very own view of the indefeasible autonomy of the ethical self in splendid defiance of every threat whether from the order of natural appetite or from highest heaven. (Of course we knew that a Kantian God does very little thundering out of heaven, and never intending to frighten the ethical self into heteronomy.)

Then along came Farrer. He, too, capitalized Creation as <u>relation</u> rather than unimaginable originating act. But with a difference that was initially puzzling. The self as moral agent comes to be through the exercise of will in choosing its goods. Thus it creates its character. Character, accordingly, is a gift neither of God nor nature; nor of history. But doesn't this virtually make self-creation out to be the grand human possibility?

Existentialist extravaganzas on this theme were already on the boards. Farrer seemed to be no more inclined to join that act than Leibniz would have been. We saw later that Farrer was prepared to defend the absolute and exhaustive prerogatives of God the Creator as heartily as any traditionalist. So character as the self-determination of the finite is ordained by God. But "ordained" is not a trip-word for a necessitating divine causality. God wills that man should acquire virtue in the exercise of fully finite freedom. Relative (related to) to moral endeavor the divine will is not coercive. God indeed has created us for himself. It follows that our being cannot be fulfilled in the enjoyment of any earthly goods, no matter how grossly they are amassed, no matter how passionately we pursue them one after another. But of ourselves we must incline our hearts to Him. And we must resolutely follow that inclination.

This seemed to put us closer to Aquinas than to Kant, but we weren't sure. There was Farrer's masterly elucidation of the Bad Will, which reminded us that Kant was much more of a voluntarist than Aquinas. And we all know that in the end Farrer moved strongly to the voluntarist side. (Cf. **Faith and Speculation,** 1967).

In the end; but what about our first encounter with Farrer? Early in **Finite and Infinite** he avowed his sympathies for Aquinas. Substance, being-as-activity, Analogy, created reality as hierarchical, <u>a posteriori</u> proofs for God's existence, and a rejection of the ontological argument: the spirit of the Angelic Doctor seemed to speak in all these. But then there was Farrer's rejection of the scala naturae in favor of the interior scale. And here came his claim that the self's knowledge of itself, that is of its own operations, outranks decisively in solidity and clarity its knowledge of the essential operations of any other sort of being. We are aware of their activities but we do not know, directly and fairly, what they are after. We do know that about ourselves. And in ourselves we know that the lower order grounds and is sublated in the higher order; which amounts to saying that we inwardly grasp how one kind of unity differs from another.

Now what keeps this from being accounted as an investment in metaphysical idealism? The primacy of interiority, especially when it is tied to esse est operari, strongly suggests such an investment. The move to operari from percipi by itself hardly suggests more than a preference for Leibniz over Berkeley.

I mentioned above something that bears on the question about idealism, namely, the epistemological realism evident in Farrer's apprehension. This does not offer much protection on the ontological/cosmological front. All that apprehension allows for is that the mind in its cognitive activities grasps something other than itself. But was it Farrer's intention to assert that what the mind grasps is the authentic formal structure of the object, the substantial principle which makes it to be what it is? Or is the content of noetic apprehension exhausted by the intuition (inference?) that the object must have some such formal structure determining its behavior?

That is one sort of question. Another one is more obviously metaphysical. What is the relation of mind to its body? What is the connection of the physical with the psychical?

I do not mean to suggest that in our judgment Farrer was grievously remiss, in **Finite and Infinite,** in not coming forward with a systematic theory of the mind-body relationship. A position could indeed be made out in **Finite and Infinite.** Wasn't it closer to hylozoism than to panpsychism? (We recognize that in **Freedom of the Will,** 1958, he occupied dualistic territory. Cf. 176). That is, whatever qualifies as an entity, a real entity, is self-activated. Substantial individuals are not inert things, they are not purely acted on. This metaphysical principle is exemplified in self-activity as we know it in ourselves. This is the cornerstone, or proper foundation, for metaphysical analogizing. But this does not mean that man is a microcosm. Nor is it supposed to turn organismic metaphors loose to overrun the universe.

Later on Farrer developed more systematically an agnosticism about the degree to which the principle of being in anything other than the self is picked up in apprehension. (Cf. **Faith and Speculation**, 108). This does not at all mean that he relinquished his grip on the principle of singular activity as the essence of any and every entity qua entity, no matter now minute its scope of activity, or trivial we may reckon its value. (Cf. **Love Almighty and Ills Unlimited**, 1962, 52).

One thing more and we shall be finished with this part of my paper. We expected that a philosophical theologian would say something about the proofs for the existence of God. The philosophers of religion had always done that. And certain large figures in our education had made positive use of one or more of the theistic proofs: Sorley, A. E. Taylor, Temple, Tennant.

I have mentioned above that Neo-Thomists had colored our expectations. They were supposed to give vigorous support to the theistic proofs, claiming that they were valid and informative when properly selected and framed; that is if one were really rational and authentically faithful. Really rational: if one grasped the way in which reason is grounded in being rather than in or through itself. Authentically faithful: if one acknowledged that the ascent of the mind to God will surely miscarry unless the God we seek is the One in whom there is no trace nor shadow of turning, the great I am That am, Totum Simul, Actus Purus, Being in whom existence and essence are identical, Necessary Being utterly inconfusable with the whole order of contingency or any inhabitant thereof.

Well, did we believe this? Hardly. We admitted hardly more than that it was a stout contender for an ambiguous crown. We had been firmly tutored in a Liberal ranking of the Proofs which put the Moral Argument at the top. The best the Thomists could do with that was to squeeze it in somewhere between Four and Five.

So when we cocked our ears at Farrer what did we hear? A philosophical theologian who tucked the Proofs into the last few pages of his performance (in **Finite and Infinite**), almost as though it were a concession to the unfortunate expectations of the audience. We did not expect him to build his case simply or largely upon the Proofs. But to use them largely as a testing-ground for an analytic of substance, well now! No doubt once he had put on his dialectical skates Farrer could cut some intriguing figures. But on the road to what or where? What did the Proofs really go to show? What was their proper function in the life of faith? We felt entitled to answers to such questions, if not to the larger question, What is the truth-value of the Proofs?

Farrer's distinction between weak forms of the Proofs and strong ones was very suggestive. But it depended on the ontological viability of the essence-existence form-matter distinction. And behind that dependency there was an important decision: the elevation to metaphysical status of the distinction between simple and composite being; which meant that it applied to all and every being except God. But what legislated against its including God? Wasn't this another anterior decision, that God is after all at least first cousin to Actus Purus?

So Farrer must be some kind of a Thomist. Perhaps that accounted for his skillful reduction of the acceptable proofs to the Cosmological; and for the ambiguous compliment to A. E. Taylor's version of the Moral Argument.

A larger question outranked these concerns. What was Farrer's view of the proper function of the Proofs in and for faith?

We were puzzled; more specifically, we were puzzled by the concluding paragraphs of **Finite and Infinite**, deeply moving though they were. Where had Farrer shown that Absolute Activity is adorable? Even if all else is grounded in the will of that God, what rightly constrains us to worship Him? That He can slay me is a poor warrant for trusting Him, let alone loving Him.

Then it occurred to us that Farrer had been too subtle for us. Perhaps he had shown that the appetite for being courses through our entire existence; and it is only when we are afflicted with religious and philosophical distortions that we try to isolate the love of adventure from the need for security, the love of power from the respect for the being of others, the fear of the Lord from the love of God in Jesus Christ, "the joy of all desiring". Alas! we are indeed afflicted: we are sinners, all in all. But since when is sin a category, or a preoccupation, of the philosophical theologian?

III

We were surprised by a number of developments in **The Glass of Vision**, 1948.

The first of these surprising developments was the remarkable weight Farrer gave (in **The Glass of Vision**) to image and imagination. Philosophical theologians were beginning to think a bit about imagination. (For example, Kroner, in **Religious Function of Imagination**, 1941). Farrer moved straight into making master images, as he called them, the medium of Revelation.

Thereupon he proceeded to do something with the then hot topic of Propositional Truth vs. Encounter Truth. Now it is hard not to feel that the friends of Propositional Truth were retreating and the Encounter company was rapidly advancing. To what were the Encounterers advancing? Surely not to occupy the trenches being vacated by the Propositioners. Forgive the military figure. The point is, what was <u>encounter</u> supposed to mean? Surely not mystical experience; remember how hostile Brunner was to that. Nor was <u>encounter</u> an appeal to an epistemology of direct realism. Well then, what about I-and-Thou? Yes, said some Encounter people; but not all. So how about the relation of <u>Dasein</u> to <u>Transcendenz</u> or to <u>Umgreifende</u>, or both, in case they are different? That's it! cried another contingent of the Encounter corps as they proceeded to examine every crack in the surface of experience to see how the Ground of Being radiated through it.

So Proposition vs. Encounter was a hot topic. Farrer refused to adjudicate the controversy in the received terms. He was convinced that the apostolic fathers must have understood how the master images of the New Testament related to the reality of God and the situation of man. God speaks the eternal Word of salvation and fulfillment through the master images, that is true. That process must be understood metaphysically, which is to say that the gift of the image is the moment in which a human mind is 'supernaturalized'. Supernaturalization is not a transaction in which a human mind moves from one ontological realm up into another one, ascends from earth to heaven. Rather, supernaturalization is a potentializing of natural human energies to accomplish not only the extraordinary but the miraculous. That is the power to show forth both in linguistic form and concrete existence the reconciliation in Jesus Christ as the revelation of God the Father Almighty, Creator of all things, Judge of all men. The power and righteousness of the Creator are apprehended in the supernaturalizing of natural energy and form.

It struck us that what Farrer was doing here (in **The Glass of Vision**) had very little in common with Encounter as the existentializing of faith. He quarreled fundamentally with the relativism of the Existential Dialectic. But on the other hand he was not contending for the sanctity, the once-for-allness of the <u>conceptual</u> system in which the apostolic fathers articulated the dogmas of the faith. For their part the fathers were not locked into a dismal representationalist theory of truth. They were not thus constrained to declare that <u>homoousian</u> or <u>hypostasis</u>, for examples, were mental counterparts of objective realities. If some mode of representation is involved, we can legitimately suppose that it was in the relation of <u>concept</u> to <u>image</u>. But there it would be far better to speak of <u>adequacy</u> rather than <u>representation</u>. For it is not a matter of <u>fit</u> but of potency (potentialization);

that is, whether the mind of the creature is rendered conformable to "that mind which was in Christ Jesus". Thus dogma returns us to New Testament image. Through image faith participates in the divine ordering and re-ordering of existence.

So scripture is acknowledged to be primary amongst all the works of men in focusing attention upon God's presence in Jesus Christ. But it is not the word of scripture in itself that contains the revealed and revealing truth. It is word as medium of image. The image lives its own life in whatever tongue it is conveyed. The dwelling-place of this living truth is the Church as the mystical Body of Christ.

What was Farrer up to? Was he on the road to Church as Magisterium, the depository of truth-as-dogma, Authority triumphant as well as militant? It was not easy to determine. We were enheartened by parts of **The Glass of Vision,** particularly by the brilliant laying-out of the place of metaphysics in Christian reflection. But was this decisively different from Thomism, say from Maritain on the grandeur and misery of metaphysics? (In **The Degrees of Knowledge,** 1938).

We weren't sure. This uncertainty was lodged in the question about the cognitive capability Farrer meant to assign to imagination. Was imagination's role essentially that of inspired interpreter in the Church? Remember the line in Cowper's hymn: "God is his own interpreter . . ." Well, does God play on the organ of imagination for the edification of the faithful, making plain to them what to Worldly Wise is arrant nonsense or hopeless obscurity?

What engaged us here was the connection between the rational truths of metaphysics and the revealed/revealing images of the New Testament. For Farrer faith is a communal reality, the faith that saves is what grasps me in the church as God's doing. But rational truths are not communal properties, so to speak. They do not reflect the history of a community grounded and sustained by special providence. Rational truths do not save us nor do they judge us. What then do they offer to the life of faith?

It is a truism that metaphysics lives on the nourishment of rational truths; even if the metaphysician has come down from the heights of speculation to dwell quietly on the plains of Description. As we read Farrer's intentions in **The Glass of Vision** he meant to set up his tent on those plains.

His subsequent rejections of the speculative ventures of Process tend strongly to support that reading. As a thinker profoundly sympathetic to the classical tradition of theism he believes and argues that God is necessary being. If we say as Christians that we simply and piously <u>believe</u> that God is necessary being but we cannot <u>know</u> Him to be such, under what sort of necessity do we make that attribution? If we take St. Anselm as tutor in this we should have to say we have not finished with <u>necessary</u> when we have said that God is necessary for the existence of the world, or for Descartes' ontologically fragile self. Which is to say we must be antecedently sure that the world unmistakably needs a Creator, we should have to be certain that the world is not a self-positing self-sustaining self-renewing Substance. That calls for some sort of cosmological analysis and dialectic. Or in Descartes' case, we must be antecedently sure that the self is really all that fragile in itself, we must be antecedently sure that we aren't deceived by the Absolute playing hide-and-seek with itself, for the moment wonderfully drenched in histrionic <u>angst</u>. That calls for some sort of ontological-anthropological analysis and dialectic.

Farrer had produced the cosmological analytic and the ontological analytic in **Finite and Infinite**. There too it was clear that he was as fully committed to the principle of God's aseity as Aquinas and Anselm; and as Barth. But did Farrer suppose that the acknowledgment of that principle was a rational necessity?

We had stumbled over a large issue, at once religious and philosophical. I have used "acknowledgment" as the trip-wire exploding that issue. Put as a question, what sort of cognitive operation did <u>apprehension</u> signify? Did it signify a direct acquaintance with God as necessary being? <u>Prima facie</u> this was unlikely. But it was at least as doubtful that Farrer wanted necessary being to function as the sort of thing Whitehead called meta-compliments paid to God. A puzzling situation.

So far as The **Glass of Vision** was concerned there was considerably less perplexity in our understanding of what Farrer was up to in his attack on certain theological interpretations of history. He put the theology of The Mighty Acts of God in history to the test; and found it wanting. The faithful must already be established in the knowledge of God before they can faithfully make out His hand in the destruction of the hosts of Sennacherib. By all means let the pious declare, "It is by the hand of the Lord we are delivered!" Theologians are not well-advised to propose the hand of the Lord as a causality substitute for dysentery, mass hysteria, or a massive all-consuming outbreak of a M-A-S-H hatred of war. As for God's mighty act in the resurrection of Jesus Christ, it is necessary to say that the Resurrection did not teach the disciples how to get into serious and relevant God-talk. We have no reason to suppose that those men would have become his disciples in the first place if they had been antecedently godless. It stands in the record that they did not know what God through Jesus would demand of them, or of him; or what they would come to be and do in sharing his life and death. So the call of discipleship in Christ presupposes a religious reality, viz., an apprehension of God the Creator. To call the Creator "Abba, Father!" is possible only through Jesus Christ the Son. Nevertheless that Christological confession makes contact with the cosmological relation in which the Creator is apprehended, as we have seen.

I shall say something later on about Farrer's subsequent engagement with history as a theological problem. Here I want to come back to the cosmological issue because of what he did after **The Glass of Vision**. What I have in mind here is what he did to Nature as Cosmos when he took up theodicy on his own rather than as an editor and introducer of Leibniz. So what then is the order of nature, what is the shape of the cosmos? Here Farrer rejected a big chunk of Christian cosmological tradition, and made short work of the notion of a fixed order in which finite entities live and move and have their being, thus behaving as decent law-abiding citizens, so to speak. Of course he did not deny that there are genera and species. He did deny that the requirements and benefits of taxonomical science ought to be translated into ontological structures and behavior-controlling laws. It is true, he granted, that no entity acts beyond its 'essence', that is beyond its budget of capabilities. It is equally true that the characteristic pattern of activity of any entity is its own--it is not legislated by a created superordinate structure that is animated by its own Soul. (Cf. "Anima Mundi" in **Faith and Speculation**). So what is the world? Not a system; not, certainly not, an organic whole. There are of course significant wholes. They are much more like mutual benefit associations founded on particular freedoms than like organisms in which a monarch-monad controls the activities of all the cells.

What kind of natural theology could be developed with such a concept of nature? The answer was implicit in **Finite and Infinite:** it was near the surface in the concluding section, "Dialectic of Rational Theology". There the Teleological Argument was allowed a very limited run, especially in any form that tried to capitalize on "one increasing purpose" tying together ostensibly discrete and conflicting entities. In Farrer's view they are indeed discrete to the point of autonomy, and really conflicting. In **Love Almighty and Ills Unlimited** he made much of the natural law, as I suppose we can reasonably call it, of conflict among concrete entities: they are bound to collide; though not by a cosmological generalization of an instinct of aggression. Put in Spinoza's terms, though hardly with an eye to serving Spinoza's interests, each finite mode strives to preserve its being and to increase in being; and thus collisions galore among finite modes are guaranteed.

What I am saying here is that on this capital issue it seemed to us that Farrer was flirting with Spinoza as he waltzed with Leibniz. Was this any way for a Christian philosophical theologian to behave?

This brings us back to Farrer's dismissal of Process. We were perplexed by this. He seemed to share some of Process's notions. such as a conatus principle, an internal engine, so to speak, by which an entity is driven. Add to this something like Leibniz's appetition, which on the level of self-consciousness is not only choice but choice under the direction of aspiration. For Farrer aspiration is choice geared to idealities transcending though not obliterating such generic values as survival, ontological coherence etc. shared by all beings.

As we read it Farrer's rejection had at least three salients. In the next section of this paper I shall sketch these. Before we proceed I owe it to you to say why so much space is given to this element in Farrer's performance as a philosophical theologian. As W. H. Sheldon saw (In **America's Progressive Philosophy,** 1942) Process makes an extraordinarily fine fit with native American attitudes in philosophy. Its theological ramifications have become an American industry. British philosophical theologians tend to slight it. Perhaps they think it is designed exclusively for colonial consumption.

IV

I identify the three salients against Process as follows: (1) The anthropological divide. (2) A largely non-dialectical reaffirmation of traditional (classical) theism. (3) Accountability to Christian experience.

(1) Farrer seemed to us to stand clearly on the personalist side of the anthropological divide. Personhood is not read out of non-personal constituents, whether the latter are construed as cells of psychical activity ("feelings"), or as the omnicompetent genetic materials of socio-biology.

Was this salient fueled and formed by Farrer's commitment to a traditional doctrine of Creation? Did he believe that the soul was directly implanted as a special creative act whereby the 'seed' of personal individuality was sowed? If so wasn't he importing something from Dogmatic (Revelational) theology into philosophical theology? Descartes was perfectly willing to make a cosmological flourish of God-the-Creator. For philosophical purposes that God plays in a prefabricated pen. What about Farrer's Creator?

Some of us found that **The Freedom of the Will** was a necessary and sufficient answer to that doubt. Just as the analytic of substance and of will in **Finite and Infinite** stands on its own feet relative to Dogmatic tradition; so the analytic of the agent-self of **The Freedom of the Will** gives off the air of a greater freedom from the trammels of ancient philosophical conceptualities. (Later, in **Faith and Speculation** he made even clearer his rejection of Aristotelian legacies).

As for the great Process assertion of the sociality of the self, Farrer treats it as a fact of experience that we are made for one another and not for atomistic existence. But he denies that this entails or in any other way warrants the claim that the person him/herself is a society of lower-grade constituents.

(2) The second salient seemed to matter more to Farrer than the first one. If the reality of God is misapprehended or misconstrued nothing else will come right for faith--except by divine intervention. Accordingly analogy has to be set up in the right way at the outset. The right way is not to build the doctrine of God on anthropological foundations themselves grounded in the uncertain sands of modern sensibilities, or cantilevered over an Existentialist abyss. The right way of analogy would be imbued with the sensibilities of the via negativa. For the philosophical theologian is not licensed to cruise the world hoping to bag similitudes of Deity. God is truly not like anything we know in and of ourselves. So God is not "the supreme exemplification of the categories". This does not mean that the categories, however ascertained constituted and certified as such, should be given summary execution and buried ignominiously in a potter's field sponsored by nominalism. The proper ontological categories, at once scalar and vectoral, rightly used provide an orientation upon Deity rather than a description of the divine nature. So we are able to think rightly about Being that is pure existence. Neither in self nor in environment do we have a model of such a being.

I have used "pure existence" here because it seemed that it was very close to the heart of Farrer's salient into the line of Process's God. Dipolar Theism endows God with an inactive side, call it Primordial Nature or what you will. God as Pure Existence (=Pure Act, Absolute Activity) has nothing of that sort. Put in an odd formula, God eternally is everything he might be. In truth, we have no empirical model of such being. But analogy is not tied helplessly to a model.

Viewed as absolute Creator--as Process cannot and would not do--God is not acted upon by any other being. Source of all that is He is changelessly the One in whom incessant change is grounded. Again is grounded rather than controlled in an arbitrary or external way. As the piety of a familiar hymn has it, "We look to Thee in every need/And never look in vain". God so addressed, importuned, and praised has himself no needs. All that he is, is poured out upon his creatures; proportionately to what they are and to/for what they hunger to become, if such be their nature to be so animated.

Then it occurred to us that Farrer's rejection of Process was more largely governed by its relation to religious experience than by anything else. So to the third salient.

(3) From Whitehead on, Process people have made a good deal of the superior sensitivity of their view to the realities of religious experience; to the phenomenological realities, of course. Among those prayer and ethical love are particularly important. Prayer: the sense and conviction of thus being related to One who hears and answers. Ethical love: If God is the highest expression of this must it not mean that his action not only per- fectly sizes up the situation of finite subjects but also adjusts itself to it? In Hartshornian terms, God's love is a function of God's ability to feel the feelings of all actual entities.

The people of Process claim, then, that classical theistic metaphysics systematically distorts or even renders nugatory the religious realities philosophical theology ought to acknowledge at their face value. So they replace traditional theism with a speculative system they hold to be incomparably more sensitive at once to the phenomenological realities of religious experience and to the sensibilities of an irreversibly secular age.

Now it seems to me that Farrer's rejection of all this was not so summary, so cavalier, as Peter Geach's (in **Providence and Evil**). But it was no less final and unaccommodating. An important nerve in this was his view of the proper business of metaphysical reflection in the Christian life. The philosophical theologian is not ordained to develop or incorporate a speculative system in which the cardinal teachings of the church emerge as figurative representations of philosophical truth, à la Hegel; or are carefully selected and sifted with a view to extracting particles of metaphysical wisdom (what Anselm knew but couldn't understand because he was born too early to be a Processer). Over against such presumptions Farrer endeavored to make meta- physical reason responsive to the truths of faith. Thus the tasks are elucidation and demonstration. Elucidation: to let the light of faith's truth fall upon the situation of the believer; particularly upon seductive philosophical errors concerning the self. Demonstra- tion: demonstrare, "to point out clearly", perchance to prove, but not as in Euclid, rather as in proving ground: to show how faith's truth stands up in practice, in the actual working-out of God's presence.

So we could hardly help but see that the 'verification' of Christian beliefs, in Farrer's view, can only be found in the Christian life. This does not mean that the prayer of humble access shows somehow that traditional theism is right and Process wrong. It means that God glorified in humble access is infinitely more, is essentially other, than the Process Poet who savingly savors and redemptively flavors the inexhaustibly fascinating texture of ceaseless flux. The God of humble access is Creator Absolute who is also Lord invincible come to redeem what has never ceased to belong to God, and He is Spirit everlastingly present to make all things new.

So also then for Christian love, that disposition and power freely bestowed through Christ upon all who will receive and devotedly seek to exercise it. The 'verification of God' indeed entails the agapistic life. Does this mean that "God" is a conventional religious symbol for the agapistic life? Does it mean that "God" is a bafflingly metaphysical cipher which properly decoded by the philosopher means that the agapistic life is humanly commended? Far from it! The promise and the constraint, the lure and the imperative, in "God is love" are metaphysical through and through. There love is not the name of a property, something that God has, something mysteriously, if not ineffably, conjoined with another property called justice. By grace we hope to have love, the crowning virtue. God is purely all that he has. In the practice of the Christian life of love, then, there is a singular apprehension of this God. Our love is not similitude, an analogy. So far as it is in Christ, it is God Himself with us. We do not thereby add something to his being. In thus becoming, here or in the world to come, wholly ourselves we come to be what God created us to be, "children of God and heirs of his kingdom".

The quarrel with Process comes down to something like this, then. It is not the proper business of the philosophical theologian to excogitate or borrow a speculative system with which to refine one or more items of traditional belief and package it or them for religious assimilation to modern sensibilities. The conceptual decisions of the faithful metaphysician are dictated by a sense for their appropriateness as instruments for relieving intellectual obscurities in the teachings of the church. There is no divine assurance of success in that; surely none of abiding or permanent success. Ancient substance language had its day. If it cannot be purged of its defects--and we see now that it cannot--then let us move on to something else. But not to a speculative system with built-in criteria for determining what is (philosophically) true and what false in the faith and life of the Christian community.

V

The conclusion of **Finite and Infinite** warned us that the philosophical theologian had better not poach in the preserves of Eschatology. I remind you that those moving lines were written in time of war, indeed at a moment in that war when the prospects of a humane or even tolerable outcome were far from certain.

The time came, as we all know, when Farrer foreswore the pursuits of philosophical theology and plunged into biblical studies.

Then he returned to important items on the agenda of philosophical theology. And to one in which much of the theological spectrum is in fact involved: theodicy.

I want to consider briefly two elements of his treatment of that venerable vexed and vexatious topic. (It is more than a locus; it is a theological world in nuce.) The first of these is the Kingdom of God. The second is Hell.

Farrer on the relation of the Kingdom of God to history struck us first off as a reversion to oldstyle supernaturalism. Naturally it was a complex and sophisticated reversion. As we have seen part of it was a rejection of Heilsgeschichte versions of that relationship. Another part of it was an equally firm rejection of Liberal views in which "Kingdom of God" stands for an utopian transformation of human existence safely within history. So God is not at work in history to transform this world here below into a fit dwelling place for himself and humankind. History and world are not only finite, they are mortal. A full stop is ahead; not dead ahead but living ahead, we might be excused for saying.

Farrer's doctrine was hard to swallow; some of us gagged on it. The gaggers for the most part were immanentists, whether or not they still wore the badge of Progress.

Farrer's doctrine was unacceptable to others among us for other reasons. Wasn't he still flirting with archaic and arcane doctrines of Time and Eternity, and thus with all the paradoxes and paralogisms which infected those doctrines?

These discomfitures reached ecstatic magnitude when Farrer came to Hell. He embraced it. He embraced it as scriptural and as ethically intelligible. Like C. S. Lewis he found that Hell is ethically intelligible because it takes with utmost seriousness the consequences of free human moral choices. Let us put it this way: If a person chooses in freedom a godless and iniquitous life, is it ethically--or rationally!--warrantable for God to over-ride that choice and miraculously transform the moral character of that deep-dyed sinner? This struck us as a discomfiting version of Kant's sturdy ethical provincialism and imperialism. If it is impermissible for God to make us good because we must make ourselves that, it would be equally impermissible for God at the Last Judgment to remake the wicked and unholy into something they had persistently chosen not to be. They deserve what they chose. Not that they chose Hell. They chose that of which Hell is but the ultimate form: alienation from God and all righteous-ness. So as there is nothing in their life in this world that even faintly suggests a passion for holiness, or much patience or con-sideration for those so imbued; so beyond this world there will be suffering that consolidates and ratifies their choices and in no wise redeems them.

Quite apart from the fact that Farrer seemed to embrace literalistic versions of Last Judgment, his revitalization of Hell offended many of our religious sensibilities. And none more vividly than what Liberalism, in doctrine and sentiment, had made of redemptive love and mercy all-encompassing. In this reaction we may have made too little of Farrer's heaven. Perhaps that was because his heaven was in large part what we too deemed it to be, a perfection of fellowship with God himself. But now wait! In Farrer's view that intimately and unavoidably involved Resurrection. And Resurrection as fact rather than symbol.

So Farrer meant to saddle us with an old-fashioned non-symbolic miracle, wrought by Love Almighty. Where we were strongly inclined to see the work of divine love as transforming every human creature into the divine likeness (=the perfection of ethical personhood), thus seeing God's love as all but exclusively redemptive, Farrer was beating back upstream to love as God's creative power. Thus love is more than the motive of redemption. It is the power with which God creates what he wills, and re-creates whom he will.

Our hearts were not made light and gay by this return to particularistic salvation. Even Barth was better than that! Could Farrer avoid now the dreadful shoals of Predestination? Did he really want to stay clear of that peril? It was not clear but we were inclined to fear the worst: that he had deliberately returned to the ambiguous and costly comforts of Augustinianism (as John Hick claimed, in **Evil and the God of Love**).

VI

Why did we expect a prophetic figure to be wholly comfortable and endlessly reassuring? Why did we hope for a clarion re-affirmation not only of Liberal moral sensibilities and commitments but also of theological doctrine to back them up? I suppose we had all been more deeply influenced by Reinhold Niebuhr, and, yes, by Tillich than some of us were ready to confess. We probably wanted a philosophical theologian to be clearer than Niebuhr on the metaphysical side (how thin there **The Self and the Dramas of History!**), and less encumbered than Tillich with the atmosphere and conceptualities and agenda of monistic idealism. Well, Farrer was certainly much clearer than Niebuhr, and very little encumbered with monistic idealism. But were we ready to follow him back upstream to traditional theism, and to the church as the mystical body of Christ and in that the living presence of God in history, and to Hell as the condign punishment for invincible unholiness? Matters for personal decision, of course.

Well then, the great thing was, Farrer made us see that there is no magic in philosophy with which we can concoct a new vision of God, self and world that will catch up, redeem, and glorify all that is suggestive in Christian tradition, inescapable in contemporary experience, alluring and formidable in the future-as-prospect. Whatever we make of the doctrines bearing on the matter there is indeed something predestinate in the Christian life and, therefore, in any authentic (=faithful) philosophical theology. What is predestinate and predestinating is God in Jesus Christ. Every faithful form and mode of Christian theological discourse is bound to demonstrate who that is. So it is the Object and the objective of that reflection that are predestinate. The Object is Jesus Christ, the same yesterday today and forever. Rightly to serve and in that joyfully to know God in him and him in God, there is the objective. Who asks for more freedom than that in the great country between that Alpha and that Omega is asking for liberty to be without God.--That, as I make it out, is what Farrer said. If so, his word was both prophetic and apostolic.

THE AGENT'S WORLD:
FARRER'S CONTRIBUTION TO COSMOLOGY

Robert H. King

Neither popular theology nor academic theology has been much given to speaking about the world beyond the sphere of the human. That is especially true of modern Protestant theology with its strong personalizing tendency. Captivated by existentialist categories of subjectivity (and no doubt intimidated by the vast body of scientific knowledge regarding the natural world), theologians have tended to limit their attention to the self. Almost alone in protesting this tendency and insisting upon a cosmological dimension to theology have been the Whiteheadians. They at least recognize an encompassing reality beyond God and self worthy of our attention. There is, however, one theologian of note who does not belong to this school, yet who has managed to include cosmological considerations in his theology, and that is Austin Farrer. Though not generally recognized, cosmology plays an important role in his later thought. [1]

Farrer does not address himself to this topic apart from others; so it is not readily accessible to anyone who does not have a general acquaintance with his work. In fact, it is so well integrated with his other ideas that it does not immediately stand out even for someone who is acquainted with his work. Add to that the characteristic modesty with which he sets forth even his most original thought, and it is understandable why his contribution in this area might have been overlooked. yet it is an oversight that needs to be corrected. At a time of environmental crisis, when the theology of nature is once more coming in for consideration, it is imperative that theology attend to the larger world within which human destiny is set and not simply limit itself to the subjective sphere.

In what follows, I shall attempt to draw from Farrer's later writings some of his ideas on the subject of cosmology and to develop from them an argument in support of a particular way of regarding the world. In the end I want to say something about the contribution which this way of thinking can make to the present task of constructive theology.

I

If we are to think intelligibly about the world as a whole, we shall need an image, a model of some sort to guide our thinking. In the modern period the most persistent, if not the most generally acknowledged model has been the machine. So great is our fascination with our own mechanical inventiveness that it has been difficult not to conceive of creation as an extension of this very power and the world as the machine par excellence. In spite of the fact that it has been scientifically discredited many times over, the model persistently recurs. It subtly infuses our thinking, even when ostensively denied. We suppose that the best explanation of occurrences is the one that permits the most control; we reduce everything we can to the level of function; we make efficiency the guiding principle in matters where it is of dubious relevance; and we protest if the world does not meet the standards of mechanical excellence. The Engineer, we suppose, must somehow have botched the job.

As this last observation indicates, one of the principal points at which the mechanical model has made its presence felt in theology is in relation to the problem of evil. [2] Critics of Christianity are wont to argue that the world does not come up to the standard of a well-tuned engine. There is too much friction, too much waste; the parts do not mesh perfectly; nor do they (to all appearances) serve a single purpose. If only persons would freely do what is best in every situation--in the manner in which pistons move freely in their chambers--there would be reason to believe that they were fashioned by a Cosmic Engineer with full mastery of his craft. As it is, they so obviously diverge from what is judged reasonable and right that we must conclude either the absence of an Engineer or one who is deficient in the exercise of his craft. What is not questioned is the ideal of perfection which takes its standard from the well-functioning machine. Thus a model generally discredited within the sciences is brought in to confound the theologians.

Farrer's tactic is to attack this model and not simply the inferences drawn from it. [3] In his view it is wholly inappropriate to the subject. That it should have been invoked as a way of comprehending the mystery of creation is understandable, since the making of machines is something we experience at first hand. The criteria of successful mechanics (such as the accommodation of means to ends, smooth and efficient operation of parts, absence of waste) are deeply ingrained in our thinking. Yet the model is grossly misleading as applied to cosmology.

In the first place, machines are artificial arrangements. They are constructed out of pre-formed material. The genius of the engineer is his ability to take the structure inherent in his material and utilize it for his own purposes. Whether he attacks the structure at the macro-level (bending steel bars, pouring concrete into molds, piling brick upon brick) or at the micro-level (as in generating molecular change through chemical reaction), there is always some structure there to work with, a fixed order that can be made to serve his purposes. The art of engineering is precisely the imposition of an extrinsic order, pattern or design upon natural structures and processes. It is inherently artificial.

Not so God's creation of the world. If "creation" means anything it means a radical new beginning, an act of unqualified originality. God as Creator does not impose an alien order upon previously ordered material, but rather establishes the order wherein things are what they are. Farrer denies that this is simply a piece of archaic dogmatism on his part. Any other view of creation would be unintelligible. Suppose, for instance, that we were to hold that God in creating the world imposes order upon previously unstructured matter. We should then have the problem of conceiving of such matter. Structureless, formless matter is simply unthinkable. For it is the structure of the thing, however minimal, that makes it what it is, gives it its identity as a distinct entity. On the other hand, to suppose that God imposes order upon some previously established order is to raise the question at what level we are to suppose the order as given. Shall we stop at the level of molecular, atomic or sub-atomic structure? Any point we choose is going to seem arbitrary.

The creative act, unlike every sort of mechanical contrivance, cannot involve the imposition of an alien order, since it is that act by which there is any order at all. Moreover, it cannot be thought of as serving some extrinsic end. For what possible end could it serve? In as much as the world takes in all that there is outside of God, there would be nothing for it to do than simply be. Yet it would be a strange sort of machine that served no other purpose than simply to be. Certainly it is no purpose of a machine that the individual parts should have the fullest possible scope in which to be themselves--yet for all that we can tell, that is the case with the world. The world serves no purpose extrinsic to itself, while the individual components of the world have their own intrinsic good. On even the most extended interpretation, the world fails to qualify as a machine. The mechanical model breaks down at all the crucial points.

An alternative model brought in to fill the place vacated by the mechanical model is that of an organism, but this too Farrer rejects. He does so by questioning whether the world is such a "totality" as to constitute a vital unity. "My body is an organism, to all evidence the world is not." [4] It is altogether too pluralistic, too internally diversified to fit this model. "The universe is indeed organized, or drawn together into a unity, but it is so organized or drawn together a million million times over at all the single points where a field of forces finds a focus; and that is wherever a single active existent is present." [5] The notion of the world as a cosmic superorganism is a "violent hypothesis," inconsistent with scientific knowledge and intelligibility, we had best begin with ourselves and generalize outward from there. The cosmological model will, therefore, be in the first instance an anthropological model. Only through qualification and modification is it given a larger application.

There are, of course, ideas of the self that would be difficult if not impossible, to develop in a cosmological direction. That is because of a built-in antithesis to nature. The self of the existentialist literature is probably such a concept. In some statements it would seem to be virtually defined in opposition to nature; so that whereas nature is empirically observable and objectively knowable, the self is not. The self is irreducibly subjective, known only reflexively--if at all. It stands radically outside the world of natural occurrence and process, the inexplicable locus of freedom in an otherwise determinate world. With such a model of selfhood it is difficult to see how one could ever get to an inclusive picture of the world (which may help to explain why Bultmann with his strong existentialist leanings has so little to say on the subject of cosmology). [6]

Farrer's concept of the self is quite different from that of the existentialists, though there is a similar importance given to the freedom of persons. Subjectivity as such is not the key, but rather _bodily agency_. I am, he argues, most fully accessible to myself and others when I perform a bodily action, when I do something purposeful that everyone can observe. "Conscious bodily behavior" should, therefore, be taken as the standard, the clue to personal being. [7] By extension it is also the clue to other-than-personal being; but to begin with it is important to recognize the role it plays simply in revealing the person. To act with intention is to give objective form to what is inherently personal (the subjective intent of the person); at the same time it is to personalize what is basically objective (the bodily behavior of the person). Whenever I act with full awareness of what I am doing, I am both subjectively and objectively present to myself. Moreover, I am present to others, present in my action. That they are able to take in my intention, and thus have access to my subjectivity, is a consequence of our common humanity, our shared concerns, and our ability to enter sympa-thetically into the viewpoint of others. But the key is the bodili-ness of the action. This gives it an objectivity for others it would not otherwise have.

Bodily action, as we have come to realize, is actually constitutive of personal identity. Yet it is not for that reason abstractable from the larger world of occurrences and processes. On the contrary, the bodiliness of a person's action assures that it will be situated within this larger context. By identifica-tion with a physical body the person is pinned down within the cross current of forces that go to make up the physical world, obliged to interact with these various forces if anything at all is to be accomplished. Sometimes these forces limit what can be done; other times they greatly enlarge and enhance the significance of an action. The point is that action, however personal, takes place in the context of other agents--some like ourselves, some different, but all with the capacity to affect what we do.

The difficulty in developing a cosmological model from this particular vantage point is in making the transition from the personal to the non-personal. What can we possibly know of agents other than ourselves? We do not have the internal perspective that we have with respect to our own action. We can only observe the behavior of animals, organisms, plants and chemicals from outside. Besides what we do observe seems less and less like action the further removed we are from the sphere of the human. Animal behavior may bear some resemblance to our own in that it exhibits a certain purposiveness, yet in the absence of a language in which to express this purposiveness can we say that it is intentional? Probably not. If we descend even further to the level of molecular behavior, we may be reluctant even to use the word "action." So perhaps we are no closer to a cosmological model than when we began.

Farrer does not think so. He contends that it is possible to qualify the model of personal agency in such a way as to discount those features which do not apply beyond the sphere of the personal, and still be left with an intelligible idea of agency. Consciousness, obviously, must go and with it intention and feeling. At the lowest level we may speak only of brute forces blindly acting upon one another within rigidly fixed pat-terns. Still there is something going on, something with which we can interact. So the analogy is not entirely lost. It may be severely diminished. We certainly do not know what it is for cells to interact, much less electrons. Yet we can at least place their action in a continuum with our own, and that may be sufficient to save the analogy.

What exactly is left after you strip away the personal aspects of personal agency? What common core of meaning remains? Farrer points to two aspects: pattern and force. [8] Beyond the realm of the personal we are likely to attend only to the patternedness of things, since we are frequently not in a position to experience their force. We may, for instance, plot the movement of planets without thinking about the force they exert upon one another. Objects within our immediate environment which stand in the way of our efforts, on the other hand, do make us aware of their force. The resistance they offer is the measure of their force. Still the force is there whether we experience it or not--and so also is the pattern. Outside of the action of personal agents this pattern may not be consciously chosen, yet it is none the less basic. Pattern is what identifies a particular movement as a discrete action.

The term that Farrer settles on for agency below the level of the personal is "activity system." It encompasses both aspects--the pattern without which there would be no system and the force without which there would be no activity. It is sufficiently general to take in the full spectrum of activity from the microcosmic to the macrocosmic, from the most personal to the least personal. It does not exclude rigid determinism at one level or a high degree of spontaneity and inventiveness at another. The degree of self determination open to any activity-system is dependent on the kind of system it is. A person in full possession of the powers of rationality is obviously going to be more self-determining than a single-cell organism; yet in as much as the person's body consists of such organisms, the scope of that person's action is bound to be limited. A bodily agent cannot do or be anything it chooses.

The notion of an activity-system is then a generalization of what we know at first hand, a broadening of the concept of agency on the basis of interaction with other sorts of agents. The absence of first-hand knowledge at the outer limits does not mean that the application of the model is entirely speculative since there is still the possibility of interaction. Whatever else we may say about the larger world it must be such as to engage our action; otherwise it really is meaningless to speak about it. The world in which we find ourselves as agents is nothing if not a field of activity. If we cannot speak of it as a unified field, we may at least speak of it as the totality of interacting systems.

III

The place in which Farrer makes the most sustained and imaginative use of the cosmological model is his discussion of the problem of evil. **Love Almighty and Ills Unlimited** though self-consciously set within the Augustinian tradition, is unquestionably one of the most original approaches to this problem in modern times--owing in large measure to the use made of this model. Whereas some recent critics have argued that it is necessary to revise our thinking about God to meet objections raised against Christianity under this heading, Farrer challenges our assumptions about the world. Much of what we call evil is a consequence, he contends, not of God's limitation or our own perversity but simply of the world's being what it is, a world.

We have already noted his argument against the mechanical model. It is simply not applicable to the world as a totality. In fact, any model which treats the world as a closed system is certain to fail since it is consistent neither with what we know scientifically nor with what we believe theologically. To all appearances the world is not a system but "an interaction of systems innumerable." He is hesitant even to call it a society, for that would suggest "a mutual regard and peaceful coexistence scarcely to be found." [9] Better to remain agnostic as to the degree of mutual adaptation and harmonization among systems. It is enough that we can find sufficient coherence within the world to justify rational action. We have no need to posit a unified system of which we have no actual knowledge and which on grounds of faith we have reason to doubt.

But now supposing we look at the world as an interaction of activity-systems too numerous to count, what light does this shed on the problem of evil? To begin with it gets us away from a narrow anthropocentricism which insists on seeing everything that happens in terms of its immediate benefit to human beings. Each activity-system has its own self-determining principle. The principle may be more or less limited, the system more or less flexible, yet without some such determining principle it would not even be a system. Activity-systems must be allowed their own identity; otherwise they are not systems in their own right but simply parts of some larger mechanism. Yet granted even a modicum of autonomy, conflict becomes inevitable. One system's interests will invariably conflict with those of another. Animals will eat plants if they do not eat other animals. Plants in their turn will compete with one another for available soil, sunlight and water. Even below the level of life there is conflict, upheaval and change. The forces that make up the world at whatever level we choose to consider them are in constant interaction--with the balance of power ever shifting. Depending upon the perspective taken, the conquest of one of these systems by another will be seen either as an evil inflicted on one by the other or as a necessary phase in the growth and development of one at the expense of the other.

If we try to detach ourselves from the vantage point of a particular system and look at the total interaction of systems, what we see is an extraordinary interdependence. For one system to prevail to the exclusion of all others would upset the balance and could jeopardize the whole. It could, as we have come to see, precipitate an "ecological crisis." The point, however, is the relativity of evil. In a world of interacting systems, each has its own particular claim; no one system has an exclusive claim. The good of one will necessarily conflict with the good of another. So unless all systems are to lose their distinct iden- tities and become means to a larger end, there will be conflict and with it loss as well as gain. That is the kind of world it is.

Perhaps we would prefer that it were not this sort of world--that there were not the mutual interference of systems that we observe. Yet it is doubtful whether we can conceive of any other. Farrer contends that we cannot think away this feature of the world without depriving it of its physicality, for what we mean by the physical world is "rudimentary inter- active energies." [10] It is fantastic to suppose that these elemen- tal forces should take into account one another's good, yet how else could they be harmonized without ceasing to be in any meaningful sense entities in their own right? Besides would we want to see the world so de-vitalized as to be utterly devoid of conflict? Gone, in Farrer's eloquent words, would be "that enormous vitality of force, which makes every system or concen- tration of energy to radiate over the whole field of space, every living kind to propagate without restraint, and, in a word, every physical creature to absolutize itself, so far as in it lies, and to be the whole world, if it can." That it cannot is, of course, because of the interference of other systems "equally reckless in their own vitality." [11] Eliminate the interference and you lose the drama of existence, as well as the viability of individual existences.

Another way of approaching the question would be to ask what are the conditions necessary for personal agency as we know it. What sort of world does our own exercise of agency presuppose? Is it not precisely the sort of world we have been speaking of, one in which relatively independent agencies oper- ating according to fixed principles interact with one another? Suppose, for instance, we were to think away the rigidity and regularity of elemental forces at the lower levels of existence. What we would have left would not be a world in which there was greater scope for intentional action, but less. Farrer compares it to the situation depicted in Lewis Carroll's **Alice in Wonderland** in which the characters attempt to play croquet with flamingos for mallets and hedgehogs for balls. Far from enhancing the agency of the participants, the relative freedom exhibited by the "equipment" utterly frustrates their efforts. The animals may succeed in not interfering with one another, but in the process the human agents are rendered incapable of achieving any indirect effects. [12] Without the ability to achieve indirect effects by incorporating within one's own action the set behavior of other agents, human agency would be severely curtailed--if not abolished. Having a world of the sort we have is a necessary condition for being the sort of agents we are.

Suppose, however, we were to forego physical existence and opt for a world that was purely spiritual. What sort of existence would that be? Not only would there be nothing on which to act or through which to act besides other spirits--a dubious prospect at best--but there would be the difficulty of distinguishing our own agency from God's. What would there be to prevent the human agent from simply being absorbed into the agency of God? In one of his most original insights, Farrer maintains that the physicality of the world is necessary to give independence to the human agent. The physical world stands as a kind of screen between finite spirits and God, providing them with a space within which to be themselves. If the first requirement of a created world is to be other than God, what better way of insuring that otherness than by rooting spiritual being in physical being through a gradual buildup of systems of limited capacity for action, systems that repetitively do whatever it is they do, and whose interaction is not the direct expression of a personalized will, but the gradual unfolding of a generalized will.

At this point we may note something of an anthropocentric concern asserting itself. The world is such as to constitute a suitable habitat for humanity, an appropriate setting for the working out of the divine purpose for humankind. We began by looking at the world "ecologically," allowing to each constituent its own viewpoint and reason for being; we now find ourselves taking a more "teleological" stance, regarding the whole sphere of interacting systems from electrons on up as a necessary staging area for ultimate human fulfillment. That Farrer should have developed so ecological a viewpoint as he does is a valuable corrective to the anthropocentric bias that generally prevails within the Christian tradition. Yet he does so without simply discarding the teleological. As is his practice elsewhere, he balances the one motif off against the other, seeking in this way to suggest, if not actually describe, the true mystery of God's creation.

IV

This brings us to the final stage of our analysis: an overall assessment of Farrer's contributions to cosmology. There are four points I would like to make.

1. In the classic divide between Augustine and Aquinas, Farrer clearly takes his stand on the side of the great medieval theologian. He regards the world as having a certain integrity, even autonomy, in distinction from God. That is probably a necessary position to take in view of the massive assault of gratuitous evil upon modern consciousness. To ascribe the Holocaust--or even natural calamities such as flood, drought, earthquake or tidal wave--to the direct agency of God offends our religious sensibility. We cannot believe that the God who intends our good could directly intend such monstrous occurrences. It is far more reasonable to suppose that God intends creatures who intend for themselves--thus providing space for independent agency. This in turn requires that finite being be rooted somehow independently of infinite being. The world, as Farrer conceives it, provides such independent grounding for human existence.

2. In respect to the other great divide, that marked off by the Enlightenment, Farrer shows himself to be a thoroughly modern thinker. The world, as he understands it, is not a closed system. It is open to chance, to purposive change, to the new and unexpected. The world exhibits such consistency and continuity as to make meaningful choice possible, yet it is not so totally determined as to render that very choice illusory. It is, in other words, a suitable field for human action. And that is necessary if religion is to have a significant ethical component. An agent's world, such as Farrer has delineated, is a world in which responsible moral action is not only conceivable but theologically mandated.

3. The present situation in theology requires that we give more attention to cosmology than past liberal biases have permitted. Moreover, we must do so in a way that avoids the intense anthropocentricism characteristic of nearly all of Western Christianity. To the extent that Christian cosmology has provided legitimacy to a ruthless exploitation of the environment, it must be corrected. Farrer's more ecological approach, attending as it does to the interaction of discrete activity-systems at all levels of existence, offers such a corrective without going

to the opposite extreme of being dogmatically anti-teleological. The world as he conceives it is such as to support a higher purpose for humanity without subordinating everything to this end.

4. What about the Whiteheadians? Is there any reason to prefer his approach to theirs? Setting aside substantive differences, of which there are not a few, I should say that the primary reason for going with Farrer is that his cosmology is the less speculative of the two. It is derived largely from reflection upon practice. Since I tend to think of religion as a fundamentally practical affair--a form of life, a way of being in the world--I do not think that theology ought to depart very far from practical considerations. Farrer's cosmology meets this test. It sketches a picture of the world that is not inconsistent with what we know scientifically, yet which serves primarily to provide a meaningful context for responsible action and thence for a life of faith incorporating such action.

NOTES

1. That would include **Freedom of the Will** (New York: Scribner's, 1958), **Love Almighty and Ills Unlimited** (Garden City, N.Y.: Doubleday, 1961), **Saving Belief** (London: Hodder and Stoughton, 1964), **God Is Not Dead** (New York: Morehouse-Barlow, 1966), **Faith and Speculation** (New York: New York University Press, 1967).

2. See, for instance, the collection of essays edited by Nelson Pike, **God and Evil** (Englewood Cliffs, New Jersey: Prentice-Hall, 1964), especially excerpts from Hume's **Dialogues on Natural Religion** and essays by Mackie and McCloskey.

3. Farrer, **Love Almighty**, 34-46, 54-56.

4. Farrer, **Faith and Speculation**, 148.

5. Ibid., 150.

6. Compare the essay by Paul Minear in **The Theology of Rudolph Bultmann,** edited by Charles W. Kegley, (New York: Harper & Row, 1966) 78f.

7. Farrer, **Freedom of the Will**, 19.

8. Ibid., 150.

34

9. Farrer, **Love Almighty**, 49.

10. Ibid., 53.

11. Ibid., 50.

12. Farrer, **Freedom of the Will**, 177.

ORIGEN REDIVIVUS:
FARRER'S SCRIPTURAL DIVINITY

Charles C. Hefling, Jr.

And to put the matter plainly, . . . the principle
of all good is drawing together and reduction
from disordered multitudes to singleness.

ORIGEN, Homilies on Ezekiel, IX, I

ACCORDING TO one of the many recent books on theological prolegomena, "the rarest phenomenon in our necessarily
specialized age seems to be a contemporary constructive theologian who is also a historical and hermeneutical master of primary
Christian texts." [1] Austin Farrer is such a phenomenon. For
besides the philosophical series that begins with **Finite and Infinite**
and continues with **The Freedom of the Will** and **Faith and Speculation,** he published a number of equally remarkable biblical studies.
A Rebirth of Images: The Making of St. John's Apocalypse heads
this second list, which includes two books on the gospel of Mark
and a further study of the book of Revelation. It is perhaps natural
to suppose that these two are separate streams, running parallel
but never meeting. This paper aims to suggest the opposite: there
are not two Austin Farrers; his exegetical and philosophical works
are parts of a whole, flowing alike from a unified vision of what
Christian theism is.

The earliest and in many ways the best statement of this
reciprocal relationship is **The Glass of Vision.** It stands between
Finite and Infinite and **A Rebirth of Images** in more than chronological order, for its theme is "the form of divine truth in the
human mind," considered in relation to both scripture and metaphysics, which Farrer in the preface calls "equally my study"
(GV 1, ix). [2] And impressionistic and rhetorical though it may
be, **The Glass of Vision** makes it clear that the highly unorthodox
approach of Farrer's exegetical work belongs to a larger context,

35

and that in the end this context is nothing short of metaphysical. His "scriptural divinity," as he often calls it, will not be considered here as a contribution to New Testament criticism in the specialized sense; rather, it will be suggested that when the biblical studies are seen in the light of Farrer's philosophical theology, they appear less capricious and perhaps more significant than has sometimes been thought. For, on the whole, they have not been taken seriously. The title here is borrowed from a review of his **Study in St. Mark** that echoes many others by dismissing Farrer as "an Alexandrian of the first water, an Origen redivivus" who insists "on turning every word of the Bible into an allegory." "I suppose," the reviewer adds, "that there is very little the rest of us can do about it." [**3**]

The comparison with Origen may be more apt than was intended. The "first principles" on which Farrer, like Origen, speculated are effectually present--though for the most part invisible--throughout his interpretation of the New Testament, because it is finally the theological meaning of scripture that is his real concern. As it was for the Alexandrians, Farrer's exegesis is part of a larger project.

I

Farrer's extended biblical works are limited to the earliest gospel and the Christian apocalypse, each of which he regards as having inaugurated a new genre. For reasons that will appear later, it is the Marcan studies that will be the starting point here. Besides the two books, there are a number of articles and also an unfinished manuscript, "Materials on St. Mark." Only the introductory section has been published, but the remaining pages show that despite a good deal of revision over the years Farrer never abandoned his major hypothesis. **A Study in St. Mark** (1951) was his first attempt to argue it in detail, but the core of this proposal appears already in his first article, published in 1933.

This early essay, "A Return to New Testament Christological Categories," discusses the life of Jesus as the definitive segment of a divine "career" in space and time. Does it follow from this notion that every one of Jesus' acts has to be thought of as "the very thing God is doing and saying"? Taken individually, Farrer answers, they are not. Only generically do the many separate incidents comprised in the "event" of Jesus constitute the expression of God's act in finite terms. These incidents are necessary to the saving "career" of God, as matter is to form, since without some specific content that form could not be real. If a ministry of healing is part of the divine plan, for example, it does not matter whether this person or that one is healed. "But then the ministry of healing cannot be actual except in a number of particular instances. So the instances are, though not individually, yet generically relevant." On Farrer's argument it is "not only a ministry of healing, but such a ministry" that counts, "and this such can only be seen in examples" ("Categories" 315).

As the unfinished manuscript shows, Farrer was still convinced thirty-five years afterwards that this such, actualized in thirteen examples, is the key to the gospel of Mark. Far from being a naive and shapeless pastiche, the earliest gospel is on his reading a complex unity. The points of articulation in its first ten chapters, which comment on and prepare for the passion narrative that follows, are the episodes in which Jesus heals an individual man or woman or child. Taken generically, these thirteen healing stories are more than "a mere list; they are a series in which there is sense and rhythm" ("Materials" 12), linked by similarities of detail. These connections, "echoes" as Farrer calls them, can be illustrated by the last four episodes of the series:

X	a deaf-mute healed at Decapolis	Mark	7:31-37
XI	a blind man healed at Bethsaida	Mark	8:22-26
XII	the healing of a deaf-mute child	Mark	9:14-29
XIII	a blind beggar, Bartimaeus, healed on the way to Jerusalem	Mark	10:46-52

Farrer holds that these are not four items; they are a double pair. In the first place, he observes that the sequence of the last two repeats the sequence of the first two: "ears and eyes, ears and eyes; or rather ears-and-tongue, eyes; ears-and-tongue, eyes" (SMSM 25). The healings at Decapolis (X) and Bethsaida (XI) are paired, not only because of the natural association of ears (and speech) with eyes, but also because of three features common to both stories: the difficulty of the cure, Jesus' use of spittle, and his command of secrecy. The pairing of the second two, XII and XIII, is not so obvious. Both are crowd scenes, however, in contrast to the privacy emphasized in X and XI, so at least they are linked by their common difference from the previous pair. These three (perhaps four) parallels or "echoes" that draw the last four episodes into a pattern can be set out schematically as follows:

This pattern is only a fragment of Farrer's analysis of the Marcan "mosaic," an analysis which in its own way is just as densely packed and difficult to summarize as the argument of **Finite and Infinite**. The way he treats these four paragraphs can no more than hint at his approach to biblical interpretation, because it rests throughout on something that cannot be defined-- similarity, the repetition of a word, a name, a pictorial detail; repetition of unusual diction, sequence, or allusion. This "simplest of all poetic devices" generates an elaborate formal structure because, to anyone who "has travelled in that region of Jewish writing which forms the background of the New Testament, it becomes almost a routine principle, if he is losing his way, to stop and count" (SMSM 19). Applying this principle, Farrer argues that the skeleton of the gospel of Mark is arithmetical.

Not that the arithmetic is simple. Working backwards, the double pair diagrammed above is immediately preceded by the episode of the Syrophoenician woman, linked to the twelfth item of the series by three details: in both, a child is healed; their maladies are respectively a "spirit unclean" (Mark 7:25) and a "spirit unspeaking" (Mark 9:17); and in each case Jesus acts at the behest of a parent. In one glaring respect, however, the ninth healing is an intrusion. Jesus' first words to the Syrophoenician woman emphasize the anomaly: her daughter is the only non-Israelite in the whole series. The inclusion of this "extra" makes the healings a baker's dozen, twelve Israelites plus one Gentile, and on Farrer's analysis there are two further twelve-plus-one patterns woven onto this framework. Jesus also calls thirteen individuals, but one of them--Levi, called in just the same way as Peter and Andrew, James and John--disappears later, when the Twelve are listed. Through the twelve apostles, Jesus distributes twelve loaves, first seven and then five, in Mark's two narratives of miraculous feeding; immediately afterwards the thirteenth, "extra" loaf appears in the boat with the Twelve, just at the point where Jesus' speech about their incomprehension dwells on the arithmetic of loaves and leftovers.

What the gospel of Mark says about Jesus it says, in part, through a web of symbolism in which the themes of calling, feeding, and healing are elaborated and clarified by comparison and contrast and by Jesus' own commentary on what he does. Throughout these first ten chapters, the paragraphs are, as Farrer admits, strung together like beads. But they are strung with poetic art; "each bead is carved by the jeweller for the place it is to occupy in the row" (Study, 30). And this is only the first layer of his argument. The second is that the formal patterning of the earliest gospel is dynamic. The story moves towards a dénoûment. Jesus' acts of calling, feeding, and especially healing point beyond themselves towards the central act of the gospel, his resurrection.

Yet, paradoxically enough, Farrer defends the rather abrupt final episode, the terrified flight of the women from the tomb (Mark 16:8), as the original conclusion of the book. In some ways, his conclusions about the Marcan ending are the goal of his whole literary, structural, and symbolic analysis. The scene at the tomb, he writes, is "a final chord which draws together, echoes, and concludes the previous music" (Study 174). To continue this metaphor, however, the chord on which the gospel of Mark ends is unresolved. There is not a full cadence. Every sentence points towards the resurrection, but the focus on which the movement of the whole story converges is not a part of the story; "the poem ends with finality at the words 'for they were afraid'. The rest cannot be written" (GV 145). Every argument for a lost or intended episode beyond these words comes down to this: a Christian writer "could not" have left off without portraying appearances of the risen Jesus. Against this supposed impossibility, Farrer sets a different one. The resurrection "cannot" be written because of the difference, which the evangelist recognized, between what is truly supernatural and what is only marvelous; between Christ's rising, that is, and the miracles that precede it. That he was raised was the cardinal point of Christian preaching from the first. What the resurrection is cannot properly be described.

Neither can it remain a bare assertion, a that without a what. Therefore, on Farrer's reading, the gospel of Mark describes the resurrection improperly--indirectly and in advance. In this sense the whole book is about the "triumph of Christ," the complex unity of death and resurrection, for the events prior to the passion are narrated so as to function cumulatively and indicate the supernatural side of Jesus' natural death. By juxtaposing events or sayings and leaving their relationship unstated, the earliest gospel sets out a series of riddles, a "systematic enigma," a repeated "opportunity and stimulus to reason from analogy" (SMSM 7; Study 226, 276). This relationship is in fact one, but it is presented in many transitions: from water to spirit, wilderness to promised land, exorcism to raising up, prophecy to fulfilment, defeat of diabolical temptation to the preaching of the gospel (SMSM 202; Study 67f). It is also the relationship of the passion to what follows but "cannot be written." This last extrapolation too is left to the reader, who has been prepared in advance to make it by the cumulative analogies of the first ten chapters.

Here then is a first link between Farrer's scriptural divinity and his philosophical theology. Considered formally, as ways of thinking, the imagery of the gospel of Mark and the theistic argument of **Finite and Infinite** are the same. Both are exercises in what he calls analogical dialectic. **A Study in St. Mark** in fact invites the comparison:

The use of the many healing miracles is to exhibit the richness and diversity of the one saving act, much as the many creatures exhibit the multiform fecundity of the one creative power. Therefore the evangelist begins from multitude. But in order to apply multitude to unity he condenses it as he proceeds. The themes of the many miracles, concentrated at length into a single sign, point on through it into the heart of the reality signified, which is the passion and resurrection of Christ (Study 52, cf. GV 46, FI 60).

Because the resurrection, like God whose self-defining act it is, "cannot be reduced to any class of facts whatsoever" (EE 11), both Mark and theistic "proof" use comparisons dialectically to take the reader through the steps of thinking towards--not about--the divine. Both move in the direction of an unimaginable point by way of what can be thought about. Neither is a demonstration; both are "persuasions" that take a kind of leap at the final and decisive moment, where "if we want to proceed further than the last stage of refinement our analogy will bear, we can only do so by standing on the extreme tip of our tapering spit of analogical description, and pointing out to sea" (GV 70).

II

At the same time, Farrer insists that the story of Jesus is more than an imaginative, pre-philosophical natural theology. It is revelation. Here too the early "Christological Categories" article suggests the direction Farrer's thinking would later take. The category of a divine "career," God's relativizing of himself to the world, presupposes another. Prior to the religious notion of God as "one agent interacting with others" is the purely metaphysical notion of God as "common ground of all agents and actions" ("Categories" 308f). The distinction between nature and grace, natural reason and supernatural revelation, is one he maintains from the first page of **Finite and Infinite** on (cf. GV 1, RF 140). It is regrettable that he never takes up the question whether revelation is something that pertains to other traditions, confining himself to "revelation par excellence," the Christian revelation he believes in (GV 35, FS 86). But even when the proximate evidence is limited to the New Testament, there remain philosophical questions; how, for instance, these texts can be understood as revelation. Since the subject of their sentences must presumably be God, they must in the first place allow of being so construed (GV 110). The gospel of Mark, specifically, may be a poem about Jesus; it is not _ipso facto_ a revelation of God, even though its formal structure resembles rational theology's use of metaphysical analogies. In the second place, revelation has usually been understood not only as a content but also as an action--God's own, supernatural, self-disclosure. So even if Farrer's literary methods make it possible to rethink the evangelist's thoughts, "to become, as far as that is possible, St. Mark in the act of gospel-writing" (Study 9), it can still be asked how the evangelist's mental acts are related to God's action. The quasi-poetical movement of images that constitutes the Marcan manner need not, in other words, be inspiration in any other sense than other creative thoughts are said to be "inspired."

(1) That the gospel of Mark is a narrative _about_ God means for Farrer that it is about the Creator. The center around which this aspect of his interpretation revolves is one of the "master images" that control the meaning of lesser images: the image Son of man. The immediate source is the book of Daniel (as elaborated in intertestamental literature), but Farrer regards Son of man as an image that belongs to "natural" rather than "revealed" theology. It is one of the primordial images that express "man's own nature, his relation to his fellows, and his dependence upon the divine power," as **A Rebirth of Images** puts it (RI 13). For Daniel's Son of man imagery draws primarily on the first chapter of Genesis, and, therefore, on Farrer's interpretation portrays a new Adam. The sequence of events leading up to the Son of man's appearance on the clouds of heaven is a new creation-week. Since Genesis itself, with its imagery of divine creativity and human destiny, is for Farrer a kind of "natural theology," his proposal that the messianic Son of man image occupies a central place in the Marcan mosaic of Jesus amounts to a proposal that Adamic Christology is "the very root of scripture. For the whole dispensation of God springs from his creation of man" (Study 287).

The pattern of Jesus' person and work is a divine pattern, which focuses what was already known about the Creator's relation to human affairs (SMSM 11, 189, 196), but which also completes it:

> That God's mind towards his creatures is one of paternal love, is a truth almost of natural religion and was already a commonplace of Judaism. That God's paternal love takes action in the gift of the Kingdom through the death of the Son of Man, this is supernatural revelation (GV 43).

What Farrer finds the gospel of Mark driving at can be stated in a number of ways. In symbolic terms, the dimensionless point on which its story condenses in the Sunday of a new creation. Having fulfilled the destiny of Adam by dying, Christ inherits the dominion over all things for which man was created in the image of God. None of this is new; it is the recapitulation doctrine of Irenaeus (cf. IB 170-175). What is remarkable is Farrer's claim that it is already the unifying movement of the earliest gospel, together with its corollary--that Jesus of Nazareth took the myth of Adam on himself by taking the title Son of man.

Not that Mark spells all of this out. The evangelist's purpose was not so much to say something as to do something; to change readers as well as inform them. The anticipatory symbolism of the gospel is indicative in so far as it condenses on the resurrection; it is imperative as well, in the sense that further commentary on what Jesus did and was consists in what his people are to be and do (Study 185). This forward-looking and pragmatic aspect is stressed in some of Farrer's later articles, where he tends to substitute parable for the less dynamic image: "those who receive revelation are called upon to live the parable that is revealed" (IB 43). And when he undertakes in one of his sermons to summarize the gospel of Mark in three lines, they are:

> God gives you everything
> Give everything to God.
> You can't.

The next line, the one that "cannot be written," has to be lived. "Christ will make you able, for he has risen" (FOO 112). And so scriptural divinity passes over into the theology of morals, for what God does in Christ is, first, to provide human aspiration with its object, the will of God, in a human life; the second, to conform the efforts of finite aspiration to this object. In theological terms, the first is Incarnation; the second, grace. Both are manifestations of the same supernatural act by which created nature is enhanced or intensified but not removed.

Appearances of the risen Jesus might have rounded off the gospel of Mark, but they would still be included under the title announced in the first verse--the beginning of the joyful message of Jesus Christ. There is no end, short of the end of the world (Study 181). Where the conclusion of the gospel is portrayed is in the Apocalypse, which, as Farrer interprets it, uses the same library of images--Genesis and Daniel in particular-- in the same way--a series of condensing spirals--to point towards another dimensionless point, the Sabbath, the last day of the new week of creation (RI 71, 308ff; RSJ 29, 197).

Has Christianity a Revelation? is the title of a book that takes Farrer's views, among others, to task. Today a number of theologians are seriously asking whether Christianity even needs a revelation. [4] What Farrer's work suggests is that perhaps these are not quite the right questions. Christianity is a revelation--begun but not finished, specific in content but universal in implication, a "truth claim" but also a demand.

(2) Even if the subject of the Marcan parable is God, materially as well as formally, the second question posed earlier remains. In traditional terms it is the question of the inspiration of scripture. It is not enough for the New Testament to symbolize the perfection of nature by grace. It must also be an instance of it. The first element of Farrer's argument here has already been given. He rejects the "divine dictation" idea of inspiration along with propositions as the medium of revelation. The only appropriate, though always inadequate language for "mystery" in the sense he borrows from Gabriel Marcel is the language of image and parable. Further, precisely because of their "excess of meaning," it is not images themselves, but their interrelations that do the work of revealing (SMSM 11, RI 20). Religion itself is transformed, he writes, when the images that clothe it are transformed, "and their transformation will determine the character of the spirituality" (RI 14).

The Christian "revolution" itself was such a rebirth, and while writing was only part of the transformative process, the New Testament is the only direct evidence for what that process was like. If it is or conveys revelation; if revelation is indeed a supernatural act; and if it takes intelligible effect in images rather than propositions, then it follows that the inspiration of scripture must lie in the enablement of imagination. A further step leads to Farrer's philosophical theology. For if writing a book is to be thought of as a supernaturalized activity, it must in the first place be a free one, since for Farrer it is only in so far as the actions of human consciousness are voluntary that they allow of being enhanced and intensified.

Farrer's exegetical principles are consistent with--perhaps consequences of--his philosophical defense of voluntarism. **The Freedom of the Will** devotes a number of pages to showing that literary creativity as such cannot be accounted for deterministically. Farrer takes the hypothetical case of Shakespeare's decision to give Hamlet a certain speech. A determinist can only account for this imaginative act by driving a "sophistical wedge" between the phrases that occur to Shakespeare, and the arrangement he makes from them. But if this split is allowed, the determinist can dismiss the "occurring" as passive, since the poet had nothing to do with it; and can then reduce the admittedly active arranging to previously established policies of rhetoric, verse, or drama. Farrer denies the validity of the initial split. Shakespeare, he argues, does not wait for something to "occur"; he fumbles for what he wants. Alternatively, what occurs to him may alter the plot he had in mind or the character he had so far given to Hamlet. The elements and their form, content and pattern, the particular speech and the direction of the play--these are complementary rather than sequential. "The two things suggest, or call for, one another; who can say which comes first, if either does?" (FW 294).

Farrer is not making a case for utter caprice. He denies only the kind of linguistic determinism that leaves no place for changes, the transformations of language that imagination brings about. Here as elsewhere, freedom consists in the introduction of something new but not in creation ex nihilo. Similarly, in the biblical studies, Farrer objects strongly to both literary and psychological forms of the "archaeological" approach to exegesis. No doubt the seven-headed monster in Revelation 13 is a reworking of Daniel 7, as Daniel itself transforms Genesis. But to trace the image further back is pointless. Perhaps Daniel's sea monsters are also descended from a still older dragon, the Tiamat of Mesopotamian myth. Perhaps; but the author of the Apocalypse "did not know that he was rehashing Tiamat on a Christian dish." The point is what he did know--the Old Testament--because the Apocalypse's transposition of previous scripture is the key to the deliberate, imaginative, self-reflective process that produced it; the key, that is, to its meaning. For the same reason, Farrer protests still more against reducing the seven-headed monster to a phantasm cast up by a dragon-haunted subconscious (RSJ 54f).

Thinking for Farrer is a real, voluntary activity. In literary composition, the work it does is formal, the integration of smaller units into larger patterns of meaning. Thus his quarrel with the New Testament form-criticism of his day is at bottom the same as his philosophical quarrel with determinism. What the earliest evangelist does with his materials is more significant than where they came from. The similarities that make a double pair of the four episodes of healing discussed at the outset cannot be satisfactorily explained by positing a standard first-century recipe for the narration of miraculous cures. Similarly, that Jesus twice feeds a crowd with a few loaves is not reducible to two different versions of the same story, both of which happened to have been available to the author of Mark.

Farrer has been criticized for dragging the Holy Spirit into his exegesis. Yet it follows consistently from his conviction that the way scriptural inspiration is understood--and this includes denying it--largely decides how scripture is used, for scholarly as well as devotional purposes (GV 36). There is a certain amount of old-fashioned piety in his own scriptural divinity, but it is backed up by the rest of his work. "Belief in inspiration," he writes, "is a metaphysical belief; it is the belief that the Creator everywhere underlies the creature, with the added faith that at certain points he acts in, as, and through the creature's mind" (IB 53). There is no better summary of his philosophical theism than the one that appears in the commentary on the Revelation of St. John: "The control of our Creator is not an alien control, preventing us from being ourselves. The more he directs us, the more we are what we have it in us to be" (RSJ 26).

III

Most of the criticisms of Farrer's biblical studies are variations on a theme: his interpretations are, in the literal sense, fantastic. On theological or confessional grounds, for example, it can be objected that he overlooks the most important truth about the Christian message, its historical factuality. On scholarly and methodological grounds, it can be objected that his "literary" approach to the Bible is impossibly subjective. Farrer's own treatment of these very real issues will also serve to suggest what his position implies for the theology of Christian theism.

As compared with the Marcan studies, Farrer's work on the book of Revelation is perhaps more successful. Apocalyptic writing, after all, is not far from pure poetry. Nonetheless he consistently argues that there is "little reason to suppose that the religious imagination of our other New Testament authors worked any differently from the Seer's" (RSJ 4; cf. IB 52f). Where there is a difference, it is due to the constraint exercised on the evangelists' imaginations by the historical actuality on which they fit their imagery (RI 17). Farrer does not deny the importance of these events; one of his objections to Bultmann is that he dissolves the historic creed into a philosophical generality (KM 220ff). At the same time, however, events by themselves are dumb; "the martyrdom of a virtuous Rabbi and his miraculous return are not of themselves the redemption of the world" (GV 43). Interpretation is involved, and in the case of the New Testament, it is interpretation of a special kind. The point of Farrer's debate with Alan Richardson in **Faith and Speculation** is that a theological interpretation of the past, a Heilsgeschichte or "sacred history," is not just a history written from a special slant. The interpretive concepts of the theologian differ from those of the historian. Sacred history is about the acts of God, and God is not an agent in the univocal sense of being a member, along with men and women, of the class of agents. What the diagrammatic concepts of theology express, therefore, is something that no historian qua historian has any business talking about. History talks about the acts of God; theology talks about God's doing them.

And while Farrer thinks it a wise saying that "in Scripture there is not a line of theology" (GV 44), there is nevertheless interpretive patterning of events. In the gospel of Mark especially, the pattern can be put in one word: prefiguration. It is, Farrer insists, a historical form and not something else, though "it is unlikely that any historian would use it apart from theological belief. It belongs to history viewed as divine revelation" (Study 184). The healings as a series are prefigurations of the resurrection or, as Farrer often prefers to say, its _types_. It is simply not the case that typological interpretation in his sense replaces events with allegory that can get along quite well on its own. It is the case that the earliest evangelist cannot be forced to conform to modern standards of historical scholarship. The very form of his gospel narrative expresses a conviction that revelation is not simply what anybody says or does, even if it be Jesus himself.

The objection that Farrer does away with the historicity of the gospels can be maintained only if history, "what actually occurred," is a pure datum "prior to those necessary evils, reflection and communication" (FS 101). On this point, too, the scriptural divinity is of one piece with Farrer's philosophy of mind, specifically his rejection of the clean Cartesian separation of consciousness from matter. Cognition as he understands it is an interaction of energies. No doubt the human contribution to every such interaction is fallible, but that will not be corrected by digging for self-authenticating givens.

Even so, it can still be argued that Farrer has read imaginative patterning into the gospel of Mark rather than out of it. Certainly both his method and its results are out of line with the New Testament scholarship of his day--and of today, for that matter. As to his conclusions, it should be pointed out that Farrer never supposed that typological symbolism accounts for everything in the New Testament (IB 58). In some ways he is very conservative. He takes the Annunciation story in Luke, the Barabbas episode in Mark, and Jesus' authorship of the Lord's Prayer in Matthew all more or less at face value, even as he hints that all of these might have been invented by the evangelists in order to fill out a symbolic pattern (IB 107ff; SMSM 15, 170; Study 169, 202ff). While he argues convincingly that there are more typological allusions in the gospels than just the ones their authors call attention to, he also denies that the formula decuit ergo factum est, "it was fitting and so it was the fact," applies. Inspired imagination can select and arrange historical events; it cannot create them (IB 117, Study 289). Yet if anything it would seem that the conclusions to be drawn from Farrer's literary methods are more sweeping than the ones he draws himself; his student Michael Goulder, at any rate, has drawn them. [5]

As to Farrer's methods themselves, Eric Mascall has suggested that Farrer was something of a prophet, anticipating the approach known today as redaction-criticism. It is true that **St. Matthew and St. Mark** is almost entirely about the redaction--Farrer would say transformation--of an existing source, the gospel of Mark, by a later author. But this book, like his other biblical studies, shows his constant stress on the priority of a whole over its parts, narrative structure over "sources," Matthew's "vision of wholeness" as compared to Mark's (cf. "Loaves" 8). It is this emphasis that sets Farrer apart even from the redaction-critics. For they regard their task, by and large, as a supplement to text-, source-, and form-criticism, whereas for Farrer even so seemingly trivial a point as the way a particular sentence should be punctuated depends on grasping how the author in question characteristically thinks ("Examination" 78f). As Goulder has discussed in a recent article, the same premise leads Farrer one step further, to the quite heretical judgment that "Q" (the ready-made source that most scholars think accounts for similarities between the gospels of Matthew and Luke that cannot be traced back to Mark) can be dispensed with as an unnecessary hypothetical entity ("Q" 55, 85). [6] Only grant that Luke the evangelist was not a scissors-and-paste editor but an author in the fullest sense, and it is at least possible to argue that the gospel of Matthew was his only non-Marcan source.

Redaction-criticism only partially removes what Farrer takes to be the great fault of the form-critics--their "positive interest in incoherence." Closer to his own methods in this respect is what the Old Testament scholar Brevard Childs calls canonical criticism, his remedy for the "crisis in biblical theology." Childs argues that it is the final, canonical shape of the biblical books that must serve as the starting point for reversing the atomistic tendency of recent exegesis. His methods cannot be applied neat to the New Testament, but they raise some highly important questions in relation to Farrer's work. At the outset, a major decision faces the canonical critic. <u>Which</u> canon will define the investigation--Alexandrian or Palestinian, longer Daniel or shorter, the Roman Catholic Old Testament or the Protestant? Either way, taking the canon as the context of interpretation involves what is finally a theological judgment about the past, namely the history of setting the boundaries of scripture.

Farrer recognizes the analogous question raised by his own more literary methods. It has become a commonplace to point out the New Testament's "pluralism," especially the variety of ways it expresses the meaning of Jesus. By examining not just what the New Testament authors were saying but also what they were doing, Farrer arrives at a very different view. The New Testament cannot be used to authorize "multiple Christologies" today if even in the earliest gospel there is, as he holds, a drive towards unity, a gathering of many images and titles into an ordered whole. Mark is a kind of commentary, prompted by the question, "How are the many words and deeds of Jesus to be understood?" The gospel of Matthew is partly a commentary on that commentary, an answer to the question, "How is Mark to be understood?" When Christian writings had multiplied, the same kind of question continued to be asked, transposed into "How is scripture to be read?"

"Naturally the process of reflection upon the paradoxical complex of things the faith contained took time," Farrer writes, "and indeed I do not see any signs of its being completed" (Study 366). But if the process of reflection, which began with choosing, using, and combining images, continued as the choice, use, and combination of texts; and if the first stage is revelation--then what of succeeding stages? Farrer answers that the formation of a canon of Christian scripture is as much a part of revelation as any other. Near the end of his important essay on "Revelation" in **Faith and Logic**, he writes that "the Church believes that she has been inspired . . . to canonize what is required for the understanding of the revelatory events" ("Revelation" 107). He adds that a sentence beginning "the Church believes," whatever it may be, is not philosophy. Yet his suggestion that inspiration continues is altogether consistent with the philosophical discussion of revelation in **Faith and Speculation.** An ongoing revelation is what follows from his contention that the "point of punctuation" between divine self-disclosure and voluntary human response is a moveable point (FS 98f). When the prophet Isaiah saw the march of the Assyrian armies, a military fact was the datum; the response was prophecy. But for those who heard Isaiah's voice, the Lord had spoken and they were called to respond by their repentance. Once this whole episode had become part of the sacred story, the point of punctuation moves again, when and where there is a "willing of the will of God" that the story reveals.

One of Farrer's critics has countered that if the revealing work of God is extended in this way into the process of reflection, the result can only be to canonize "everything Apostles or Church Fathers, not to name lesser or later authorities, have said or written" (FS 101). This objection is only partly fair. It is true that neither Farrer's philosophical treatment of revelation, nor his study of the texts he believes to be the medium of revelation, lends support to the notion that after a certain point--the death of the last apostle is the usual one--the process ceases. It is also true that he thinks it suicidal for Christian theology to retreat from scriptural inspiration, just as it is for believers to disclaim present illumination in their believing. It does not follow, though, that every development in between is of equal importance or value. Farrer understands revelation as "the work of the mystical

Christ, who embraces both head and members"; on the next page he goes on to say that "[d]evelopment is development, and neither addition nor alteration. The first and decisive development is the work of the Apostolic age" (GV 41f). If "we are believing enough to accord validity to the revelation," revelation in Jesus Christ, "we must be tough enough to claim validity for the parable as well as the event"--the interpretation, in this case, of the New Testament writers (IB 45). There is no way to get around and "behind."

Theology can only move forward, and only if it constantly overhauls its reinterpretations "by the standard of Christian origins; and 'Christian origins' can only mean in practice the evidences we have for Christian origins; and they come down pretty nearly to the New Testament writings" (IB 158). It follows that the relatively recent emergence of historical scholarship, including New Testament criticism, can be regarded as the newest of the many criteria by which revelation has been sifted and refined. Yet there is no scholarship de novo. Everyone starts from assumptions of one sort or another, though the initial premises are often broken as inquiry proceeds. What has sometimes been taken as Farrer's hostility to historical examination of the New Testament is really his repudiation of one possible assumption, namely that "there was nothing supernatural about what happened in Galilee and Jerusalem round about the year 30, and nothing theologically surprising about the interpretation placed on the events by the chief participants in them" (Study 366).

His own assumptions are, perhaps, a little too obviously orthodox for many. This paper will have done its work if it has suggested that they are by no means unexamined assumptions. They inform and are informed by his philosophy--as well as by his prayer. "Scripture and metaphysics," equally his study, are no more separable than Farrer's scholarly work is from the Christian theism he preached.

NOTES

1. David Tracy, **Blessed Rage for Order** (New York: The Seabury Press, 1975) 240.

2. In addition to the abbreviations cited at the beginning of this volume, the following citations and abbreviations are used in this essay:

EE	"Introduction," 11-16 in **The Easter Enigma** by Michael C. Perry (London: Faber and Faber, 1959).
FOO	**A Faith of Our Own** (sermons). (New York: The World Publishing Co., 1960).
KM	"An English Appreciation," 212-223 in **Kerygma and Myth,** edited by H. W. Bartsch (London: SPCK, 1953).
"Categories"	"A return to New Testament Christological Categories," Theology 26 (1933) 304-318.
"Examination"	"An Examination of Mark XIII. 10," Journal of Theological Studies, n.s. 7 (1956) 75-79.
"Loaves"	"Loaves and Thousands," Journal of Theological Studies, n.s. 4 (1953) 1-14.
"Materials"	"Materials on St. Mark" (unfinished manuscript).
"Q"	"On Dispensing With Q," 55-88 in **Studies in the Gospels,** edited by D. E. Nineham (Oxford: Basil Blackwell, 1955).
"Typology"	"Important Hypotheses Considered. VIII. Typology," Expository Times 67 (1956) 228-231.
"Revelation"	"Revelation," 84-107 in **Faith and Logic,** edited by Basil G. Mitchell (London: George Allen & Unwin, 1957).

3. S. Vernon McCasland, review of **A Study in St. Mark** by Austin Farrer, Journal of Biblical Literature 72 (1953) 201f.

4. F. Gerald Downing, **Has Christianity a Revelation**? (London: SCM Press, 1964) 200, 253ff; Basil Mitchell and Maurice Wiles, "Does Christianity Need a Revelation?" Theology 83 (1980) 103-113.

5. Michael D. Goulder, **Type and History in Acts** (London: SCM Press, 1964) and **Midrash and Lection in Matthew** (London: SPCK, 1974).

6. Michael Goulder, "Farrer on Q," Theology 83 (l980) 190-195.

AUSTIN FARRER AND THE ANALOGY OF OTHER MINDS*

Charles Conti

Recent excavations on the Cartesian foundations of knowledge have confirmed the difficulty of reaching that bedrock from which our knowledge of things can be deduced. There is, in the estimation of one penitent foundationalist, no level 'below' which one can dig with ratiocinative tools more basic than the consciousness that conducts the enquiry. Neither do facts exist as brute or atomic particulars, physical artifacts. In asking "How or what do we know? it is naive to suppose either the pure deliverances of sense-data or the neutrality of the investigator. Conversely, "what things are" is layers thick with predilection. There are no physical "posits"--as Quine describes them--lying in a pristine state in the beds of experience, as yet uncorrupted by interpretative response: "a fancifully fancyless medium of unvarnished news." [1] Ontology has a personal as well as cultural basis, a conceptual bias.

This admission of theory-ladenness not only undermines the Cartesian methodology, it also affects the positivist ideal of finding an indubitable "core" of verifiable facts around which to construct the solid ediface of empiricist belief and, by implication, grounds for eliminating spurious metaphysical abstractions. It is now generally agreed, since Wittgenstein, that there are no epistemological "givens" in this primitive sense: no "objective" evidence compelling the belief in a real world or presuppositionless approach to the logic of other minds. Finding a "neutral" substrate of brute facts from which to infer the belief in objects and others was the product of radical reductionism, Ayer now admits; accord-

* I am indebted to Edward Henderson and F. Michael McLain for encouraging me to rethink the essential continuity between **Finite and Infinite** and **Faith and Speculation;** also to Wayne Proudfoot whose misrepresentation of the evolution of Farrer's thought, in **God and Self,** provided me with the stimulus of a rebuttal.

ingly, was abandoned for the more "architectonic" the theoretical features of language. In the house built by linguistic philosophers, sense-percepts and observation-reports lose their status as building-blocks of theory of knowledge. Physical paradigms--the touch, taste, see of sentient life--merely reflect ingrained prejudices of what reality must be like, an empiricist's Wonderland. There are, then, no evidential simples in the Cartesian sense, low-level fodder for high-level interpretation. Language plays an active part in the constitution of facts. Concepts determine content.

This denial of primitive data affects what I have to say about Austin Farrer in two ways. First, it suggests what is right or wrong with taking a "foundational" approach to religious belief: finding the evidence of faith. (Is belief in God its own evidence?-- or must one prove the existence of God prior to the belief? Fideists would affirm the former; rational theologians, the latter.) Founda-tionalism is also relevant in that the "more up-to-date" account Farrer gave of himself in **FS** (1967) came about precisely by reassessing work on Descartes done in **FI** (1943) and in a way that anticipated how recent philosophers emended the Cartesian epistemology. One thinks of Stuart Hampshire and P. F. Strawson. The former shifted the epistemological center from cogito to ago, evaluating thought in terms of intentional action, performed in a world-context; the latter re-examined the presuppositions of what it means to be a person, thereby resisting that dualism which would also isolate the cogito-consciousness from the world of its concern. Hampshire's book, **Thought and Action**, was pub-lished in 1960; Strawson's **Individuals**, the previous year. Farrer employed both tactics to similar effect; in **FI** and **FW**, the Gifford Lectures for 1957. Though written from a theological perspective, these books also aimed to broaden the effects of an austere positivistic empiricism; showing our author's work to have some-thing in common with these philosophers of action serves a dual purpose: setting his work in the larger context of recent linguistic philosophy, "placing" him philosophically and revealing his theo-logical method.

What, then, prompted the writing of **FS**? Was it merely restatement of the idiom and Aristotelian premises of his former book?--or was Farrer, like Wittgenstein, motivated by a new insight into the nature of philosophy and, by implication, rational theology? To decide this question is important in evaluating Far-rer's contribution to philosophical theology since it is not obvious why the author of **FS** seemingly denounced "cognitive theology" in that book when the path Descartes set him on in **FI** headed in that very direction; defining the ideal of philosophical theology and the goal of the book, in the Preface, as "a reflective cognitive activity appropriated to the knowledge of God from universal grounds." (xi). Was the "later" Farrer, in adopting "pragmatic theology", also moving towards a "no-foundations" approach to religious belief? We are to do the will of God, not cogitate on it. The purpose of this paper is to resist that conclusion; certainly in its bald form--foundationalism versus fideism. Any about-face on rational theology is apparent only; FS was written to strengthen the format of his early book rather than seriously alter or discard it. This is not to deny change, only to resist overstating it.

Farrer was, to be sure, constantly rethinking his position--he remarked to a friend that he wrote his major books twice--and there are subtle shifts of emphasis in his final work. However, FS must be set in the context of that early work, if only to avoid the imperception of one reviewer who described it as "a series of fireside chats with an avuncular companion of urbane wit and theological whimsy. Austin Farrer has written books of major importance in our time. This is not one of them . . . The main pity is that it was published as a book and so subjected to critical standards that can do it no kindness". [2]

To dispel this misconception--more widespread than it ought to be, even among his learned readership--I want to consider that argument central to the book, but the analogy of other minds; instructive not only because contrary to critics, it is critically informed, it also illustrates Farrer's unique ability to "bridge" the alien camps of philosophy and theology, divided this century as never before. Although he used this analogy to reassess the logic of theistic belief, loosening up the disjunction of "finite" and "infinite" in much the same way Wittgenstein discarded the conscious analogic inference to other minds, the shift from entailment-relations to what is presupposed in (credited to Hume) "natural belief" is also evident in FI, especially the central chapters, a book within a book, as one reviewer put it. This was further brought to fruition in FW, where Farrer specifically debunked that Cartesian dualism, consciousness versus body-predicates, responsible for creating the problem of other minds in the first place. Establishing this fact of continuity serves two functions at once. First, it demonstrates the error of discounting the "later" work as philosophically slight, since it incorporates and builds on the "early" work. Second, it shows Farrer thinking with integrity out of the past, his own and the rationalist tradition in which this aspect of his work was steeped. The result was a rare synthesis; combining traditional metaphysics--in a scholastic mode--with recent analytical insight in a daring and resourceful attempt to revise an argument for the existence of God.

In part I, I brush off foundations lying half-exposed in that early metaphysical treatise, showing why, in the Cartesian conjunction of finite and infinite, Farrer found a divine similitude: "made in the image of God". "Finite," he argued, implies the "crypto-apprehension" of Infinite Act since limitation points to a "transcending archetype" responsible for being in its lesser or finite mode. Closer to home, we are also made in the image of each other; and in Part II, I compare the belief in God with the logic of affirming other minds. Does this simplify theistic belief?--the "fact" of God presupposed in the practice of piety? Belief in God, like belief in our neighbors, is obviously appropriate if God exists, but can we trust him to exist? If not, even on Wittgensteinian fideist premises, the existence-question is relevant to a full statement of theistic belief since, apparently, dispositional belief requires an "object" of attachment, socially and/or theologically.

Given that conclusion, I digress now and again to compare Farrer's philosophy to non-foundationalists Alvin Plantinga and John Hick. [3]

I

Starting from the solipsist's premise of scepticism is self-defeating, we learn from Wittgenstein's argument against private language. This is not because we can draw no meaningful contrast between "public" and "private," allowing "privileged access" to our feeling-states, but because even the ability to refer to one's own sensations is bound over by such communal or positional concepts as are naturally inclined to carry the weight of the premises being denied. Thus, talk of certainty "here" as opposed to dubiety "there", self contra others, conjurs up a whole network of associations, weaves a virtual "web" of intersecting or overlapping doubts. In formulating the sceptical hypothesis, the solipsist--wittingly or otherwise--relies on such network of relational concepts as show personal identity more continuous with the world than its polar opposite; a continuity-thesis which naturally affects the logic of arguing "from our own case". Social interaction is the very form of personal awareness. Strawson writes:

> There is no sense in the idea of ascribing states of consciousness to oneself, or at all, unless the ascriber already knows how to ascribe at least some states of consciousness to others. So he cannot argue in general 'from his own case' to conclusions about how to do them; for unless he already knows how to do this, he has no conception of his own case, or any case, i.e. any subject of experience. [4]

"Already" establishes the logical conditions of predication, going beyond mere temporal contiguity or anteriority. In order, that is, to explain the ascriptive/descriptive functions of language, we must have already solved the related problems of identity and identification--how we recognize other beings as "like" ourselves, parcel out predicates, describe pain, etc.--and this can only be the case if there is a "case": a social category to which we lend our meaning as language-users and from which we have drawn the requisite criteria for identifying others. Otherwise put, selfhood establishes a principle of co-presence. "I am a person among others", Strawson writes. [5] Being cognate with others, the concept "I" functions as a "compound subject", linking self and others by the common bonds of language and providing just that principle of differentiation Hume needed to escape phenomenal egoism. "So the concept of a pure individual consciousness--the pure ego--is a concept that cannot exist." [6] There can be no principle of unity internal to the self apart from external comparability and social differentiation. The individual is logically "secondary" to the social construct "person".

Two corollaries follow from (or underwrite) this: (1) reflection on oneself is subsequent to awareness of others. (Children sometimes speak of themselves in the third person before acquiring the first person convention.) (2) Although we primarily speak to others, for their information, we sometimes talk to others to further self-understanding. (This may be dubbed "the Alice syndrome", "How do I know what I mean 'til I've said it.") Privatism is therefore strictly untenable.

One finds a similar communitarian strain running throughout Farrer's work as well.

> Mentality . . . is a social product. Thought is the interiorisation of dialogue. We should not think at all, were we not mutually aware. Speech is the standard case of mutual communication; but speech is merely a specialised form of intentional action directed at one's fellows, and the understanding of speech presupposes acknowledgement of other-personal activity as such. It is not possible to be a mind which neither accepts nor has accepted other-personal activity for what it is. [7]

This statement (virtually a précis of chapter 8 of **FW**) epitomizes the more linguistic treatment personal identity received in Farrer's later work. But the social dimension of language also played a part in the early work as well; chiefly as antidote to the solipsistic tendencies of Positivism. Even taking "bundles of sense-presented stuff" as the fundamental world-unit for reconstructing the doctrine of substance, Farrer nevertheless challenged the adequacy of interpreting reality by physical paradigms, pointing out that we personalize the "raw" stuff of what is presented in experience by constructing a "pseudo-genus" to include "self" and "others" in one epistemological continuum. (**FI** 65f). Nor was it pure constructionism, what Strawson has criticized "revisionary metaphysics". The revisionist errs, he suggests, in passing a piece of linguistic legislation as <u>apriorist</u> in its commitment to abstract entities as Positivism was committed to concrete or "verifiable" things. Farrer was equally hard on abstractionism.

> We grow up in a field where individual lives are in mutual relation, each functioning in a way that will maintain it in the face of others or at their expense, unless the laugh happens to be with the others. Our conscious experiences find themselves framed from the start by this system; the organism or quasi-organism is from the start the natural unit of our thought, and not those sense-elements with which a sophisticated analysis first makes us acquainted. (**FI** 67)

Calling sense-datum philosophy "sophisticated" is, of course, irony. Interference-capability (or co-operative effect)--not the deliverances of <u>sense</u>--conveys the "being" or doing of others; consequently, our sense of what is real or not takes its cue from the mutual impingement of interactive <u>agents</u>. This interactionist-epistemology stands in stark contrast to those "blessed givens" much beloved of English empiricism and explains why Farrer, like Hampshire, took exception to those passive theories of perception descending from Locke, Berkeley and Hume, crediting touch, not sight, with the basic sentient capacity. [8] Interaction thus laid the groundwork for a "religious" epistemology in **FS:** "a god about whom we have something to do" (as Farrer paraphrased the author of the Hebrews). But this empirical mandate grew directly out of the epistemological portions of **FI.** [9] In chapter 20 Farrer argued that interference and "disturbance-effect" generate our fundamental sense of "thinghood"--"the immediate experience of being up against that with which we interact in some manner on a level and which must thus be known as to some degree <u>in pari materia</u> with our own activity and being." This Latin tag which makes the point that "mind" is a logical extension of world and "world" an ontological construction of mind--subject and object, logically co-terminous--appears in all Farrer's major philosophical books and should have warned Proudfoot against reading, worse presenting, Farrer as a metaphysical "individualist": as guilty of constructing a world-view that betrays a basic <u>discon</u>tinuity between self and others. [10] We are aware, and <u>only</u> are aware (Farrer maintained) in relation. "For we are social beings, and in a thousand other ways dependent on what is outside us for the data of our proper and indeed our highest activity." (**FI** 58).

Although the context in which this passage appears is primarily theological--Farrer is speculating on whether there is any basis for conceiving God on the analogue of "society", as a "trinity" of relationships, and concludes there is, provided such characteristic features of life-in-society as "accidental collocation" and "mutual externality" are not allowed to mar the "divine self-sufficiency"--what he has to say about interaction as fundamental to persons is consistent with that stand he took in the central chapters of the book against Hume's passive, piece-meal and "atomistic" analysis. In light of the charge of metaphysical solipsism--what Proudfoot calls "theological individualism"--a digression is perhaps in order.

The self is, as Hume would allow, primarily aware of itself in relation to things--"a bundle of concernments with that outside world" (FI 225)--but the self is also aware that this awareness is itself, not as a pure concentrate of activity (man is what he does, no more) but as the "being" responsible for that activity. The unity of the self is thus "best seen when the self is opposed to external things, not to its own constituents." (FI 229). This much to Hume. However, what the "unified self" expresses "is not as aspect of the self, but the self expressed in all its aspects." (FI 221). And this comes closer to the transcendent subject school of Kant. Between Hume's causal-sequence view and Kant's "self-in-itself" Farrer proposed a via media using the logic of intentionality. Consciousness is "placed" by our acts of intending apart from which it would be neither conscious nor an "act"; but it is a placement à propos the real world. "Always [in analyzing intentional action] there appears an agent, something he is concerned with, and the act in which he deals with this thing." (FI 225). Consciousness is thus only possible in the interplay "between awareness of facts and effective reaction to them." (FI 235).

What about the standard Cartesian picture that persons operate an intentional headquarters from which acts are decreed and projects mandated? We shall always be baffled, if we look "inside" the self for our fundamental unity, Farrer warned. By stressing "unitary selfhood", we cannot mean an unawareness of distinctions as would result from taking an interior view of will-activity. Our awareness derives essentially from "an act of mind which opposes its own self to another." (FI 222). As such, the principle of personal identity is social differentiation. "We do experience interaction, because as conscious agents we have it with ourselves." (FI 245).

Here Farrer is quite close to Strawson. "When I experience myself coming into action against another self, substantial unity is something I am aware of." (FI 221). It will not do, then, to regard the self as socially discrete. Nor is consciousness a mere epiphenomenon of activity. For the mind is able to rise above the piecemeal manner of its operations and "intuit the <u>unum</u>". (**FI** 220). There is, then, a "real connexion" between what we <u>are</u> and what we do. It follows that self-understanding is not as Hume portrayed it, a relative unity held together by the inductive "glue" of fleeting, momentary perceptions. Nor does personal identity depend on retaining a faithful memory-image of ourself. Given that the mind views its proceedings in the world simultaneously as actor and monitor-self, it directly participates in the action it intends; in consequence, the self knows itself immediately, in the mediacy of will-activity. The unity of the self is not, therefore, an arbitrary feature of conscious life, "but that which has these." (**FI** 229).

In talking like this Farrer admitted the mind's "slight tendency . . . to hypostatize." (**FI** 222). Nevertheless he raised "the ghost" of a "residual" or "transcendent self" in **FI** (as if anticipating Ryle's **The Concept of Mind**) to frighten off behaviorists; those who would take a "pure onlooker" or facade-oriented approach to personal identity. Behaviorism errs in effectively reducing the role of the agent in <u>choosing</u> his course of action to the vanishing-point.

> Hence the . . . salutary illusion . . . when we look within the self--we are convinced that something essential has been omitted, the very thing indeed, and so we find ourselves assuming a transcendent unit, the self in itself, the pure subject, unanalyzable and related externally to the data which we have been industriously analyzing. Empiricists then complain that the self is nothing but the ghost of the total empirical self viewed externally and taken in the lump; and they are right--(with a reservation of the sense of the word "externally"). But their inference is wrong. They say: "We analyze the self, and you admit the analysis; you only save the self from disintegration by restating the still unanalyzed datum as a metaphysical <u>Unding</u> transcending the analysis. (**FI** 221; cf. 223, 224).

If the behaviorist draws the wrong conclusion from the "illusion" of transcendence--denying, in effect, the efficacy of will-activity-- what is the <u>right</u> inference? The illusion of transcendence is indeed an illusion, Farrer admitted; but the appeal from the "many" sides of sensation to the "one" unifying and integratory concept of intentionality is "right and necessary". Why?--because a phenomenal account of will-activity omits precisely that intellectual or spiritual "bond", <u>das geistige Band</u>, which, when we are <u>aware</u> of our activity, acts as overseer. <u>A fortiori</u>, intentions do not precede action accidentally--merely by Humean coincidence, according to a phenomenal rule-of-thumb; but are "ingre-dient" in the action. Our activity "is something positive in itself, even though it never to our knowledge exists by itself." (FI 241). We are, so to speak, inside ourself as "author" of our activity (Farrer's metaphor), not merely the Humean-appointed executor of that property-estate taken by consciousness unwittingly; an authorship which is anxious to transmit its causality in the world with a view towards calculated means or anticipated effects. (It was his denial of the will as reflective under-laborer that allowed Hume the splendid irony that he could never catch himself without a perception or distill from it the pure ego substance.) The self only knows itself dynamically, Farrer countered; in "giving rise to events." (FI 107). Consciousness thus realizes itself teleo-logically rather than by rote or random sequence; e.g. Hume's Kaleidoscopic sensatism. As such, the self stands in a "metaphysi-cal" relation to itself: it can abstract from its immediate situation in order to monitor and project its activity. In philosophers this love of abstraction has been turned into a profession, viewing themselves "as from the vantage-point of a fly on the ceiling" (recalling a similar point made by Wittgenstein). But we do not abstract for the sake of abstraction; we ruminate with a view towards action. Therefore, to "metaphysicalize" philosophers, "catch them in the posture of vigorous action (since philosophers, off duty, are agents too) and get them to introspect before they know they have introspected; before, that is, they have time to retire to their fly-pitch on the ceiling." (FI 109). Ask them, in effect, what "animates" or motivates their decision-making; and what they will conclude, if they give due consideration to the morally deliberative nature of their choices, is that value-judgments and dispositional attachments are built-into the very capacity to act.

The move to theology was a short step away. As intentional agents, we enjoy the right of self-determination; being uniquely "placed" to plan and execute actions. However, we find that the will "paradoxically qualifies" its autonomy by "patterning" itself after acts and values other than those defined by self-interests. [11] Thus in seeking "the object of right appetition," finite agents (a) give the lie to ethical utilitarianism, being "after the good"; (b) pursue an ethical ideal which carries them to the brink of theology. "Ideals are either made by men, or else they are evoked by God." Since we cannot believe our will deserves measureless respect, the ideal "must be proposed to us by God." (FI 298).

So FI leavened "the lump" of an "empirical self" with just enough "transcendental ego" to dutify action, thereby resisting Humean "piecemeal" phenomenalism, while at the same time introducing, in the form of an enlightened social conscience, a theological conclusion to the analysis of will-activity. The will "is an implicit theologian," Farrer wrote. (FI 51). Although self-originative, it acts under theological constraints. To the extent that the will denies itself the right of self-determination-- although clearly it is entitled to such by virtue of its causal capacity--it gives way to the "cosmological idea," creature as defined by a Creator. We sense our derivativeness, "caused" to be by another; intuiting sanctions transcendental in origin and universal in scope. "Are we not here experiencing God's ordaining in the actual happening?" Farrer asked; in the homage the divine will extracts from its finite counterpart; in the unconditionality of ethical obligation? (RF 73).

Mutuality is thus both a function of community and an aid for conceiving God. On the one hand, it mirrors the finite/infinite relation; extending the idea of a "creation." We are to treat our neighbor as "a piece of divine handiwork in the making," not run roughshod over this creatureliness. On the other hand, it establishes the fact; informing us that we are creatures of a creator. Persons are not merely "co-existent" with a world of others. Important as mutuality is to personal identity, they regard themselves as theologically "composite" as well. (FI 262). Finite agents act as though the maxim of their behavior had been willed for them by a universal law-giver, hence betray the belief that they have been made in the image "of a high and finer perfection"--the will of an Ordainer-God.

Thus, in a single stroke, Farrer thought he had provided the evidence of theistic belief, in the nature of an absolute categorical demand, as well as the basis for life-in-society: "claimingness" sanctifying human responses. Moral regard flows from the giver of every good and perfect gift--the origin of life itself. One might call it communitarian theology; though Farrer preferred the label "cosmic personalism." To the extent that we use the human model to think theistically, co-extensiveness provides just that intelligible basis for conceiving God's involvement with men. We love him because He first loved us and made us in the image of an extended concern: our neighbor's good. Reading it in the reverse order (the only avenue of reasoning open to the creature) the "measureless respect" owed our neighbor alerts us to the essentially commissioned nature of things; as derivative from a Supreme Good. Thus FI used the scholastic distinction between the ordo cognoscendi, the order of knowing, and ordo essendi, the essential order of things, to construct a cosmological argument, using moral sensibility as the prod.

Finding an idea of God appropriate to our self-understanding as social beings which functions as a paradigm or model for thinking theistically, is what Proudfoot finds lacking in Farrer. One wonders how he missed it. It is central to the dialectic constructed in (what Farrer described in FS) "the best part" of his old book. (Here endeth the digression.)

Interaction carried other "social" implications for personal identity in **FI**. In intentional activity, consciousness touches the nerve of its own immediacy: becomes self-aware. Not in the act of consciousness _per se_: consciousness _is_ consciousness _of_. (With this much of Sartre's philosophy Farrer would agree.) Apart from the _activity_ of the person, consciousness would be "analogous to mirror phenomena"--narcissized by its powers of observation; an epistemological error Farrer avoided by substituting _esse est operari_--to be is to act or interact--for a passive Berkleian _esse est percipi_.

By aligning consciousness with activity, and activity with effective or contingent interaction, Farrer extended the Cartesian boundaries of selfhood _necessarily_ to include the context of a world. The self is an "unrealisable abstraction," he wrote in **FS**, if cordoned-off from the world of its concern. **FI** had something similar to say. The relation between "self" and "world" is not only an "if/then" contingent mingling. Mind is logically co-terminous with its world-surround. "The self is not easily intelligible without supposing things," he suggested. (**FI** 230). Even the simple act of walking "is relative to the ground over which one moves" and, therefore, presupposes knowledge of _where_ one is in order to express _who_ one is. So **FI** aligned consciousness with "movements in a field of space . . . which make it the sort of field for movement which it is. It is primarily, _his_ field, the field of action, and it is the _extent_ of his action that determines the extent of his field." (**FI** 233; italics added). Intentionality and extensionality thus combine to make any act what it is. Intentionality is the appropriation of an extended state of affairs; extensionality marks the limitations of "my world"; delimiting what is conceivable, according to Wittgenstein. The person _qua_ agent "is not swimming in a perfectly featureless medium; he is walking the earth among all sorts of obstacles." We find out what things are by running our will up against them; we discover where our limitations lie by trying to claim a world-space. "Hence the monstrous unnaturalness of Cartesianism, which confronted many selves with one extended substance, thereby overthrowing the nature of the substance it asserted" (**FI** 68)--which is, _by definition_, socially interactive and contextually aware.

The cogency of the "cogito" argument is not, therefore, that the capacity to doubt proves the (reflective) "I" exists (nor, for that matter, that introspection is the "privileged" case of what it means to be an existent), but that the person who (even only) _thinks_ his doubt could have no sense of self-identity _but_ for the fact of occupying a world of impinging objects which define him in relation to things, providing him with a framework for formulating or rejecting that doubt. More simply, the "I" represents a conceptual as well as existential starting-point. Thus the certainty Descartes overlooked (and where the foundational model admittedly goes wrong) is that the sceptical question "Does anything exist besides myself?" is put in a form of language which presupposes the existence of things: nouns to designate objects; verbs to announce what we intend to do about them-- whether to honor or malign; in scepticism or in health. Language not only courts ontology; it is isomorphic with it: word and world in one "compendious" embrace, as J. L. Austin put it. There are, then, logical grounds for refuting solipsism implicit in language. Because it cannot be formulated except in terms of common concepts, it is impossible to put forward any theory about the nature of reality which does not automatically, as a matter of logical necessity, employ an alphabet of objects and others. A fortiori, the person who denies others contradicts himself; for that denial is a social act, the very intelligibility of which depends on the premises being denied--viz., that we live in a world we share with others and have the means, language, of putatively describing (for the benefit of others) or, if solipsis- tically inclined, of incoherently denying (stultifying even ourselves). For any denial à propos language merely confirms the positive side of its own negation. We can only extract (i.e. philosophically abstract) ourselves from our social situation by performing a linguistic act juxtaposing "the self" with "the self's opposite number"--mutual partners in the ontological dance as Farrer paired them; hence the epistemological significance of the "thing/ self" genus mentioned earlier on.

This explains why, in all three major philosophical essays Farrer fashioned a "metaphysic" out of concepts of action and interaction. For when the self is not taken in solipsistic isolation (as Proudfoot misreads Farrer), but is set against a backdrop of others--in relation to a "world" of finite, interactive selves--the prospects for drawing a cosmological conclusion are considerably enhanced.

> /M/en will more and more observe that the proximate determinates of those factors in their lives which they cannot determine for them- selves are other finite agents with whom they share the world. At the same time they will be coming to see that none of these other agents is more self-determining than they themselves are, and most of them vastly less so; and the undetermined Determinator, the Sovereign Will and ultimate Power, is acknowledged to stand behind or above the whole series of finite determi- nants and determinates. (FS 123; cf. 168-169).

Although Farrer recognized "the leap" (even called it that) from social indeterminacy to Divine Determinator, he thought he had justified it by arguing that the will "demands" of us one metaphysic rather than another. We have, in effect, a preferable way of regarding ourself; imposed by conscience. "Precisely at this point at which we are able to make the experiment of playing at being God Almighty, and decreeing what we choose, we find that we cannot, but are under mysterious ordinances." (RF 44). Thus by showing the will in transcendental bondage, analogous to Kant's categorical imperative, Farrer thought he had located that point where divine causality makes its impact felt in finite effect; hence justification for the theological interpretation "begotten," not self-made. Finites live out a sense of appointment, seek a transcendent ground for moral aspiration.

But in that it claimed to be motivated by a quest after perfection--"the proper perfection of its type," as Farrer incorporated the Aristotelian idiom (FI 254)--the will seemed overly keen to hurl itself across that ontological divide separating finite from infinite in a desperate attempt to establish a bridgehead on the dark shore of our knowledge of God. The "nerve" of the argument, Farrer wrote, "really lies in the indemonstrable implicit knowledge that there is a Being in whom the ideal and actual essences are identical." (FI 298). And such a being would be God: "who is all the good He sees, and sees all the good He is" [12]; "standard of what one might expect being simple to be." [13]

Eventually Farrer presaged a more natural metaphysic in will-activity. In the revised Preface to the second edition of FI (unchanged apart from these few paragraphs) he restated a theory of "being" on linguistic premises, reminiscent of the position Wittgenstein took in the Investigations.

> Speech is the very form of our linguistic activity, and linguistic activity is but a specialised type of intentional action in general; which, as it were, attains to explicitness in the spoken mode . . . /B/ut speech is human being, and uniquely revelatory of the rest of it. And as I trust I was able to show in this book, we both do and must think of the being of all things through an extension of our self-understanding. (FI ix-x).

This articulates that two-fold truth of action-theory which, in FI, Farrer saw as the proper culmination of Cartesian voluntarism and as marking the demise of the subject/object distinction (what philosophers now refer to as a "bi-polar" relationship [14]). Ironically, it was Descartes' withdrawal of the vital kingdom of consciousness interior to the self--to protect against the inroads of a mechanistic, deterministic science--that set up the bifurcation in the first place. Commensurability is, however, just as much a fact of mind as it is of physical interaction, body mechanics.

Apart, that is, from the experience of being "bound over" by objects external to us, we have no capacity to be an agent, because we forfeit weighing results. "Weighing results" is shorthand for "an agent-assessing-activity in light of its distributive effect in the world." This limits the divisibility of body and mind, reunites person and world. Just as one cannot deny the capacity to act without indirectly owning up to it--because it takes a speech-act to discharge oneself of responsibility--neither can one deny the world as arena for self-expression without bankrupting the idea of an act as an accomplishment. For will marks the capacity to act which, when taken in conjunction with an actual impinging world, reinforces the desire to act. Actions are, therefore, commensurate with the world of their mutual affection; point to and away from the person as actor/agent and towards the world as outlet and stage.

The same epistemology was in force in chapter 20 of **FI**, but in the Gifford Lectures, Farrer realized that the two-sided nature of the knowing-act becomes clearer in language--in any statement of intention--than talk of the "pseudo-genus" of "thinghood" stretched to include the differentia of self and others "immediately known." (**FI** 245). In intentional action, the agent is performing his explanation; an explanation which, when offered in advance announces the likely outcome of any act. It is not only that stated intentions are the paradigm of personal meaning--"I mean to do such-and-such" informing us what the person had in mind--but that, since intentions are designed to be performed in the amphitheater of a world, they also function as object-designators as well: a personal testimony to what we think we are doing. (Hence the appeal of autobiography, the "inside story," publicly revealed.) There is, then, an ontological commentary implicit in will-activity, made explicit by a statement of intention. Consequently one doesn't have to superimpose a metaphysical interpretation of will--as did **FI**, "appropriating a pattern laid up in heaven" to sew a more noble garment for our actions--it is there to begin with: in the agent's experience of world-conditionedness, in the "causal texture" of will. The will evolves pari passu with things, Farrer wrote in "Causes"; [15] meaning with equal pace, therefore, simultaneously. This too was implicit in the voluntarist metaphysic of **FI**. But there, Farrer compromised interaction-epistemology with talk of autonomous beings, or "substance-selves," ostensibly complete in themselves, yet tangibly lured in the direction of the "supreme archetype" of their own causal capacity--a pure or Perfect Will, synonym for God. In later work Farrer discarded the reified extrapolation of a scale of substance--from partial to "pure" being; using action-concepts to determine the nature of what is real: the idea of God as revealed in his effects. This led him away from the Aristotelian luminary of a self-motivated Mover to an involved Deity; an idea of God as suited to the practice of religion as to its philosophical defence, bringing Thomas's "third way" in line with the philosophy of action: the logic of grace as creative or contingent interaction.

Interactionist epistemology thus led the way into theology in the later work, whereas the early work subjugated it to traditional theism. As he admitted in a letter to Edward Henderson, FI used the doctrine of substance to prop up "the only theology worth holding" [16]--God as Absolute Being, the supreme form of Autonomous Substance, whose existence is synonymous with his essence: in short, a Necessary Being. FS took Aristotle's logico-metaphysics to task; substituting a "linguistic" philosophy. "The verb defines the noun, the action reveals the agent." (FS 144). God's voluntary action "is a synonym for God Himself; for what is a person but his voluntary action?" (FS 57).

By the time he could write this in the Deems Lectures, an empiricism of language had overhauled substance-talk. The corrective to "chasing wild metaphysical geese" (he admitted in FW), set in flight by commissioning an Aristotelian telos to fly close enough to a Platonic heaven in order to "catch a glimpse of the Divine Being out of the corner of the mind's eye"; [17] moreover to "read our true calling out of the pages of the divine mind" (FI 253) is "to be found in responsibility towards an object of supreme respect, our neighbour's being, and our own." [18] To be sure, FI prompted a similar form of moral theism--"the creation, preservation or enhancement of being, whether one's own or another's." [19] But, in the Gifford Lectures, Farrer disassociated moral aspirations from that "quest after perfection," which seeks the "imitation of Deity as far as our nature permits," being in danger of succumbing to the Aristotelian stasis of a prescribed nature, raising the question whether the soul is endowed with goodness (naturaliter deicola) or crippled with corruption. The ideal of love is epitomized by an incarnation, he concluded in FW: hence arises from our compassionate involvement with others, "God in our neighbour, our neighbour in God," a sense of duty which establishes the practical bearing of theology and condemns the "self-making" ethic of Existentialism. [20]

Accordingly, the constraints freely imposed on the will "grounded" the high-flying Aristotelianism of FI, reinforcing the strain of realism already apparent in the epistemological sections of the book. "For the physical is known to us by the way it conditions our physical motion; and the divine will, which is God himself, is known to us in limiting or evoking our dutiful action, through all the persons with whom we have to do." (FW 309). FS was to do the same for theology completing the "purge" of "Aristotelian leaven" from the abstract idea of God as a self-subsistent Being. [21] We refer to things as or if we engage with them; we assess existential claimants in terms of the value-judgments or emotional responses they elicit from us. This allowed Farrer to convert the latent activist epistemology of **FI** into a full-blown voluntarist metaphysic in **FS**. In grace we sense the presence of an "Other" having all the hallmarks of that beneficial and creative dependence characteristic of our interaction in a world of others.

> I test environmental activities by seeing what I can do with them. I determine what I think of environing agents by deciding what to do about them. God is not to be placed in our environment; but mutatis mutandis, the two sides of our active assessment which relate us to our environment are also present in our knowledge of God. (**FS** 60).

Creative or contingent interaction thus provided the empirical stimulus for revising the argument a contingentia mundi. "To be contingent, you now suggest, is to be passively determined by agency other than one's own; and all contingents must ultimately be determined by the wholly free or self-determining agent, the sovereign will." (**FS** 120). Whether on philosophical or theological premises, the inventory of action still functions as metaphysical census-taker; in the "early" as well as "later" work. For it was this central contention of **FI**, that we can only know agents "in and as" activity, that Farrer drew upon in **FS** arguing the logic of grace implies "by some Other." (I shall have more to say about this in Part II). .

What conclusions do we draw from the inescapable sociality of the self?--the ontology implicit in a moral code, transcendentally conceived?

Although Farrer tended to overstate the theological interests of will-activity in **FI**, standing theology on the slim hope that people would recognize "goodliness" as close to "godliness" and "leap" from there to the divine goodness God is, he was right to see moral or ethical inclinations as constituting the practical refutation of solipsism. In that we qualify our activity on behalf of others and, if we are believers, in deference to a Divine Other, we show that the self regards itself not as something solipsistically simple in itself, but as co-habiting with the "must-solicitation" of others (using Farrer's telling phrase). "What I do with my life, what I do to my neighbors, comes under the claim of something I cannot but hold sacred, their humanity, my integrity." (**FW** 308). Moral responsibility thus falls under the aegis of a sacred trust. In judging our lives not ours alone to make, rather as made in the image of a transcending good--the gift of life shared with others, from the author of life itself--mutuality informs us of our derived status as subservient beings. "Humanity claims our succour," Farrer suggested, building a moral argument for the existence of God. This not only establishes a precedent for thinking theistically, it also creates a moral environment in which the fragile flower of humanity may flourish. We take, so to speak, an "overview" approach to morality; viewing our acts, whenever possible, from the god-like perspective of what is expected of us--"to do justly, and to love mercy, and to walk humbly with God." (Micah 6:8). There is, then, a natural theology in "the good that I would"; a sense of duty which, Farrer observed, finds itself "at home in a world where existence is the expression of the divine will." (FI 298).

Thus, **FI** paved the way for cosmological interpretation by expounding the theological interests of the moral will: "too rich" to be reduced to "naturalistic" description. The will carries with it "a whole bundle of associated meanings," contrary to Hume's "bundle" theory of the self. By subjugating our autonomy as free and rational agents to what believers have come to regard as the "will" of God, conscripted will defers to Unconditioned Will, showing the idea of a Supreme Being not far from us and as providing a concrete instance where the finite/infinite conjunction pertains. Where divine causality "passes over" into finite effect, duty sounds in reason's attentive ear an echo of the voice of God, commanding our presence for another. Thus by reversing the solipsistic sin of Adam, our mythical forebearer, imago Dei theology finds its focal point in the analogia relationis. "In the image of God created he them, male and female"--in a societas of two. There can be no more "social" or un-solipsistic way to conceive of God.

Mutuality is also indispensable to personal identity. To say that man is a social creature and that these "quasi-natural [i.e. moral] formations" arising from life-in-society are fundamental to self-understanding (as well as religious perception) is, Farrer concluded, "to say the same thing." (FI 188). Moral sensibility thus has an important part to play in making us aware of the divine presence in the world, further aiding our conception of God, a Supreme Good: "anthropological dialectic," Farrer called it; being designated to carry the mind from world to God by a rational or reasoned inference.

Compare and contrast Hick. "In each instance," he writes, speaking of our consciousness of the world and our consciousness of God, "a realm of putatively cognitive experience is taken to be veridical and is acted upon as such, even though its veridical character cannot be logically demonstrated." [22] Hick makes this move in deference to solipsism, which, though "theoretically possible," is judged by the majority of people to be sufficiently stultifying to be rejected. [23] From this practical lesson in ontology, he concludes that the belief in other minds has more of a psychological than logical basis. "It is a belief on the basis of which we live and the rejection of which, in favour of a serious adoption of the solipsist alternative, would so disorient our relation to other persons within a common environment that we should be accounted insane." [24]

This argument--that solipsism is logically possible, though psychologically untenable--is misplaced. Ideally Hick would argue that, although the veridicality of neither social nor religious belief can be logically demonstrated, "it is as rational for the religious man to treat his experience of God as veridical as it is for him and others to treat their experience of the physical world as veridical." [25] But if the denial of our physical and social environment is not perforce open in the way that Hick supposes, theistic belief cannot be regarded as practically more acceptable, logically upgraded, by virtue of downgrading the theoretical requirements of the belief in other minds. Conversely, if there are logical conditions related to the belief in other minds, either theistic belief must produce similar arguments, or acknowledge that the belief in God runs along other lines: requires a different sort of justification; e.g. a Kierkegaardian "leap of faith."

It is, for this reason, misleading of Hick to subsume the existence-question in the intensity of religious experience per se. "It seems," he writes, "that a sufficiently vivid religious experience would entitle a man to claim to know that God is real. Indeed if his sense of the divine presence is sufficiently powerful he can hardly fail to make this claim. He is sure that God exists." [26] In its pure form, Hick compares the intensity of religious experience with being in a physical environment, the "twenty-four carat" hallmark of faith. To the Biblical authors,

> God was known . . . as a dynamic will inter-
> acting with their own wills; a sheer given reality,
> as inescapably to be reckoned with as destructive
> storm and life-giving sunshine, or the hatred
> of their enemies and the friendship of their neigh-
> bours. They thought of God as an experienced
> reality, rather than an inferred entity. [27]

Rather than relieve ordinary believers of an awkward confrontation with foundational philosophers, Hick's "either/or" puts them at their mercy. How many believers can claim an experience of that degree of intensity?--or make it last a philosophical lifetime? Is it not more likely to be eclipsed by the starkness of everyday events? Basil Mitchell, shunning perceptual theism, maintains that it is possible to gain access to this realm of "subjective certitude" Hick posits at the core of religious epistemology, by piecing together an interpretative mosaic which, to the best of our ability, does justice to the facts as we tentatively or probingly discern them: inference abreast of experience rather than its adversary or antithesis. [28] Overstatement aside, Hick's position seems vulnerable to the following criticism. The "strong form" of the argument from compelling circumstances seems to suggest that one can disregard the existence-question altogether; the "weak form," that one can dismiss it provided one is in a suitably "pro-affective" attitude towards the object of religious worship. But if one is not in that state of mind, how does one get there?--presumably by having an experience "sufficiently powerful" (according to Hick) to allay sceptical doubt. But when is it "sufficient"? Here the believer is on the horns of a dilemma. For it follows from Hick's "experiential" premise that if he, the believer, is in any doubt about the existence-question, it must be discussed, since the mere presence of doubt would suggest that he lacks the requisite experience to dispel unbelief. And if the believer is not in the least troubled by doubt, how can he be sure that what he has subdued (in himself or as a result of the probing questions of others) is not a thin-lipped, overly critical scepticism but--can he allow it?--valuable philosophical curiosity? Is it not the case that the durability of faith is proportional to the difference between squelching and quelling doubt. If so, some doubt is needed to distinguish between that doubt which precludes faith and that which, in Luther's case, "made" the monk.

Hick's experience-model, for all its advertisement as implicit in the faith of the ordinary believer, shows itself disadvantaged precisely at this point--viz., in its inability to contend for a form of belief wherein most of us (I suspect) would recognize ourselves as tentatively feeling our way along corridors of doubt, urged on by half-beliefs and intuitive judgments; often believing against the facts or through the dark night of the soul?--surely as important to the psychology of belief as the "twenty-four carat" form of faith. In short, we stumble, and, therefore, cannot afford to walk philosophically unaided, after the truth. Nor do we (to change the metaphor, in keeping with Hick's use of Wittgenstein's "seeing-as" analogy) often bask in the sunlight of an unshadowed perceptual belief. By emptying out the reflective element in religious experience, Hick takes away the assurance of correctness; in consequence, he is left with no choice but to turn agnosticism into a virtue. "The theistic believer cannot explain how he knows the divine presence to be mediated through his human experience. He just finds himself interpreting his experience in this way." [29] But is it not the case that the rationality of religious belief is placed in jeopardy by likening faith to a cognitive mode analogous to sight when the reflective element in religious experience has so much more work to do? Farrer spoke of the "contextual" support of a theology of nature--"seemings of divine purpose" in the things that are made--which have the effect of "stretching" the mind in the direction of an Infinite Source and Sustainer: "evidence" in the weak sense that the believer's experience of creative dependency in grace is compatible with the contingency running throughout all things. Grace and natural theology, Farrer concluded, has the advantage over religious experience per se.

The situation is no better in the "strong form"--the idea that given certain experiences, one cannot help believing in God; cannot disbelieve. This thesis is likely to become (Paul Helm notes in The Varieties of Belief) the claim that the existence-question cannot be discussed; is therefore irrelevant to the exercise of faith. But the existence-question does affect the credibility of religious belief; its philosophical credit-rating. Of the reasons for not discussing it--the believer is not sure whether God exists; on the contrary, he is so very much aware of it, he has no need to articulate it--Hick concludes, having loaded the options, that it is surely the latter which characterizes the attitude of the Biblical writers. They "lacked incentive to assert that God exists because they (at least sometimes) seemed to themselves [a slip of the self-convincing tongue?] to be as conscious of God as they were of their physical environment or their fellows." [30] But the range of options, between agnosticism and tacit assumption, narrows if one takes up the positive side of the question as Farrer did. Of the reasons for discussing the existence-question--it underwrites the "blessings"; alternatively, clarifies the content of a transcendent belief, establishing to whom or what one refers--one cannot ignore the cognitive hopes that God actually exists by citing the practical presumption that "the blessings bless." For unless these blessings emanate from actual divine Beneficence, they are not what they purport to be, "of" or "from" God; a sense of other-origination implicit in such impetratory acts like praying for things to happen. [31]

And what is the lesson of Biblical authors? They did not assimilate the existence-question to a dispositional response by ignoring it; they assumed it and, on occasion, articulated it loud and clear. According to the Psalmist, "The heavens declare the glory of God," likewise St. Paul: "For the invisible things of Him from the creation of the world are clearly seen." Even in that eloquent faith-chapter of Hebrews which takes us on a Cook's tour of those Old Testament exemplars Hick cites, evidence is implicit. By faith Abraham went out not knowing whither he went, received the promise of a son, etc.; by faith Sara received strength to conceive past age; by faith (and virtue) Joseph was rewarded with the task of protecting her offspring, and Moses was granted a visa, against all odds, to deliver them from Egypt; and so on. Stuck right in the middle of "so great a cloud of witnesses," as the first verse of the next chapter puts it, evidently piling-up the evidence, we read: "He that cometh to God must believe that He is, and that He is a rewarder of them that dili-gently seek Him" (Heb 11:6)--a dual "that-clause" substantiating the fact that the existence of God, if not logically prior to dili-gently seeking after him, is certainly presupposed by the fact of spiritual provision. Here then is a rock of ontology of God on which the non-foundationalist's ark of belief must sooner or later come to rest and which seems to put dispositional belief in the larger context or some form of natural theology.

If, then, the Biblical authors did excuse themselves of the existence-question, was it not because they thought they had so much evidence to go on they could afford to leave it unannounced?--evidence which, to the dismay of the demytholo-gizers, they did not altogether leave out of their scriptural ac-counts. Here, as we have seen in **The Myth of God Incarnate**, Hick throws his lot in with the rationalists; those who would separate the husk of a pre-scientific, miracle-ridden surfeit of evidence from the kernel of a supra-cultural, timeless truth; expunging what seems to them like excessive supernaturality in the gospel accounts by weighing the evidence for and against what is being claimed. Since this often involved the appraisal of ontological assumptions--e.g. whether Jesus was the God/man according to the Chalcedonian formula; whether there was an actual bodily resurrection--such a rational format seems readily extendable to the foundational claim "that God exists." Hick declines to make this move, doubtless for fear of falling prey to the old-styled "proof-mentality"; setting out to prove the existence of God and, by implication, denigrating the need for faith. But between "proof-positive" and "experiencing-as," one can (as did Farrer) argue for the appropriateness of religious concepts, establishing theism's inference-license.

II

Still, it may be protested, Farrer's approach in his later work is not much different from Hick's. Turn from the admittedly impressive treatise of **FI** to the more manageable **FS** and one is seemingly confronted with a statement of belief unblushingly unphilosophical. "How did religion get into our heads? It was taught to us, was it not?" **(FS** 3). Speaking further on behalf of this "unphilosophical believer," Farrer reasoned: Since under the guise of a "neutral" investigation philosophers may be inclined to pursue the chimera of their own a priori expectations, the examination of religious belief should begin with motives for believing rather than the more usual "reasons as grounds"; for who knows better what a belief must be like than those who practice it?

Even as _obiter dicta_ for the inarticulate, Farrer seems in danger here of overstating the capacity of a practical belief to dispense with philosophical questions. However, it is significant that, whereas the "practical believer" of chapter 1 of **FS** rests his case on _assumed_ knowledge of other minds--we take it as fact that we know our neighbor in "dealing" with him--Farrer uses the same analogy in chapter 8 to probe the rational foundations of faith; drawing the inference to a Divine Other.

> We take it as axiomatic that the straight path of rational theology must be the prolongation of that basic theism which precedes all philosophising. It is a movement of thought which the simplest of minds can make; the rational theologian's justification must be that it calls for the developments he gives it. As much, after all, can be said about our knowledge of our fellow-beings. (**FS** 122; cf. 11).

Applying the analogy: "From first infancy our elders loved us, played [with] us, served us, talked us into knowing them; and so the believer claims that he has been brought by mediated divine initiatives into the knowledge of God." (**FS** 129).

Claiming that the inference to other minds is elementary-- even a child can manage it--does not mean it is unsophisticated, utterly lacking in "logic." We do not believe in our neighbors "_because_ it is self-stultifying to deny their existence, but because we are involved with them." Interaction it may reasonably be concluded, is also "the cause of our belief in God." (**FS** 174). Here Farrer is sorting out priorities; putting logic in its _proper_ place, not just "in its place." To the practical-minded, the provision of spiritual benefits is "motive" enough to set aside the question of formal demonstrations for the existence of God; and although to the more discerning, such "benefits" naturally find their place in the larger framework of cosmological belief--a Being that can _only_ be known as the agent of finite "effects"--the warning against treating such "effects" as a convincing proof of the divine reality is logically the equivalent of not over-philosophizing the inference to others. How many believers--Farrer reminds us--have walked humbly before their God without being able to follow Anselm's ontological argument. Nor did Russell's sudden appreciation of that argument--"Great Scott, the ontological argument is sound!"--have any lasting or significant effects on his _ir_religious sentiments.

Does this mean that the inference to others can't be philosophized? Not necessarily. Simply because one has not bothered to identify the grounds on which belief rests, or can discuss competently the logic of theistic affirmation, does not mean

(a) that belief has no grounds--Pectus facit theologum, we are non-foundationalists at heart--or (b) that the grounds can't be excavated by those who, literally, have a mind to. "The logic of thought which allows a small child to appreciate his mother as a personal subject can be no miracle of complexity; it gives philosophers plenty to enlarge upon, nevertheless." (FS 122). Notice, Farrer said "enlarge," certainly not discard, nor even perhaps dramatically improve. It is incumbent on those who would construct a convincing argument for knowledge of other minds to honor the precedent set by experience. And surely this is what is right about non-foundationalists' attempt to get away from the acid-bath of Cartesian doubt. It is apt to melt the baby of experience away.

Neither, of course, should one overdress the child in fancy logical lace, like a Victorian picture-postcard. Those who, like Plantinga, would construct an analogical bridge here--from person-disclosing bits of behavior on their own part to comparable or allied instances in others--are unduly hesitant; not as far from Descartes as they might think. [32] Except in unusual cases when, befuddled or amused, we struggle to put ourselves in another's place, our understanding takes no detour through analogical back-alleys or across rickety inferential bridges. "What would I have meant if I had said or done such-and-such?" is not the height of philosophical wisdom but the grim echo of a solipsistic disquiet. Ordinarily we take each other's meaning straight. "In personal understanding we do not analogize at all," Farrer wrote. "We make a direct use of powers which are de facto analogous with our neighbour's powers." (FW 323). In a rare footnote, he added: "Never mind how we come to be so [connatural with others], whether by identical constitution, common education, or mutual infection." (FW 152). This is playing coy. Much of the Gifford Lectures were devoted to showing that this "common infection" can be traced directly to language, intentions being in principle intelligible and expressly so in speech. Intentions are the common property of a community of discourse; and actions, our clue to other persons.

But how does the "clue" of intentionality work? Do we "leap" from vantage-point "inside" the self to an immediate "outside" appreciation of others? There is no need to. Personality is part of that common social and linguistic core we share with others; in consequence, behavior does not merely confirm the criterion "person"; it establishes it as a criterion: a commonly-shared modus operandi for the intelligible transmission of personal meaning. An intending agent intends a meaning and, like playing charades, delights when his audience grasps it. To be an agent, then, is to perform an act so that others recognize the twin of their own intentions; or at least the foundling of deserted ambitions. The trick depends on producing a mirror image, showing others to themselves, or <u>vice versa</u>. The same holds true for language, primary instrument of meaning-making. The social commodity of language, being purchased from a common store of concepts, therefore ensures reference-success by virtue of mutual applicability. We describe <u>our</u> sensations by observing what <u>others</u> predicate of themselves; we modify <u>their</u> descriptions by reference to our <u>own</u> experience. "Articulate speech may fairly be reckoned the foundation of the mentality we call distinctly human," Farrer wrote in that supposedly unphilosophical first chapter of **FS**. "The tribe which invented speech might be fairly said to have invented human nature." (**FS** 5-6). But, strictly speaking, we don't "invent" speech; we share it, patenting our use of it with others, finding our coveted audience in a society--and so may conclude, with Wittgenstein, from the emergence of "mind" to the untenability of a "private" language.

Consider pain; ostensibly the most private of experiences; yet clearly not without a social dimension. We <u>teach</u> appropriate pain-behavior by responding to it; conversely, <u>learn</u> by following the stoical or demonstrative examples of others. (E.g. we gasp when we want to dampen a child's reckless antics, giving advance warning of pain and notification to the effect that hurt, if incurred, carries social consequences; alternatively, we pooh-pooh whining when we deem their misery incommensurate with the facts, rationing the milk of human kindness according to strict social codes, e.g. a stiff upper lip.) What makes the supposition of other-personal activity so compulsive then, is that <u>we have a part in determining it</u>. In consequence, we don't <u>start from</u> the logic of our own case; rather, in the ability to predicate (or empathize) successfully, confirm that we carry the conviction of the other in the very form of language we employ. In the capacity to respond to instances of pain in others, we show that we <u>immediately</u> understand what he or she is feeling at the moment.

There is, then, an "evidential relationship" (as Anthony Kenny described it) built-<u>into</u> the meaning of the predicates we use to describe our intentions; a relationship neither "discovered" to the surprise of the intending agent by observing causal consequences (how could one be an "agent," setting out to perform an act?) nor arising from trial-and-error experimentation with our acts (how long, beyond infancy, would society stand for inductive experiments?) but which is, <u>contra</u> Cartesian dualism, parasitic on bodily implementation plus the fact that intentional behavior has a social dimension <u>in principle</u> intelligible. (Hence the point of Strawson's claim that "person" is a mutually <u>inclusive</u> category, related by the common patrimony of shared predicates.) In consequence, we don't use behavior in the strict deductive sense as "evidence" of other minds since behavior, <u>qua</u> informative pantomime, is indicative of having <u>already</u> internalized "public" criteria: living proof of being able to operate with the standards of others. Intelligible behavior informs us of agents "like" our-selves, with whom we share our world and whose mimetic behavior, when it doesn't embarrass us into silence, forms the basis of social or communicable acts. When, therefore, we recognize in ourselves the development of a specific self-consciousness able to communicate in words or deeds with others, this entails the recognition of a commensurability between self and others without which intentional activity would have lost its raison d'être in the first place, as shared meaning, i.e., to promote mutual understanding. Farrer put it simpler: When adults talk to children they evoke or implant the very mentality which com-prehends their speech. Conversely, when children answer back, they echo the sentiments of others. Our belief in others is, accord-ingly, of the "lend-lease" variety. Humanity is a social fact, he concluded: "We need other men, to be human ourselves." [33] The investment of others is appropriately at the heart of what it means to be a person. As such, life-in-society is not lived in terms of deductively or inductively valid inferences. We take "persons" to exist if and when we have something to do with them. The existence-question is, accordingly, the natural conse-quence of the fact that we interact with agents and things; whose existence we acknowledge by virtue of their impact on us and whose reality is judged intrinsic to the practical response they elicit from us. Thus, what looks to the child or common-sense realist like the obvious fact that, given the nurture of others, they must exist, can, to someone weaned on formally valid criteria leave the question of solipsism open, intensifying the problem of other minds. But (just to remind us) who has been weaned on formal logic or suckled a syllogism? This does not mean that the child is acting illogically, or a-logically, in accepting the belief of others. To those who enjoy the benefits of life-in-society, they have the existence-supposition as part of their immediate or intuitive experience of others. Thus, the philosopher who lets his criterion of other-personal activity be shaped by de facto canons of rationality escapes dependence on analogical inference by living the belief; a practical mandate which, he may insist, has an ontology built into it. Life-in-society is both premise to and consequence of the experience of mutuality; mutuality both yields and nurtures the belief in others. In similar fashion, the religious believer may contend that the "spiritual tonality" consequent on the belief in God provides prima facie evidence of the investment of a real Other, the life of faith carrying the conviction of supreme Being, analogous to the existence-presupposition of life-in-society. "Illusions do not nourish so richly, so powerfully, so deeply." [34] Both forms of nurture imply a nurturer.

But a prima facie justification is not the full case; and it is not difficult to imagine what a foundationalist will say about "form-of-life" theology. With our neighbor we are seldom in doubt whether he or she exists, although it is possible to refuse to have anything to do with him; whereas the lack of obviousness of the object of religious worship makes the existence-question all the more imperative. Moreover, the foundationalist might add, we can only know God in _affirming_ God; adopting--not a frosty--but a friendly stance towards the divine neighbor. For, as with those in the human realm upon whom we have come to rely, only by casting our care upon Him can God reveal Himself a very present help in time of need. Not only foundationalists take this line. This is Farrer's position as well. Granted religion begins with practical or non-theoretical concerns--"a commerce with saving powers"--to avoid the prayer of the agnostic, "God (if you are there), save my soul (if it exists)," the believer should be able to give (as admonished in the Scriptures) a _reason_ for the hope that lies within him. This means taking into account the _assumptions_ on which belief is based, even if these assumptions, being presupposed by the form-of-life in which he participates, are hardly tentative in the sense suggested by that term. Accordingly, Farrer's "foundational" approach cites a precedent and posts a warning. If all thinking based on uncriticized assumptions is groundless, those who, from _living_ a life-in-society, _assume_ knowledge of others, must be deprived by the stringent demands of logic of what experience has taught them they have good reason to accept. (This sense of logic is responsible for those sudden, dithyrambic outbursts to the effect that life is larger than logic.) But, equally and reciprocally, if a belief has worked its way so deeply into human consciousness as to form the backbone of society and is at the heart of what it means to be a person--a man among men, self _cum_ others--such an entrenched belief can hardly be presumed _une_vidential and should not be left out of any attempt to excavate the assumptive-base on which experience is built. Should not be left out, but _may_ be included in the following way.

If, to explain what persons are, we find ourselves committed to certain realist assumptions--to wit, that there is a real world "given" in language which forms the basis for life-in-society and provides the cornerstone of personal identity--it follows that these assumptions are neither extraneous to the belief in other minds, nor merely superfluous to the conviction of an external reality but logically and ontologically commensurate with the beliefs they engender. Objects and others thus represent the logico-empirical conditions of what it means to be a conscious, cognizing mind. More simply, the belief in objects and others is what it means to be a person. As such, these "realist assumptions" are less like assumptions, optional extras to our world-view, than they are presupposed in the form of experience we have of the world. Without objects and others, there would be nothing to say and no one to say it to. Worse still, no mind to know the difference; or _sans_ mutuality, individualism founders.

Turning the results of holding these beliefs into a consciously formulated reason for adopting them, we might say: As social dividends underwrite the belief in other minds, so does our mobility in an object-cluttered world confirm the surefootedness of language--the fact that our concepts refer; signpost an external reality; identify things to be avoided, persons to be acknowledged, etc. One must take care not to overstate foundational logic: If our concepts have purchase, the world exists; _if_ our social interaction is rewarding, persons exist. This is philosophical philistinism. It represents a strained attempt to reap the ontological rewards of the buried premise by a too-strict, syllogistic inference; an "if/then" approach to objects and others. Right way round, we insist that only by virtue of the fact that we have already accepted a real world, well-stocked with persons and things, can we explain that we are language-users, sociable beings, inventively creative with our environment, etc. The form of reasoning thus implied in drawing inferences from such natural or practical beliefs is _from_ the presuppositions implied in holding them; alternatively, _to_ those ontological facts required to explain them. Given that we are _already_ the beneficiary of extra-mental reality, these facts or presuppositions must be presumed to have deeply embedded themselves in human experience; indeed, are _responsible_ for experience. The belief in objects and others may thus be brought to the surface, if at all, by retroductive inference--from consequence to underlying premise; their logic does not belie simple entailment, from premise to conclusion. Not all beliefs, then, come about by the conscious application of inductive or deductive inference. Some beliefs, perhaps the majority, have a more natural "base" in ordinary experience; and if we try and "cash in" the ontological subsidy of these beliefs by converting the buried premise into an hypothetical contingency--"If life-in-society is rewarding, that is reason to embrace the belief in other minds"--it is not only at risk of over-commercializing our commerce with others but also of debasing their more fundamental logic: viz., _de facto_ validity. We simply _live_ these beliefs (Farrer reminds us) and "are the selves we are" by virtue of this fact. **(FS** 127). This does not mean there is _no_ logic at work in affirming others-- only Hick's practical ontology--but that the "logic" follows the grooves cut by experience.

Consequently, we seldom live or think solipsistically; having to _argue_ ourselves out of disbelieving in others because--and this is as much a logical truism as it carries the weight of experience behind it--we recognize the oddity of inferring others in the narrow sense, from premise to conclusion, since in the form of our mutual humanity, we have no good reason to doubt them. The rejoinder of solipsism, therefore, need only be "foundational"

enough to eliminate spurious inference; calling us back to a different sense of fundamentals, not to no fundamentals. And what
is fundamental to "self" is awareness of others. In this regard,
Wittgenstein reminds us that to be able to formulate the question
of "grounds" for affirming others, is to think in a form of language
we share with them so that the very hypothesis of scepticism,
verbal exploiter that it is, is logically self-defeating. Here, then,
is an "archeological" or presupposed bed of experience, based
on the conceptual contribution of others, as opposed to a freshly
poured Cartesian foundation, reinforced by the lattice-work of
doubt. Jung's "collective unconscious," if true, provides a case
in point. In the cellar of any individual psyche all the collected
remnants of our ancestral past; incipient personhood drawing
on the parentage of others. In a similar vein, Farrer wrote: "Humanity is an inherited deposit taken on trust." [35] Social belief,
we may conclude, turns on the assumption of others rather than
the dubitatio of evidence "for" and "against" them.

The conclusion, then, to which we are ineluctably drawn
by examining the logic of our language is that we can't help
but accept the fact or "givenness" of others, since to be a "mind,"
a talking, thinking being, is already to have done so and presumably
before we were conscious of the capacity to do otherwise. The
child is indeed father to the man; the simple-minded believer
to the philosophical sage. The "logic" by which a child grows
to adulthood is not a provisional code of analogical resignation--"as
good an answer as we have to the question of other minds,"
as Plantinga admits [36]--but the practical realization that others
"exist" in the form of nurture thus provided. (Infants who suspect
poison in the milk-bottle do not grow to be the next generation
of sceptical philosophers; in milder form, lack the language in
which to propagate their own poisonous doctrines.) In presuming
to reason to the belief in other minds, we actually reason from
it--from our experience of and exposure to others; a foundation
of considerable breadth. By underscoring the prepositions, we
express the awkwardness of casting a natural belief in philosophical rectitude. The philosopher who concludes to other minds
has the evidence for that belief on his mother's breast; though
it is not until he becomes a philosopher that he is apt to view
it as evidence.

Can we apply this type of de facto argument to religious
belief?--reasoning, since it is a condition of experiencing the
nurture of family and friends that, somewhere along the line
which perpetuates the legacy of the human race, we must have
affirmed their existence, so the theological believer is entitled
to hold it as corollary to the kind of person he has become that
God exists. Not without qualification, Farrer admits. Religious
nourishment does not indicate "divine person" as "unmistakably"
as does social nurture our fellow-man. Nevertheless, as one may

use the enriching effects of the belief in others to fend off that Pyrrhonistic scepticism which seeks after signs in the social realm and will desist putting one's neighbor to the test, so too, the believer who _lives_ his belief in God may use "the founding, steadying, invigorating, illuminating and enriching" aspects of faith to resist the comparable sceptical accusation, "no evidence that God exists."

Here Farrer improves on the analogical format of Plantinga. After criticizing the positions of Wittgenstein, Malcolm, Shoe-maker and Strawson--odd, because these philosophers also wrote to cure the slab of fresh-poured foundationalism--Plantinga con-cludes: "Of course, there may be other reasons for supposing that although rational belief in other minds does not require an answer to the epistemological question, rational belief in the existence of God does. But it is certainly hard to see what these reasons might be." Hard?--these reasons are, in a manner of speaking, capable of articulating themselves, in the perplexed amazement of _non_-believers. People who do not see the point of religious belief, at any rate not as readily as Plantinga, _would_ seem to require an explanation, if only because, as puzzled or sceptical friends, they have the capacity to confront us with an existence-presupposition _dis_-analogous to the belief in God. Ignoring these walking, talking contradictions--those capable of asking why he doesn't consider their existence any more obvious than the _Deus Absconditus_--Plantinga ends his book exactly where he begins: "If my belief in other minds is rational, so is my belief in God. But obviously the former is rational; so, therefore, is the latter." [37] What is the force of the "obviously" here?

Farrer attempts a more discriminating _apologia_, even building on the quicksand of experiential premises. Because the believer lays claim to "a gospel of salvation"--call it, if you will, an effica-cious belief--he is led to postulate the existence of God as premise to the consequence; as required in the _weak sense_ by the fact of spiritual provision. For if God were deemed _not_ to exist, the experience of nurture "by some Other" must be delusive, the product of wishful thinking; and to the believer who experiences "divine causality" firsthand--in the enabling of grace--this account is as unacceptable as that the gifts of personality are somehow self-induced, manufactured out of our own psyche, rather than, as they appear to most who enjoy life-in-society, the internalized legacy of others: a minor miracle of social engineering. But in no sense can he, the believer, maintain with Plantinga or Hick that the logic of affirming God is on all fours with the logic of affirming others. To deny others in a form of language they (likely) taught us is a blatant contradiction, insult added to injury if they are within earshot; whereas to deny the existence of God is to be deprived of only _a certain way_ of being human, for which the evidence is neither unambiguous nor the results unassimilable to psychological explanation. However, the death of the soul, from denying God, may be as real and telling in its effect as being deprived of the society of others, albeit more imperceptible in taking hold and more disastrous in consequences, therefore, the more carefully to be guarded against. In Pascal's terms, given the prospect of an infinite loss, the indemnity of a finite gamble may strike the believer as comparable to the absurdity of denying others, a trust better risked (even in light of logical impurity), than lost. And when it comes to religious renunciation, one doesn't have to go "beyond" life, to the here-after, as an example of spiritual loss _in_ life.

The point, then, of denying that the rationality of the belief in God turns on a strict (or analogical) equivalence with the belief in others is not to deny religious inference altogether, only to let it arise where it is naturally inclined. And where is that?--Surely in the believer's experience of grace, Farrer reasoned: "an effect referred to God as to its creative source and underlying subject." (FS 128). For this raises the question of _who_ or _what_ is responsible for "effects"; and if "the good that I would" I reckon myself to be incapable of in my _own_ strength, I may conclude, with St. Paul, that I am what I am (when or _if_ I am good) by the grace of God: the "personal dealing" carrying the conviction of that other's enablement.

This "voluntarist metaphysic" had its origins in the inter-actionist epistemology of **FI**. "My affection by another being is concretely experienced as an interaction of beings; I feel the force of that other as an ingredient in the interaction, so far as the interaction expresses it; and that may be very abstractly or incompletely." (**FI** 231). **FS** simplified it: "Only an experience analogous to personal dealing with some other can carry conviction of that other's self being." (**FS** 172). When, therefore, the "later" Farrer rhetorically asks, "What is a person but his voluntary action?" en route to reminding us that the creative transformation of grace "is a sort of efficacy," revealing _divine_ agency by (seem-ingly) _supernatural_ "effects," he is not (after the manner of Plan-tinga) plumping for a straightforward equivalence between the social and religious belief; "in the same epistemological boat." Nor is he, in recommending "a god about whom we have something to do," merely a dispositional well-wisher, advocating that we practice our religion until our convictions come alive; stamped with the "twenty-four carat" hallmark of faith. He is claiming that principle of identity first laid down in **FI** and subsequently refined in the Gifford Lectures by which we acknowledge the "being," that is the doing, of others. Activity _is_ the form of our common humanity (a conclusion supported by the philosophy of action). If, then, we sense a power or activity in us "working for good," a _divine_ "doing," we have, on the premises laid out, the supposition of divine agency in the molding and shaping of our personal destiny. But only the "supposition."

Is this a philosophical argument? Not in the sense that, from the mere fact of "effect," one is compelled to accept the believer's account of "Beneficent Causality." It is only to be expected (someone may say) that such beliefs work themselves in the living. To the extent that we consciously choose our beliefs, they provide us with a practical mandate: the praxis of credo. Provided then, the sceptic can offer an alternative account of "spiritual provisions," he can (a) allow the practical consequences of religious belief--"undoubtedly efficacious"--while (b) denying they have anything to do with God--"nevertheless false, not from God" (in any literal or metaphorical sense of the word "from"). However, reasoning from "effects" back to underlying (or transcendent) Cause might be given a hearing, Farrer thought, if a similar form of inference were found at work in the world of common experience. And it is his contention that, in the belief in other minds, we do have an analogy for the inference to a Divine Other. But only an analogy; so he took care not to over-drive the argument. The form of reasoning involved in inferring Divine "Cause" from supernatural "effect" is similar to inferring "person" from nurture; but the logical intensity of the yield is dissimilar. "[L]ife-in-God has not the indubitable evidence of life-in-community." (FS 130).

Therefore, by holding the existence-question consequent on the religious "form-of-life," all the "unphilosophical believer" can hope to achieve is that, since the initial response is dispositional, "If any man will do the will," the credibility of theistic belief be drawn from the fact of its effect; its impact on the lives of its adherents rather than (as in the classical theism) what would count as indisputable evidence for the claim "that God exists." For given the alleged difficulty of locating the empirical grounds of transcendent belief, a "pragmatic criterion" seems better-suited to test the validity of the belief in God than, say, positivist truth-telling. And if the believer is up on his philosophy, he may observe that Wittgenstein employed a similar form of practical reasoning in undoing some of the logical problems complicating knowledge of other minds. Personal consciousness presupposes a community of discourse; therefore, the Cartesian starting-point of radical doubt is untenable. In a similar fashion, the religious believer may conclude that the evidence of the belief in a Divine Other, since resting on the fact that it creates an environment that nourishes, establishes religious belief as having a practical rather than philosophical bearing.

Here the danger is on the other side. One must take care to avoid the beguiling simplicities of non-foundational logic. Even the man who petitions God in prayer holds certain assumptions about the capacity of this being to "hear and answer"; and so he conceives of God as an "agent," "over-against" him, and able to "act" on his behalf. In short, the "thatness" or "thereness" of God is presupposed by the fact (or promise) of prayerful sustenance. This led Farrer to conclude that the existence-presupposition is "the flattest platitude of elementary reflection." (FS 122). Nevertheless, because the believer does not so much reason himself into faith as respond reasonably and as a whole man to the life of faith, he may draw philosophical nourishment from that pragmatism which concludes: It is more likely that God exists rather than not, given that those who "stand on the divine promises" do not readily topple over. Basil Mitchell leaned less heavily on the pragmatic sanction: "If what Christians believe is true, there ought to be a detectable difference here." [38] All this attests, the unbeliever may reply, is that there is a pleasing commensurability between the sincere attempt to do God's will and a certain intangible quality of living. This quality may still be discounted or discredited. ("Gentle Jesus, meek and mild," is no posture to adopt in the 20th century.) Spiritual effects may also be denied as religiously appropriate. ("Give Sister Serene, who sits in her prayer-cell all day interceding on behalf of mankind, a house to keep clean, two difficult children and an inadequate budget," a housewife wrote to the editor of Time magazine, "and see how serene she stays.") Finally, these sensitizing "extras" may be credited to other sources--the result of a deep, psychological self-understanding. Nevertheless, such is the impact of certain personalities upon us that we may feel it implausible to maintain that the strength or durability of their belief derives from just a pleasing or appropriate commensurability between the disposition to believe and a resultant quality of life, concluding that the lives of the Saints, rather than tending towards fundamental delusion, give ample evidence of "conspicuous sanctity." [39] While no-one supposes that a well-integrated personality is either a necessary or sufficient reason for believing in God, or that God can be proved from the availability of spiritual resources, spiritual endowment in the form of extraordinary gifts of personality does seem to allow for the possibility of theological explanation since the palpable absence of such qualities is often made a reproach to believers. If, that is, theistic belief is undercut by its ineffectiveness--the fact that, in the estimation of some, it puts a person on the lunatic fringe of society rather than seeming to enrich him--by the same token, positive results, if they could be agreed upon, must count for the validity of religious belief.

It is perhaps with the "belief-worthiness" of religion in mind that Donald MacKinnon has reasoned: If theistic belief makes possible "a view of the world that is fertile and illuminating, a posture for men . . . that vindicates itself," [40] this must be some measure of its truth; livability being one of the tests of truth. Farrer echoes MacKinnon's sentiments. "On the supposition that God is truly what we believe him, it would be odd if our giving ourselves to him made us on the whole more restless, more frustrated, less able to manage our relations with others or to discipline our own passion, less generous or outgoing, less alive all over." [41] Conversely, if beneficial results do seemingly accrue from the life of faith, this may tend to elevate the "supposition" that God is responsible from the status of hypothetical to probable fact. Elliptically: most false beliefs have dire consequences: the result of the belief in God is not at all dire. Ergo. theistic belief is likely true; certainly not false in the conventional sense.

The logical loophole (or philosophical escape-clause) is in the "likely." How "likely" depends on the unlikelihood of any alternative explanation, and supernatural explanation to some (e.g. Flew's Stratonicians) seems disadvantaged from the start. Nevertheless, if we do find it odd that a reputedly "false" belief can produce good results, because truly false beliefs usually cancel themselves out in the living--to imagine oneself Napoleon is likely to end up certified, rather than Emperor of Europe--this disinclination to fault a "workable" belief may be turned into a positive reason to suppose it true. Practical belief would thus nudge us from the unlikelihood of a belief being false, yet efficacious, to the possibility of its being true because efficacious. Beneficial effects are no guarantee of truth. Neither does the criterion of plausibility probabilify belief in the eyes of all. For what one person may plausibly gulp down is poison to another and some (to Lewis Carroll's capacity to amuse) do not so much as raise a metaphysical eyebrow over the vast improbability of a world evolving unaided from a raw concatenation of physical forces; finding "no logical difficulty in regarding Nature as a process of involution, passing from definite coherent homogeneity to indefinite incoherent heterogeneity." [42] From the practical point of view, then, the issue is onus probandi: on whose shoulders does the burden of proof lie? And the point of Chapter 1 of FS (as I understand it) is to take both naive foundationalists and soft religious practitioners to task. The sceptic by his recriminations of "no hard evidence" oddly promotes himself to be a better judge of what theistic belief entails than those who, by living it, draw its veracity from its applicability. The fideist, by citing a "feel" for authenticity, treats reason too much as the stumbling block of faith and is deprived of that "keen nervousness" which, according to William James, is capable of deepening faith. Against the former, Farrer argued that the believer is in a privileged position to weigh his dispositional investment against the evidence it alone is capable of engendering. Against the latter, he argued that without faith being able to be thought, how is it to be lived? since man is both heart and head. It is not only a matter of matching belief to the evidence (as Locke advised, with his economical approach to belief); attitudes of approval, censure and the like affect the nature of our investigation, maximize or minimize our findings. Faith does not <u>substitute</u> for evidence, but it may (Farrer concluded) put one in a favorable position to judge it.

Whether in the final analysis this pragmatic appeal is philosophically acceptable depends, I submit, on the companion-assumption that theistic belief calls attention to <u>the way things are</u> in being belief-worthy. That is why, although Farrer began the argument of **FS** defending the <u>right</u> to believe, he hastened to include an argument <u>a contingentia mundi,</u> the right <u>way</u> to believe. The believer's experience of creative dependency, in grace, picks up and amplifies that creative contingency running throughout nature; transmitted and brought nearer to home in the interactive "web" of society. None of us, we may observe, is any more self-originating than any other, and most men vastly less autonomous than those capable of articulating their contingency, which, extending the tremulous web of cosmological inference from part-determining causes to causes more fully realized, brings us ultimately to the determining act of a <u>Divine</u> Cause, an Absolute Being judged responsible for "being" in its proximate or finite form, whom believers, investing in this dependency-relation with worship and prayer, have come to acknowledge as a Sovereign or Ordaining Will. "Our simple theist, with whom we began, knows himself a being both posited and self-positing. Looking for the simply self-positing positor, he cannot see him in his fellows, still less in his inferiors; ·he looks above his own head. He is perfectly philosophical, whether he knows it or not." **(FS** 169).

Therefore, as regards the "commerce" which believers claim with Deity, this only excuses them from the pretence of objective evidence; it does not altogether dispense with evidence. For that, a more penetrating dig around the foundations of faith is in order, which the man we are gathered here to commemorate was never reluctant to roll up his sleeves and try. The analogy of other minds provided him with a sharp and ready instrument of excavation: a practical precedent for claiming the assurance of faith's object; a philosophical justification for assessing the life of belief, in terms of a latent existence-question. Faith and philosophy. Surely this is the model.

NOTES

1. **Word and Object** (Cambridge, Mass.: M.I.T., 1960) 2; see also **From a Logical Point of View** (New York: Harper, 1963) 44.

2. Frederick Ferré, Theology Today 25 (1969) 269. He was not alone. Michael McLain catalogued some of the consternation generated by **FS** in "Austin Farrer's Revision of the Cosmological Argument" in the Downside Review 88 (1970) 270-9. The TLS reviewer (Aug. 24, 1967; 767) also commented on Farrer's dazzling feats of dialogical dexterity "leaving the reader breathless and often slightly puzzled . . . It may even be true that the formal qualities of Dr. Farrer's thought and style make the most serious enquiries seem a little too much like Mozart's music--the intensity of feeling and intellect may go unobserved under the felicities of the facade."

3. It is, perhaps, misleading of Plantinga to espouse non-foundationalism in "Is Belief in God Rational?" C. F. Delaney ed., **Rationality and Religious Belief** (Notre Dame: Notre Dame U.P., 1979). In **The Nature of Necessity**, (Clarendon: Oxford, 1974) 213f. he uses the logic of self-evident propositions to construct "A Victorious Modal Version" of the Ontological Argument. If, he argues, "unsurpassable greatness" is equivalent to "maximal excellence in every possible world," what exemplifies this property in any possible world is just that ontological measure of completeness that counts as rationally probative in this actual one p. 216. Plantinga thinks he avoids the discredited leap from "maximal greatness is possibly exemplified" to the status of necessary truth by holding the universalizability principle as merely "rationally acceptable," not provable: i.e. if and only if maximality pertains in every possible world.

The empiricist in me is unconvinced. Positivism notwithstanding, the relation between propositions and actual (i.e. provable or observable) states of affairs must be such as to disallow or, at the least, place certain restrictions on any inferentially valid comparisons between these type statements and their more speculative or merely logically possible counterparts. (This was Strawson's bone of contention over revisionary metaphysics.) Otherwise expressed, it does not seem possible to convert the logic of possible worlds into ontological actuals any more than it is legitimate to translate a virtual impossibility into a finite improbability. (See D. Adams, **The Hitchhiker's Guide to the Galaxy** 69.) More seriously, J. L. Mackie insisted, in his review of **The Nature of Necessity**, (TLS, Nov. 14, 1975) that Plantinga's ontological premise lets in too much, including the propositional obverse "no-maximality is possibly exemplified." Exemplification, in his estimation, requires more than the logic of universalizability to instantiate existential claimants; otherwise the ontological disproof of "maximal greatness" equally draws its cogency from the highly abstract nature of the concept of God presupposed, as unsurpassably and inconceivably beyond comprehension, which is where J. N. Findlay left the challenge some years ago in "Can God's Existence be Disproved?" in A. Flew and A. MacIntyre, eds., **New Essays in Philosophical Theology** (London: S.C.M., 1955) 476.

4. **Individuals** (London: Methuen, 1959) 106.

5. Ibid., 103.

6. Ibid., 102.

7. FS, 126. An excerpt from a letter to Edward Henderson, 24 March 1966, is relevant here; especially in light of the criticism that Farrer's conception of God in FI is not compatible with our self-understanding as social beings:

> [O]f course I agree that personal "existence" is a function of the community of discourse, and that (transpersonal) talking comes before (interior) thinking . . . (You mention, by the way, my trivial work 'Love Almighty . . .'; how strongly I embrace the view that 'humanity (in the "person" sense) is a social product'). [I]s the activity of any agent conceivable without a field constituted by other agents? The relation is constitutive of the existence we (and other finites) enjoy. The traditional theology amounts to denying any analogy of it to God, while asserting of him an analogy of interpersonal relations (relations of discourse) in the Blessed Trinity.

A footnote added: "I have touched the point in a popular book called **Saving Belief**."

Far from denying any analogy of "sociality" in God, Farrer relied on "the 'cosmological idea'--the scheme of God and the creature in relation" (FI 16)--to provide the grounds for knowing Him. Since, he reasoned, God is not an instance of a type of being commonly experienced elsewhere, any description we give of Him cannot "be independent of the ground on which we propose to believe in Him," viz. the function He performs for finites--e.g. as "maker," "sustainer," "redeemer." God must--logically must--be understood as the agent of some "effect." "If our predecessors have not grasped this function they have not known God at all." (FI 4).

This would make Farrer's retreat from traditional theism, which holds it possible to say Deus est, the flattest platitude of theistic reflection, separating the nature of what the Being God is in himself from our knowledge of Him as 'creator,' etc. quite early. However, his draping of the "rational theology" of FI in an "Aristotelian garb" (FI 247)--being before becoming, essence determinative of activity--left him in two minds; divided between a formalist and voluntarist conception of Deity, thus prompting the 'purge' in FS.

For the passages cited, see **Saving Belief** 63-7; **Love Almighty and Ills Unlimited** 150; also **A Science of God**? 100.

8. Cf. FI 232; **Thought and Action** (London: Chatto & Windus, 1959) 48, 88-9.

9. Farrer might have made the connexion between books clearer by not describing the empirical principle of FS--"no thought about any reality about which we can do nothing but think"--as "newly defined" p. 23. It appears, nearly verbatim, in FI 74, 292, and is characteristic of that (Strawsonian) abhorrence of speculative metaphysics announced in the Preface. "[T]his centring of metaphysics in the act of thought is vicious." p. x.

10. See **God and the Self** (Lewisburg: Bucknell U.P./Associated University Presses, 1976) esp. ch. 3. For the expression in pari materia see FI 230-5; **FW** 183; **FS** 134.

11. FI 248f; 290-2; also RF 43. "There is a pattern of our true destiny to which we know that we are called, and to which we are bound to show a measureless respect."

12. RF 44. He used a similar formula in FI 58. "God wills and knows all He is, and is all He wills and knows."

13. RF 45; cf. FI 266 where the "proper form" of existence "must be a maximum": "the maximum intensity of esse" being the Aristotelian principle by which FI endeavoured "to fill an empty form [of godhead] with content." FI 37, 271, 191.

14. E.G. Anthony Kenny, **Wittgenstein** (London: Penguin, 1973) 195.

Using "voluntarist" insights to break down the subject/object distinction may be traced to the legacy of scholasticism, according to Kenny, **Aquinas** (Oxford: O.U.P. 1980) 22. "The importance of the study of human dispositions (habitus) was lost sight of with the decline of scholastic philosophy at the Renaissance, and was rediscovered only in our time by linguistic philosophers such as Wittgenstein and Ryle." In **Wittgenstein** 124, he makes the link more explicit: "In the **Bemerkungen** his [Wittgenstein's] attack took the form of saying that Russell's method ignored the element of intentionality (Intention) in language. This term he appears to have taken from Husserl, who in turn took it from Brentano, and scholastic tradition; but he explains what it means in language drawn from the **Tractatus.**"

15. See RF 200f.; esp. 209.

16. Farrer wrote: "You ask me whether I think that the traditional theology I uphold in **Finite and Infinite** is any necessary implication of the substance-doctrine I defend. I would say, No: in fact I wrote the book the other way round. That theology seemed to me at that time the only theology worth holding, and I saw that it could not stand without such a doctrine of finite substance as I set out to reconstruct. How many theologies are compatible with that doctrine, I will not attempt to say. I no longer wish to define God as Actus Purus (though I wouldn't want to say he was Actus Impurus!). I would define him rather as the Being who wills to be all that he is, and is all that he wills to be, which comes nearer to Causa Sui than to Actus Purus.--I make no concessions to those who wish to relativize God or to qualify his Prior Actuality." (letter, 24 March 1966).

17. **FI** 158; **RF** 45--an expression connected with the perfectibility of noesis (see **FI** 287f; **RF** 50-1) and the early "theology of apprehension" of **FI**, subsequently dropped.

18. **FW** 329. Farrer's criticism of Aristotle, in "metaphysical limbo," mocks up too striking a contrast between **FI** and **FW**. The "cat of aspiration," after Aristotle's good, purred as pragmatically in the former as it did in the latter: Cf. **FI** 146, 192; **FW** 305f.

Farrer's appreciation of Aristotle is more evident in "Grace and the Human Will" **RF** 192f. Augustine sees the deliberative, volitional capacities of man as fixed by the appetites of a fallen or depraved nature--an a priori psychology that (Farrer noted) "has little to commend it." p. 196. To Plato and Aristotle, the instincts are capable of aspiring beyond self-interests--"A true education . . . or a consistent exercise of the rational faculties" can liberate us p. 195--to a point where choices are not dictated by passiones ("Da mihi castitatem et contientiam; sed noli modo") but are simultaneously most free and most truly our own; a working-model for the complementarity of grace.

> According to the distinction with which we started [Was it I or the grace of God?], the way to experience grace is to find ourselves occasioned to do good by influences and forces outside ourselves: for then it will not be we who act. According to the thought-form we are now using, the way to experience grace will be to exercise our highest powers in the freest and most truly personal way: for by so doing, we shall touch the point of transition in the hierarchy of being, where the divine action actively comes through into the creature. (p. 197-8).

19. **FI** 254; also 58 " . . . the ideal of love is to be a steady care for all being in so far as it is, or can by us be helped to be." This "communitarianism" significantly comes in the most essentialist section in the book, discussing the divine "self-sufficiency."

20. See **FW** 297f.; esp. 299-300 for one of the most moving passages in the Farrer corpus.

21. "Whatever we may think of the life of God in God, we are obliged to admit his action in his creatures, apart from which we should know nothing of him." **FS** 159; cf. 59.

22. **Arguments for the Existence of God** 110. It is, perhaps, significant that Hick reads Descartes and Hume opposite to Farrer, commenting on the failure of Descartes . . . to provide a theoretical guarantee that our senses relate us to a real material environment, and . . . the success of Hume . . . to show that our normal non-solipsist belief in an objective world of enduring objects around us in space is neither a product of, nor justifiable by, philosophical reasoning

but is what has been called in some expositions of Hume's thought (though the term does not seem to have been used by Hume himself) a natural belief." (italics added).

23. Ibid., 111.

24. Ibid., 110.

25. Royal Institute of Philosophy Lectures 2 (1967-8) **Talk of God** (London: Macmillan, 1969) 35.

26. **Faith and Knowledge,** 2nd ed. (London: Macmillan, 1967) 210.

27. **Philosophy of Religion** (Englewood Cliffs, N.J.: Prentice-Hall, 1963) 60-1. Near verbatim versions abound in the Hick corpus; e.g. **Christianity at the Centre** (London: S.C.M., 1968) 52; **The Many-Faced Argument,** J. Hick and A. C. McGill, eds., (London: Macmillan, 1968) 344.

Gordon Kaufman's reading of the Old Testament is more perceptive; in **God, the Problem** and his article, "On the Meaning of God: Transcendence Without Mythology," in Harvard Theological Review, April, 1966. Given that the Hebrew vocabulary does not have a term corresponding to our word "nature," it is unwise to conclude from the absence of "natural" theology in the O.T. either to its unimportance or to a theory of "divine action" which blurs the distinction between God and world, obliterating the autonomy of nature or losing sight of the "activity" of the Creator. To a mind-set that conceived God and nature in one divine continuum, doubtless everything counted as potentially revelatory, "divine act" amply showing itself in the most mundane of events (e.g. Hosea's marriage to Gomer). This does not mean that what is necessarily implied in the theophanic view is an interventionist or spectacularist Deity. If so, Biblical belief is on a collision course with natural science; the concept of a supernatural God edged out of the secular picture as science increases its explanatory holdings. What is needed is a concept of "divine action" which does not overtax miraculous expectations nor reduce God to nature; is therefore compatible with our current understanding of natural process; a "half-theology" of "theistic semi-naturalism" Kaufman admires in Farrer.

For further discussion, see "Farrer's Concept of Double Agency" by Maurice Wiles in Theology, July 1981; 243f. and "A Reply" by David Galilee and Brian Hebblethwaite, with response by Wiles in Theology, January 1982, 7-13.

28. See **The Justification of Religious Belief,** (London: Macmillan, 1973).

29. **Faith and Knowledge,** 2nd ed., 118-19.

30. **Faith and the Philosophers** (London: Macmillan, 1964) 240.

31. See Peter Geach, **God and the Soul** (London: Routledge & Kegan Paul, 1969) ch. 7.

32. Plantinga doesn't deny it, arbitrating the issues that divide Strawson and Descartes more on the side of the latter, **God and Other Minds** (Ithaca: Cornell U.P., 1967) 207-11; 229-30. Cartesianism, the "luminous obviousness" of the idea of "maximal greaness," also played an important role in his "modal" version of the ontological argument--see 3 above.

For a general discussion of analogy, see **God and Other Minds** 180f.; especially 191-2, and 268f. where he admits that analogical arguments to other minds are, to some extent, malady-ridden.

33. **A Celebration of Faith** 89; also 104-5. Sociality thus provided the basis for conceiving God.

> He made man in his own similitude, and it is in the face of man that we must look for the countenance of God.
>
> Or rather, not in the face of man, but in the faces of men, turned towards one another; the light of understanding that passes between their eyes, in a sense that sounds through the interchange of their speech, in mutual liking kindled from heart to heart. Man's mind, not his bodily frame, is the similitude of God; and mentality always was a social, not a solitary, thing. We learnt to talk, because they talked to us; and to like, because they smiled at us. Because we could first talk, we can now think; that is, we can talk silently to the images of the absent, or we can pretend to be our own twin, and talk to ourself. CF 74.

In the case of God, it is not "the image of the absent" but the image of the present; the ever-present who has invested himself in human consciousness: the root of personality being divinely based, as Farrer once put it to me. Thus what makes us most truly ourselves also "mirrors" or "enacts" the divine reality. There can be no more "communitarian" base on which to construct theology. (Cf. **Love Almighty and Ills Unlimited** 123-9).

34. Norris Clarke, **Faith and the Philosophers**, ed. J. Hick, p. 59.

Antony Flew criticized this in **God and Philosophy** (London: Hutchinson, 1966) 131 as "breathtakingly parochial and uncomprehending," weighing its intrinsically "subjective" appeal against the mighty mass of "objective" facts--a contrast which, in light of post-Wittgensteinian philosophy and the breakdown of the analytic/synthetic distinction in its many permutations, itself appears rather quaint.

35. **Faith and Logic**, ed. B. Mitchell (London: Allen & Unwin, 1957) 87.

William James, in **The Will to Believe** (London: Longmans, Green & Co., 1909) used the context of human development to propose a modified foundationalism, acknowledging the "bottom-certitude" of the consensus gentium. G. E. M.

Anscombe seems to have had James in mind when she wrote: "The greater part of our knowledge rests upon the belief that we repose in things we have been taught and told." ("What is it to Believe Someone?" in **Rationality and Religious Belief**, ed. Delaney, p. 143). On a slightly more philosophical level, but making the same "communitarian" point, John Taylor wrote: "The individual is an abstraction; man is a family." **The Primal Vision** (London: S.C.M., 1974) 93.

36. **God and Other Minds** viii; also 192, 268.

37. Ibid., 271; cf. viii.

38. **Faith and Logic** 165.

39. The expression is Mitchell's; see **The Justification of Religious Belief** 41f. In "The Grace of God," in **Faith and Logic** 166 he explained how the logic of "grace" might shift the onus of proof to the sceptic. "The strength and graciousness of his [e.g. the saint's] personality is somehow incommensurate with what we know of their natural antecedents." "To call a man 'holy' is not to praise him or to prize him but to recognize and respond to something in him that commands respect rather than deserves it."

40. **New Essays in Philosophical Theology** 183.

41. **A Science of God**? 110. The life of faith offers "believer's evidence," Farrer maintained: recipitur secundum modum recipientis (its effect is measured by the receptivity of our wills). Hence "the disclosure [of God] is full in proportion as the response is holy and the inspiration deep." 117; cf. Price's "sensitivity model" in **Faith and the Philosophers** 22f.

42. **Sylvie and Bruno** (London: Macmillan, 1898) 258.

AUSTIN FARRER ON LOVE ALMIGHTY

Ann Loades

This essay is about Austin Farrer as preacher of the gospel of divine saving judgment; for this purpose the Farrer of the sermons, the Lent books, the paragraphs for use at the Eucharist; even the Farrer who taught the use of the rosary. The thread of the essay is provided by some of Farrer's remarks in **Love Almighty and Ills Unlimited** (1962). The title reminds us of P. T. Forsyth's [1] exposition of divine love as that which "has absolute power to give itself eternal and righteous effect." [2] Behind Forsyth lies a long tradition of discussion of theodicy, notably the challenge to Christian theology thrown down by Bayle at the end of the seventeenth century, and Leibniz' attempt to console those who like Bayle expressed inconsolable grief at the way in which "evil" is woven into the entire cosmic texture. Farrer seemed to summarize this tradition when he wrote: "The very intensity of the indignation or grief which we feel over the affliction or destruction of God's creatures is a testimony to the esteem in which we hold the happiness and the mere life of the creatures affected." **(SB** 49) Farrer's masterly appreciation and criticism of Leibniz sprung both from his own brilliance as a philosopher, and from his thorough grasp of the Christian gospel.

How may we as it were provoke Farrer to speak to us, so that he is not merely the elegant philosopher and theologian of a generation ago, but a living voice? Perhaps we can deepen our sympathies and refresh our sensitivities to those features of Christ's passion reflected in Farrer's presentation of the gospel by paying attention to two profoundly moving modern "passion stories". One is Rosemary and Victor Zorza's recently published account of the death of Jane, their twenty-five year old daughter, [3] a situation of extreme physical evil, in which moral evil is not allowed to proliferate, despite Jane's death. Another is Rolf Hochhuth's account of a German love story, [4] which ends in utter tragedy. Neither of these stories were written to further the interests of any religious apologetic, so it is by accident

93

that they give us a sense of what might be meant by the claim that the passion of Christ is of universal significance. Both stories, like the passion stories of the gospels, are retold by "interested parties"; that is, by the parents of the girl who died, coming to terms with her death, and by Hochhuth, attempting to comprehend the country of his childhood.

As Farrer remarked, to Christians, "The mixed character of the world is not so much an honest enemy as a treacherous ally, changing sides in the heat of the battle. It supports us in our proof of a Creator, but turns against our endeavour to understand him." (LA 11). Nevertheless, a theology which "stops short at creation, and disinterests itself in the conflict of evil with the divine goodness, handles a one-sided abstraction, which is not even the diagram of an actual belief." (LA 13). Farrer first turned to an examination of the dualist heresy in order to refer his hearers and readers to Augustine's defence of the single origin for the world. "A good God created good sorts. The problem remains, why he should let them go so rotten." (LA 30). [5]

Farrer invites us to consider "any range of actual creatures in all their intensity of being, their intricacy of action, their mutuality of relation; and then think of the divine appointment on which their existence rests. Think of the will that can will such things, and you may experience the awe which authentic deity commands." (LA 75). We cannot (pace Leibniz) [6] conceive the conditions, or rather, the unconditionedness, of the divine creative choice. (LA 62). "All we can do is make up our minds whether or no we are grateful for the creative acts which have made us what we are, and put us where we are." (LA 75). And yet he sounds this note of realism for those willing to express their gratitude, for "in the many and various interactions of the world, there are innumerable misfits, vast damage to systems, huge destruction and waste" (LA 52). With this remark in mind, we can begin to pay attention to the account of Jane Zorza's last months of life, and her parents' affirmation that "She met her end surrounded by love, with all emotional debts paid and the pattern of her life complete." (9) The treatments failed, she was brought home, and was able to accept her approaching death, yet "turn back to life," not least because her doctor guaranteed to help her all he could. She now knew that her painkillers would not be rationed, and she never spoke again of taking her own life. She even began gradually to help her own father to come to terms with his own terror of death, terror born in wartime Poland. She insisted that her death was natural, and asked, "what am I but a speck? What's the earth but a speck? Why should my dying be so unacceptable and so difficult to bear? . . . What's so special about me? . . ." (117-8). She matched her possessions to her friends, so that each would have something to remember her by--something that would please them and be useful. When the time came for her to go to a hospice, her mother thought "that the most terrible moment of all had come, and she was overcome by a sense of failure--conviction that she had failed to preserve the child she had given life to and nurtured for so many years." (127) When she was settled in as best she could be on her first day, one of her nurses did something simple and obvious for her in swabbing out her mouth. "In all her months of illness, when her mouth was often dry, sometimes foul-tasting, no one had ever done this for her." (134). They gave her enough diamorphine to break the cycle of pain and fear, and she was able to go on helping her father face the prospect of his own future death, his fear for himself prompting his fear for her, for "she could retain her serenity about her own death only if she could make him share in it." (178). She became very happy:

> She had no guilt about being helpless and dependent on others. She had always loved to give, but she seemed at last to accept that she could now only receive. Perhaps she realised she could only give by taking--with gratitude and without guilt. Her needs were fulfilled without question and without resentment. In return she lavished praise on everyone who served her, and did so with humility. (234).

It was at this point in the story that her mother said, "I know she's not religious, so I hesitate to use the words, but it's almost as if she were in a state of grace." (235). Her death was described as slow and gentle, a natural end to life. "The waning of her body was easy to believe and to accept. Her retreat had been strangely beautiful to watch. We felt no fear." (241). The concluding epilogue contains some of the most moving passages in the book. It opens with the words, "We had a promise to keep. 'It'll be a fun place for my ashes,' she had said of the garden of Dairy Cottage. It was a hard thing to do, to open the small box and to touch the pale grey powder." (242). But one morning her parents scattered her ashes, halting at the places she had stopped at in her last walk round the garden. And one of her friends said, "I don't need a 'thing' to remember Jane by" . . . "Jane taught me how to make bread. Whenever I make bread, I think of her." (244). Jane had hoped that she would live on in the memories of those she knew, and her parents seem to ask for no further consolation. Should one expect more? One would have to be convinced by what Farrer says in his chapters "Man Redeemed" and "Griefs and Consolations" to want to say more, and as Farrer himself says, "however believing we may be, we hesitate to offer open consolations, unless we have an equal right to grief." (LA 170).

Hochhuth's narrative adds to the dimension of grief; this

time recounting the terror of death born of man's designs, not nature's accidents, which so afflicted Jane Zorza's father, a terror that Farrer understands very well. First notice that Farrer carefully relates what he has to say about "Adam and Lucifer" as symbols of willed evil in **Love Almighty** to his earlier remarks about the "chaos of non-rational forces, each acting of itself with inexhaustible energy," (**LA** 147) and his persuasion that we must:

> accept the order of nature as a system which, the more it is looked into, the more it defies our power to think it otherwise. The world is the natural habitat, not of our bodies only, but of our thoughts. Our lungs can breathe no other air, our minds can move in no other universe. The alterations we can meaningfully propose are only of the sort that we might ourselves be imagined physically to produce; the general lines must lie as they are, or we have no foundation even for our fantasies. (**LA** 158).

Moral and physical evil, then, surface in related fundamental conditions. [7] It is clear, judging from the abundance of examples in his various writings, that Farrer was as deeply disturbed by the second world war as Forsyth had been by the first. Seventeen years after the conclusion of world war II he reminds the readers of **Love Almighty:**

> There is nothing men will not do to one another under the pressure of supposed necessities. I remember discussing the rules and conventions of civilised warfare with a friend in 1939. 'It's no use talking,' he said. 'We shall stick at nothing. There's nothing too bad to be true in war. When we think we've reached the moral bottom, another depth will open, and down we'll go.' (**LA** 178) [8].

And if Anselm's "Et hoc es tu, Domine Deus noster" struck Tillich as astonishing in the particular logical intricacies of **Proslogion** 3, [9] what are we to say of the conclusion of **Finite and Infinite**?

> As I wrote this, the German armies were occupying Paris, after a campaign prodigal of blood and human distress. Rational theology will not tell us whether this has or has not been an unqualified and irretrievable disaster to mankind and especially to the men who died. It is another matter, if we believe that God Incarnate also died, and rose from the dead. But rational theology knows only that whether Paris stands or falls, whether men die or live, God is God, and so long

as any spiritual creature survives, God is to be adored. (300).

Haunted as Farrer was by man's inhumanity to his fellows, Hochhuth warns about "the abject creature lurking in each and every one of us, everywhere and at all times." "Isn't it released or repressed, variously and in varying degrees, by virtue of personal and social standards alone?" And he goes on to "mythologize" this abject creature in a way which Farrer refused to countenance. (IB 81). For Hochhuth said of "the abject creature", "Isn't it the ever-recurrent, sometimes rampant, sometimes latent monster from the deep?" (217). Farrer maintains that we may not cast the origin of sin, perversity or malice into the limbo of the unimaginable. To attempt to do so "is merely to evade the effort of thought or the moral courage required for understanding it in the place where we can come to grips with it, that is to say, in ourselves." (LA 138). Sometimes "we come upon a spiritual stench which wakes ancestral terrors," (LA 144) but have no reason to suppose that the resources of science will prove inadequate to cope with phenomena of this kind. On the other hand there is no ground for ill-founded confidence in our own rational processes; and furthermore much to fear from psychic forces in our own souls which may wear "the guise of a subhuman malice and of an instinctive cunning; forces of which the minds housing them may be largely unaware." (LA 147) Elsewhere Farrer asks what we do to one another by co-existing, by simply being what we are, when, without the least intention "we infect and heal, encourage and depress, poison and purify the people about us, and receive from them a reciprocal influence?" (LIB 35) Not even Farrer, saintly man that he was, dares invoke Heaven to extend his action, "full as I am of a poison and a mischief I cannot control . . . if the walls of my heart were made glass in answer to my prayer, the hurt to my neighbour's eyes and the shame of my conscience would be equal."

> My words and deeds, my neglects and interferences are enough to answer for . . . But even when I see myself in the pupils of the eyes of God, shall I be made aware of all the poison that has flowed from me, not by what I did, but by what I was? Will even the rigour of the last account exact so much? (LIB 37).

Hochhuth's story of "abject creatures" tells of their reactions to the love of "Pauline", a German country woman, for a man fifteen years her junior, a Polish prisoner of war who arouses first her maternal compassion, then her love. She is typical of many of the men and women of her village, a couple of miles from the Swiss border, with no qualms about accommodating prisoners of war in their homes, never for one moment regarding them "as a source of ethno-political danger . . . The effects of ethno-political education are completely nullified by the work of the Church, which asserts that prisoners of war and foreign workers, too, are Christians and human beings." (7). Actions which infringed the prohibitions on consorting with prisoners of war included offering a prisoner of war a cigarette or some bilberry juice. (40) And:

> The courts have often had to pass sentence in the case of trivial offences such as eating at the same table, offering a cigarette and a light, rendering first aid to the injured or giving water, pain-killing drugs and the like. But very often--and herein lies the danger of letting small kindnesses go unpunished--familiarities which at first seem quite innocuous can very quickly develop into love affairs. The vast majority of the cases under review originated in contacts which were innocuous and hardly punishable in themselves. (99)

Engaging in caresses merited a minimum sentence of twelve months in a concentration camp for the women (243) and prisoners of war released for work were warned that they would be hanged if they slept with German women. This particular pair were eventually betrayed by someone Pauline mistakenly regarded as a friend. Hochhuth says that it remains doubtful whether the story can be told at all, given that nearly all its witnesses are still alive. "Their accounts are triumphs of will-power over memory: I did it, said their memory; I can't have done it, said their self-esteem." (49) Such prisoners as Stasiek Zasada had to be hanged by other detainees, where possible by a member of their own ethnic group, for the price of three cigarettes per execution. (178) Another Pole, imprisoned for wearing a pair of shoes left behind by a runaway, was bullied into hanging Zasada in return for his own freedom. Victorowicz was filled with hysteria and panic, but before he could hit on the idea of killing himself, or at any rate of injuring himself so badly that he would be useless the next morning, his wood carving tools were quickly removed and Zasada pushed in to share his cell. (185) Pauline was imprisoned whilst awaiting transfer to a concentration camp, and that fact afforded her some consolation in her agony of self-reproach for having brought her lover to "this"--"this" being what Hochhuth paraphrased as "the cautious euphemism she needed to quell the dread that was beginning, nonetheless to assail her for minutes on end . . ." (187) Her husband added to her shame by his spontaneous readiness to forgive her and resume their life together, though as it happened, he vanished in the Russian campaign. She managed to catch sight of her lover in the exercise yard below and pleaded for his forgiveness. His face was first transfigured as he caught sight of her, though as he called that he was happy to die for her, the light drained out of his face at the realization of it. (192)

Zasada was sustained in his death cell with his companion by his patriotism, (why should he be so presumptuous as to hope that he might survive when so many others had perished?); his memories of Pauline; by trying to console his own executioner, who desperately tried to devise a scheme by which he could die with him; and by the elemental anger both men experienced when they discovered that Zasada was denied even a farewell letter to his parents. Sheer physical courage kept Zasada on his feet in the truck taking him to his place of execution, when the alternative was to ride sitting on his own coffin. Mercifully he did not know that there was no grave for him, as his body was destined to end up on one of the slabs in the dissecting room in a nearby university. On the grassy hillside near the quarry where he was to die, hundreds of people had come to watch, some suffering the blood-lust of the non-combatant, some to express sympathy which only their physical presence could express. "Some were inwardly riven with compassion and others--a very few--numbed by the certainty that their native land would have to pay for this--this too . . ." (266) Victorowicz had memorized Zasada's last message to his mother: "Tell my mother I stopped feeling frightened once I told myself they couldn't inflict half as much pain on me as she suffered when she gave birth to me." (264) Victorowicz became almost as faint as his victim when the moment came, and because he was after all an amateur as an executioner, Zasada suffered death by strangulation, and screamed for his mother again and again. According to Hochhuth, the perpetrators of the event were appalled by what they had done, unanimously claiming to have forgotten how it came to pass--some measure of their inability ever to forget it.

It is to situations of this character that Christian Theodicy must, in the extreme case, address itself. It does so, as Mackinnon puts it, with the claim that "no manner of thing human could possibly be well save for a deed done as concrete and ugly as any hanging of a condemned criminal," and of course, "crucifixion takes longer than the 'drop'." [10] Human protest at either hearing of these stories is questionable, tainted, incomplete, so he says. It has value only as it somehow points to the deed which is held to purify and fulfill our protests against what appears to be irremediably pointless suffering. That deed is proclaimed in the church's liturgy. It is the primary moral response of the praise of God in the liturgy which persistently demands the acknowledgment of the authority on which human life depends, and the source of the believer's nurture, and of the ultimate cleansing of imagination, protest and action. Farrer remarks that "true religion crumbles the structure of selfish invention" (SS 33) and would, I believe, share Mackinnon's conviction that though our theology often limps, we are possibly kept from falling because of our liturgy.

> For liturgy is always thing done rather than thing said, action drawing its sense and power from the action of God in Christ, and by its very character as action preserving for the individual the sense that it is by deed that he is saved and held in the truth. It is by the action of the Eucharist that the life of the individual is, in its daily movement, rooted in and held to the source of its redemption, the action of Calvary and the empty tomb. [11]

Certainly Farrer held the Eucharist to have had its origin in the very words of Jesus himself: "you must expect the most pressing occasion to draw from him the most significant act . . . Then, if ever, things were said and done of which the significance was inexhaustible." (CR 63) The pressure derived from the imminence of Jesus' death--a deprivation of life "exacted by malice, accompanied by ignominy, and executed with torture", (SB 103)--nevertheless the source of redemption for those who harm and kill, as well as for the transformation of the meaning of suffering and death. The Holy Communion, Farrer informs us, "is not a special part of our religion, it just is our religion, sacramentally enacted."

> Of course God is not served only by the celebration of sacraments, but much more by an obedience to his practical commands. But in so far as our religion receives sacramental enactment, it is all summed up in the Eucharist, no aspect of it is left out. For the whole of our religion is summed up in Christ, and the sacrament presents Christ, his birth, death, resurrection, and his present existence: his manhood and his godhead, his being in himself, and the service of his Father. (CF 184)

Here perhaps is one reason for Farrer's interest in the book of Revelation--it sets forth the pattern of a "celestial liturgy performed by Christ and the angels," heavenly actions spilling over in earthly effects, ending with the total conquest of the earth by heavenly grace. (RSJ 23) [12]

Apart from the Eucharist, two other moments in the liturgical year meant a great deal to Farrer, namely, Holy Saturday and "All Souls." **Love Almighty**'s final chapter is an exposition of the theme that "God brings good out of blackest evil." (LA 79) As Farrer said elsewhere, "God leaves no factors out of his reckoning, nor does he plan for an imaginary virtue we haven't got, he plans for the very men we are." (**SS** 19) Farrer stands with those who refuse to concede that the price is too high, as against those who would prefer to return the admission ticket. (**CF** 182) This indispensable theme of what he has to say is in effect a paraphrase of what Leibniz had referred to in "older writers" when they called "Adam's fall felix culpa, a fortunate sin, because it had been redeemed with great advantage through the incarnation of the Son of God." [13] The allusion is to the exultet passage of the vigil of Holy Saturday [14] which goes back at least to the time of St. Ambrose, and which celebrates Christ's victory over the forces of darkness and death. (**SB** 155; **IB** 123) Also, the liturgy of All Souls includes one of two great Franciscan hymns (the other being the Stabat mater), that is, the somber Dies Irae, to which Farrer frequently alludes in his sermons, and of which he provided a superb translation. (**SS** 9-10) These two, together with the Eucharist, indicate the foci of his understanding of "saving judgement."

It is also worth noting that C. S. Lewis had recently re-minded his readers that the biblical texts were put together by the church as a unity, and a sense of the unity of scripture was fostered not only by doctrines of inspiration and by a version bearing the stamp of one age, such as the Authorized Version, but by the liturgical context in which the texts were read and heard as from a sacred book, "a book so remorselessly and continu-ously sacred that it does not invite, it excludes or repels, the merely aesthetic approach." [15] And the creed identified the map of meaning in terms of which scripture is to be read. Farrer held that

> without the creed to guide me I should know neither how to call upon God, nor on what God to call. God may be the very sap of my growth and substance of my action; but the tree has grown so crooked and is so deformed and cankered in its parts, that I should be at a loss to distin-guish the divine power among the misuses of the power given . . . So I take refuge in that image of God which we have described as branded from outside upon the bark. Here is a token I can trust, for he branded it there himself; he branded it on the stock of man when he stretched out his hands and feet and shed his precious blood. The pattern of the brand was traced on me by those who gave the creed to me; God will deepen it and burn it into me, as I submit my thoughts to him in meditation. (**LIB** 14) [16]

So Farrer represents in his varied writings a determination to recover the coherence of metaphysics and history, symbolism and meaning, comparable to that of some of the great French theologians engaged in liturgical renewal. The liturgy is inseparable from theology proper: "God can convince us of God, nothing else and no one else can: attend the mass well, make a good communion, pray for the grace you need, and you will know that you are not dealing with the empty air." (CF 59) From that center he wrote his biblical commentaries and his other theology, employing religious imagery and ideas not to enhance the sense of the capacity of human beings to transform themselves and their awareness of the world, but as Mackinnon comments to enlarge perception by giving us a vivid sense of that absolute by which our conduct is judged. [17]

We can begin from his reply to those who might ask how the free-for-all of physical processes came to achieve the oases of system and delicacies of structure we observe. His instructions were first, consider science, and if scientific enquiry leaves one with a sense of dissatisfaction, because one wants to know why it should all happen at all, he suggested his second answer, creative will, "and why not the will that wrestles with the praying mind?" [18] Equally of course, the praying mind wrestles with the idea of God as will:

> When we pray, we must begin by conceiving God in full and vigorous images, but we must go on to acknowledge the inadequacy of them and to adhere nakedly to the imageless truth of God. The crucifixion of the images in which God is first shown to us is a necessity of prayer because it is a necessity of life. The promise of God's dealing with us through grace can be set before us in nothing but images, for we have not yet experienced the reality. When we proceed to live the promises out, the images are crucified by the reality, slowly and progressively, never completely, and not always without pain--yet the reality is better than the images. Jesus Christ clothed himself in all the images of messianic promise, and in living them out, crucified them, but the crucified reality is better than the figures of prophecy. [19]

Love Almighty reaffirmed Farrer's conviction that "God is the living, self-justifying truth, and to plead for him can only be to say what he says, to capture an echo of his meaning in the idioms of our stammering speech." (LA 16) He disclaimed the prophetic voice, but offered theology and philosophy--nothing new, except freshly phrased argument. (LIB 13)

man life." (FL 24) The human histories cited at the be[ginning of]
this article fall within this "tissue of figures." As matt[ers] a[re]
lection they must be seen in relation to the self-reve[lat-]
ion of love, Christ's incarnation and redemptive sacrific[e]
[e] of "obedience to inspiration, a waiting for direction, an ac[-]
[an]ce of suffering, a rectitude of choice, a resistance to temp[ta-]
[io]n, a willingness to die." (BM 20) If we can believe that G[od]
[i]s everywhere, by ceaseless creative energy and providenti[al]
[gui]ding, we may also say "that he added this above all, that h[e]
[act]ally identified himself with one of his physical creatures and[d]
[pe]rsonally acted in and by that creature's life." (BM 109-10) Here
[i]s a man who had no need to say "There I was not myself,"
[T]B 43) living and thinking himself into being God's Son (TV
[..]), with an ability to converse with his divine Father (IB 136;
[..] 103) and to persevere in loyalty and dependence on him,
[e]ven when failure was the reward, torture the price, and death
[th]e end." (EM 70) And as Farrer asked, "Is it not a more profound
[hu]miliation to be incarnate in death than in any life . . .?" (CF
[..])

> Never was there a man whose words and
> actions were more utterly his own. The spontaneity
> of his compassion moves us to tears, the blaze
> of his indignation shocks us: his speech is an
> unforced poetry, the coinage of his heart: the
> sacrifice on which he spent his blood was a deci-
> sion personally made in agonies of sweat. If any
> man made his own life, Jesus did; yet what was
> the impression that he left on his friends? That
> his whole life was the pure and simple act of
> God. What Jesus did was simply what God did
> to save us all. (CF 148)

[H]ere is a reality supremely important, though too intangible to
[be] proved, (EM 156). Intellectual honesty may either discount
[or] embrace it; for it is as difficult to make out the theoretical
[c]ase for the trustworthiness of this reality as it is to make out
[th]e theoretical case for belief in providence, God's use for his
[gl]ory of everything that happens, however unhelpful it seems,
[w]here people trust him (CF 216)--or even, we must add, where
[th]ey do not. In the matter of redemption, extreme demands will
[b]e made upon thought, imagination and the understanding of our
[e]xperiences. In this case, did the creator make the tormentors
[o]f Jesus, and his fugitive disciples instruments of his will, (IB
[1]75) and does he so deal with comparable circumstances so that
[th]e believer wants to say something about death which could
[n]ot otherwise be said? For example:

The sheer elegance of Farrer's writing and pr
nd the particular kind of biblical exegesis which enga
eave him open to the charge that he was directing his
owards types and figures thereby avoiding the horror of th
narratives. However, Mackinnon rightly saw that the
schemes and types elucidated by Farrer from the text of St
Gospel "enable man to penetrate the deeps of a judicial
and find in them the steadfast mercy of God." The aim is
at the context in which "the transcendent is revealed an
accessible to men, as an action, as a deed and not a
speech." Words and deeds alike in the gospels "are held t
by the great deed of the Passion, which gives them the
sense, and from which the power that is in them derives." [2
it would almost seem that Farrer went out of his way to c
some of his critics about their mistaken views of his int
not only by tackling their comments directly, but by th
great care he evidently took to put all his verbal skill
disposal of the object of the attention of his hearers and
and especially in his clarification of the theme that God
good out of blackest evil. In Chapter 6 of **Love Almigh**
defends the claim that God raises the dead. However, "
God, it is not enough to die; we must be made to look
place where he has lodged himself, and at the created
with whom he has clothed himself," (**LA** 125-6) and in part
at that person nailed to his claim. "The agony brought h
his cry of abandonment, but the placard hung over his
(**LA** 175) Crowned and naked, the contrast was perfect,
56) a self-offering put beyond possibility of recall, nail
alive, immovable, dragged through the breakdown of the
to the breaking of the mind, of which the last fragment
leavings were verses from the psalms. (**LIB** 93) The sting of
fixion was that "You nailed your man to the beam like a
deal plank, and there you had him," able to move just e
to breathe with pain, suffering the detestation of pain an
norror of death. (**LIB** 53) [21] And yet Christ's eternal F
aw these inescapable agonies as "accidents and distract
eeing the current of Christ's will "steadily turning in it
direction." His Father "knew that he was praying for the salv
f mankind with the whole weight of his sacrifice." (**CR** 33)

Here, then, is the core of Farrer's theodicy: "I can
ut to you a self-revealing action of God in which he jus
is claim to almighty goodness." (**FL** 97) Almighty love
is human creatures a vestige of his likeness, and "inter
ith incarnation and redemptive sacrifice to save them from
l perishableness and unnatural perversity." (**FL** 98) The d
ve which animates creation and redemption is a parable
iman kindness. More particularly, "Creation is a parable
iman invention or manufacture; redemption is a tissue of fig
om various types of deliverance and restoration met wit

O good Jesus hear me
Within thy wounds hide me,
Suffer me not to part from thee
From the malicious enemy defend me
In the hour of my death call me
And bid me come to thee
That with thy saints
I may praise thee for ages everlasting. (**LIB** 50)

The idea of death, "our being stripped of all bodily conditions, and taken out of the whole comforting, reliable system of created things" horrifies us, defeats imagination, baffles philosophy:

> Yet by this horrifying fate, and by no other, we fall into the hands of God, <u>not</u> of his creatures. We are placed at God's free disposal, for him to do with us according to his great mercies, and not according to the requirements of a vast physical system, this world God has created, and which he is, as it were, committed to uphold. (**CF** 113-4)

Here is Christ, brought to his death not by physical accident, but by his own self-offering and the activities of the creator's creatures, yet "the careful searching fingers" (**CR** 40) found their clay in his sepulcher, clay "prepared for the potter's use by sacrificial obedience; by flogging, crucifying, death." (**SS** 82) Here, as Farrer says, believers are brought to the acid test of faith, (**EM** 4) which attaches hope to Christ in his sepulcher, and makes him an image of hope, stretching between sacrifice and life renewed by the creator. (**CR** 26) We cannot claim that 'evidence' for the resurrection of Christ is conclusive, and its supreme improbability may, as it were, tip our mental scale against it.

> The believer's mental scale tips the other way. And why? Not because he is a more, or a less, scrupulous historian, but because to him the miracle, though naturally improbable, is divinely appropriate. His predicament is much like that of the apostles whose faith he shares. They knew that the return of the dead is the proverbial case of that which does not occur, and that those who meet the departed are deemed to see visions or to suffer delusion by spirits. Yet they allowed themselves to be convinced, not only because the event had the marks of reality, but also because it was the divinely appropriate conclusion to a train of events in which they had begun already to recognise the divine. (**FL** 101-2)

The resurrection justified the goodness of God not by explaining how every evil could be cured but by revealing a power and a love that promised total victory. (BM 7-8) In a "Kierkegaardian" image Farrer expressed this as the power "to carry us all through the same motions; and so, what we have to do is not simply to imitate, but to adhere: to take hold, by faith, of this strong swimmer in the gulf of death, who not only supports us, but makes us swim with him." (SS 68) By "faith," Farrer meant our determination to accept, or to trust, what draws our love and by "prayer" the actual exercise of faith, giving us the objects we are to pursue. (EM 156) It is our achievement insofar as "by sympathy and by well-controlled use of imagination we identify ourselves with Christ's act or attitude in the narrative set before us . . . We make his action ours, or rather (as we think it truer to say) he takes our action into his own." (TV 11)

I mentioned earlier Farrer's attention to the theme of divine judgment in Christian theology. The sense of accountability to a divine judge, or of facing a "last judgement" (the latter a periphrasis of the former) is integral to the question of the connection which may hold between the life one lives now and any alleged "life after" death, that unavoidable reminder that one's life is not in the end secure. One cannot inculcate "divine judgement" as integral to belief without argument (which Farrer provided) for the truth of the body of belief of which it is a part, nor inculcate it without fostering in oneself a particularly uncomfortable form of self-appraisal, developing the habit of attention to past action and present desires. The pretence and self-protection of Job's comforters have to be abandoned in the face of a judgment which destroys them without possibility of mistake. (IB 191) Farrer sounds as though he were confronted by Nathan: "I am the man who abdicates control and embraces self-pleasing veiled by self-deceit, and is there a worse man to be found?" (LIB 66) Without this acknowledgement in conscience of God's judgment (EM 161) we cannot "be most sovereignly ourselves."

So Farrer's view of the mistake of those (as in Hochhuth's narrative) who will want to claim that their actions, however terrible, were justifiable by political, moral or religious rules is that they are opposing the purpose of almighty love. There is no comfort in the extenuations that can fairly be offered for their all too natural actions. What will console men at the hour of God's judgment will be the discovery, "that though they fought against God, they did not prevail; and when they seemed to have crushed His kingdom, they were putting victory into His hands. But more than this it will console them, that, if they can be reconciled, they are forgiven." (EM 14) We may have to suffer the truth of our condition, albeit assured of mercy, "when we see what a God we have, and how we have served him," (SB 154) but beyond that Farrer does not choose to speculate.

In conclusion, then, Farrer invites us to acknowledge that "we can do nothing positive which does not give effect to ever-lasting love." Thus he can propose that "the more creative we are (if we must use this arrogant word) the more we give expression to his will; for he is the sole creator, and to create through us is his design." (BM 99) It is in this connection again that Farrer deploys his verbal skill in his attempt to capture the echo of the divine self-justification":

> You have a poor opinion of the God who made you, for you do not let me justify myself to you by coming to you, as I desire to do, and living with you, and being your God. How can I justify myself to you, unless you let me do these things? I commended my love to you, in that while you were still in sin, I gave my Son to die for the ungodly; so I sought to justify myself. But I have not justified myself to you, not to you, until you let me treat you as part of my dear Son, and be to you that Father that I am. (EM 123)

So Farrer indicates what sense can be given to phrases such as "incorporation into Christ." (IB 99) For when the believer prays, "the hand of God does somewhat put aside that accursed looking glass, which each of us holds before him, and which shows each of us our own face. Only the day of judgement will strike the glass for ever from our hands, and leave us nowhere reflected but in the pupils of the eyes of God." (CF 122) Insofar as the glass is pushed aside, the believer realizes that "instead of the mirror-image taking form from the gazer's face, the gazer's face takes form from the image," that is, what the believer and the Father see is the projected image of "sonship." "Love shares flesh and blood with us in this present world, that the eyes which look us through at last may find in us a better substance than our vanity." (CR 8) The incarnation is the means by which God brings good out of blackest evil and loves and saves whatever there is to be loved and saved. (LA 190)

108

NOTES

1. **The Justification of God** (London: Duckworth, 1916).

2. Ibid., 3.

3. R. & V. Zorza, **A Way to Die** (London: Deutsch, 1980). The Zorzas are writers and journalists.

4. R. Hochhuth, **A German Love Story** (London: Weidenfeld & Nicholson, 1980).

5. We can bypass Farrer's discussion of Gnosticism, noting its connection with other concerns, for instance in the work of D. M. Mackinnon, **The Church of God** (Westminster: Dacre, 1940) 48, writing on the 'contemporary Gnostics' who had tended to make the scholar the 'arbiter of Christian truth'. Cf. **IB** 138, 162; **CF.** 37, 41. Also V. White, **God and the Unconscious** (London: Fontana, 1960) and **Soul and Psyche** (London: Collins, 1959); **IB** 195-6.

6. Farrer's introduction to E. M. Huggard's translation of Leibniz' **Theodicy** (London: Routledge & Kegan Paul, 1951) 32-3; **LIB** 72-3.

7. Cf. J. Baillie, **Natural Science and the Spiritual Life** (London: O.U.P., 1951) 32-3.

8. Cf. D. M. Mackinnon, **God the Living and the True** (Westminster: Dacre, 1940) 20; and H. D. Lewis, **Our Experience of God** (London: Allen & Unwin, 1959) 294; **R** 34, **RSJ** 164.

9. P. Tillich ed. C. E. Braaten, **A History of Christian Thought** (London: S.C.M., 1968) 163.

10. D. M. Mackinnon, 'Prayer, worship and life' in ed. D. M. Mackinnon, **Christian Faith and Communist Faith** (London: Macmillan, 1953) 245, 253.

11. Ibid., 246.

12. Cf. **EM** 133, **BM** 73-6; and E. Lampert, **The Divine Realm** (London: Faber, 1944) and A. G. Hebert, **Liturgy and Society** (London: Faber, 1935).

13. Leibniz, **Theodicy** 147.

14. H. A. R. Schmidt ed., **Hebdomada Sancta, volumen alterum: Fontes historici, commentarius historicus** (Herder, 1957) 639f. Cf. K. Rahner, ET. Bourke, **Theological Investigations** (London: Darton, Longman & Todd, 1971) 7:I, pp. 145-150.

15. C. S. Lewis, **Selected Literary Essays** ed. W. Hooper (London: C.U.P., 1969) 144. Cf. his **Reflections on the Psalms** (London: Fontana, 1956) dedicated to the Farrers, and Farrer's introduction to **A Short Bible** (London: Fontana, 1956) **IB** 10, **EM** 159.

16. Cf. **FL** 91; **SB** 151; **CF** 169; **IB** 118.

17. D. M. Mackinnon, 'Coleridge and Kant' in ed. J. Beer, **Coleridge's Variety** (London: Macmillan, 1975) 199, 202.

18. **Theoria to Theory** 1 (1966) 75.

19. H. W. Bartsch ed., ET R. H. Fuller, **Kerygma and Myth** (London: S.P.C.K., 1953) 222-223.

20. Mackinnon, 'Prayer, worship and life,' 243.

21. It is clear that Farrer does not make the mistake of thinking that pain can be related to the will of God as an evil wholly turned into a moral instrument. 'Pain is the bitter savour of that mortality out of which it is the un-imaginable mercy of God to rescue us. When under suffering we see good men go to pieces we do not witness the failure of a moral discipline to take effect; we witness the advance of death where death comes by inches.' P. 40 of Farrer's essay in J. Gibb ed., **Light on C. S. Lewis** (London: Bles, 1965). It is also important to notice that Farrer displays deep affection and compassion in his various writings for the creatures whose habitat was his garden, and never makes the mistake of minimalising animal pain, **LA** 77-105.

'APPREHENSION' IN <u>FINITE AND INFINITE</u>*

Rodger Forsman

INTRODUCTION

In **Finite and Infinite,** his first major work in philosophical theology, Austin Farrer attempts to reconstruct the cosmological argument. He adopts the same basic epistemological strategy as is found in every form of the cosmological argument, namely, to exhibit a certain highly general fact or set of facts about the world as evidence for the claim that God exists. Thus Farrer argues that rational conviction of the existence of God rests upon grasping the dependence of finite being upon the creative act of infinite being, a dependence made evident by an analysis of finite being (262, 265). This analysis consists of a description of finite being in terms of the categories of essence and existence.

Farrer departs significantly, however, from the usual under-standing of the logic of inference from world to God. Right from the outset he argues that the existence of God can be established neither deductively nor inductively. On the contrary, he argues, since God cannot be inferred he must be "apprehended" in his effects if he is to be known at all (8). In his view the function of argument for the existence of God is not to lead us to the conclusion that God exists by showing that that conclusion follows either deductively or inductively from a certain description of finite being; rather, it is to describe finite being in such a way that its dependence upon divine creative activity can be grasped and the creator "apprehended".

---

* I wish to acknowledge an SSHRC travel grant which helped make it possible for me to attend the Princeton Conference on the thought of Austin Farrer.

Now if theistic argument is understood in the way just outlined the notion of "apprehension" clearly has a central epistemological role to play in relation to the problem of showing how belief in God is rationally justified: for despite the claim that belief in God follows neither deductively nor inductively from the description of finite being, that description nevertheless is the basis on which belief in God rests, and the notion of "apprehension" signifies at least that there is some kind of evidential relation between belief in God and the description of finite being. What, then is "apprehension"? What does Farrer mean when he says that we "apprehend" God in his effects if we know God at all? And just what is the evidential relation between belief in God and the description of finite being by virtue of which the latter can be said to justify the former? It is the primary purpose of this paper to answer these questions.

I shall argue, partly on the basis of Farrer's actual use of 'apprehension' and partly on the basis of the way in which he conducts his main and subsidiary arguments in **Finite and Infinite**, for the following conclusions:

1. 'Apprehension' is Farrer's general term for non-inferential awareness, and in abstraction from particular contexts carries no implications about the modality of such awareness.

2. In certain contexts, namely those in which Farrer is dealing with the main issue of how we know that God exists and also with the subsidiary issues of how we know that the self is a substance, that there are substances other than the self, and that there are value-characteristics in things, 'apprehension' signifies the satisfaction of an epistemological criterion by virtue of which judgments of these kinds are warranted.

3. This epistemological criterion can be analyzed as a rule of evidence which defines the conditions under which we are entitled to believe that God exists, that the self is a substance, that there are substances other than the self, and that there are value-characteristics in things.

I shall proceed as follows: First I shall survey what Farrer himself says about 'apprehension' in **Finite and Infinite** and briefly outline some of his uses of the term. In an attempt to get further light on the role of 'apprehension' in the special contexts indicated above I shall then describe the epistemological problem which the notion of apprehension was introduced to solve. Finally I shall set forth two ways of interpreting 'apprehension', namely, an intuitionist interpretation, and secondly what I call a criteriological interpretation. I shall argue that the latter best accommodates the epistemological demands which Farrer places on 'apprehension'.

I. 'Apprehension': Some General Remarks

Farrer does not make it altogether easy for us to understand what he means by 'apprehension'. The closest that he comes to defining the term is to describe apprehension as "objective grasp of realities" (45). As he does not explain the metaphor, it is quite futile to launch an analysis of 'apprehension' from his definition. We are only slightly better off when we turn from his definition to an investigation of the contexts in which the term occurs. The most cursory inspection of **Finite and Infinite** discloses that Farrer uses 'apprehension' in a bewildering variety of ways. To cite just a few examples: we are said to apprehend God (27), will activity (130), the moral quality in men (76), metaphysical structure (18), and ordinary sense-perceptible qualities, shapes, and relations (ix, 75f., 80). It is also readily noticeable that Farrer glosses 'apprehension' with terms plundered quite freely from the ordinary vocabulary of perception and cognition, such as 'see' (17, 71), 'appreciate' (ix, 100), 'aware' (61, 65, 75ff), 'recognize' (27), and 'feel' (231). We discover also, from his discussion of the nature of rational theology, that apprehension as a way of coming to know that God exists, is to be distinguished from demonstration and induction and from certain other commonly recognized criteria for the acceptability of hypotheses, such as logical coherence and clarity, and adequacy in description of phenomena. It appears in the light of such facts that 'apprehension', for Farrer, is the most general term for non-inferential awareness; it ranges from perception of one's own experiential states (288), through ordinary sense perception as indicated above, embraces memory (108), and the understanding of words, (27), and includes awareness of value attributes, substantial connection, and divine activity, which are not usually thought to be accessible to sense perception.

Some of Farrer's uses of 'apprehension' are, of course, quite clear, such as those that imply awareness of some object of sense perception; but unfortunately, such uses of the term are of no help in furthering our attempts to understand 'apprehension' when what is at stake is a claim to knowledge of divine activity, substantial connection, and value attributes of things. Since these latter objects of apprehension are our prime concern here, it is of little help to know that ordinary sense perception, for example, is a kind of apprehension. It seems that in order to make progress toward understanding what it is to apprehend such objects as divine activity, substantial connection, and value attributes in things, we must look for data different from that which could be supplied by a mere list of the occurrences of 'apprehension' or its synonyms or near-synonyms.

What kind of data would be relevant to this inquiry? I suggest that we can achieve a satisfactory understanding of 'apprehension' only if we are able to describe it in relation to the episte-mological burden which it is intended to bear. On the assumption that this approach will supply the necessary data, I shall now proceed to describe the epistemological tasks which Farrer requires 'apprehension' to perform.

II. The Task of 'Apprehension'

What philosophical problem or problems does Farrer seek to solve by appeal to 'apprehension'? Within the framework of the central argument in **Finite and Infinite**, Farrer employs the notion of apprehension in four contexts which are especially signifi-cant for helping us understand the notion. First, of course, he speaks of apprehending divine activity in or through finite being. Second, we are said to apprehend the substantial unity of the self in and through rational activity. Third, we apprehend the substantial unity of things other than the self in and through our experience of moral obligation or the way in which our field of operation is conditioned by other things. Finally, we apprehend value-characteristics in things, again through the way in which they condition the field of our operation. As the basic structure of argument is the same in all four cases, I shall discuss in detail only the first--because the question of how Farrer thinks we come to have knowledge of the existence of God is our chief concern-- and the second, because Farrer himself places great weight on the importance of being able to claim that the self is a substance. I shall begin with the latter.

Farrer's argument that the self is a substance consists essentially of three moves. First he analyzes 'substance' in terms of the notion of activity or operation, with special stress on the causal properties of a substance whereby both the coherence of a substance into one unit and its persistence through change are to be explained. A substance, he says, is "a unit of activity" (28), or "a unit of operation which is sufficient for a certain sort of independence" (30). A substance is a complex entity whose mode of unity is such that it is a thing in its own right rather than being a thing whose thinghood, like that of a house or a heap of sand, consists merely in the convenience to us of regarding it as a thing and which rests only on regular sequence and contiguity of phenomena. A substance, by contrast, is a thing in its own right because it has the capability of bringing about its own succeeding phases and of operating or acting as one dynamic whole despite its complexity. 'Substance', thus designates a thing in virtue of a mode of relation between its successive phases or among its constituent elements. This relation Farrer calls "real" relation (or sometimes "substantial relation" or "substantial connexion"), by which he means a relation which is not merely fortuitous nor analyzable in terms of observed regular sequence or contiguity. To call something a substance, then, is to say something about the kind of unity which makes it one thing. Furthermore, to call something a substance is to apply to it a description which is metaphysical in the sense that the correctness or incorrectness of the description is not to be decided by reference to regular phenomenal sequence and contiguity. Plainly Farrer's account of substance is formulated with an eye on Hume's reduction of causality and thinghood to regular phenomenal sequence and contiguity; everything thus turns on Farrer's ability to convince us that there are instances of a relation which makes a thing one thing but which is not analyzable on Hume's formula. Where are such instances to be found? Farrer points us to the self, particularly to acts stemming from rational choice.

The second move in the argument, then, is a long and detailed description of will and self. Beginning with an account of the single act of will it ends with a description of the self as a unified center of activity (**FI**, Part II). The point of this description is to focus our attention upon certain events--human acts--in such a way as to invite philosophical interpretation of them in terms which enter into the analysis of the notion of substance. In other words, the somewhat ordinary description of the self as a unified center of activity is intended to enable us, in some way, to come to accept the analysis of substance as the correct philosophical account of what we are aware of in our exercise of rational choice.

The third move is the crucial one: Farrer holds that the description of the self engaged in voluntary activity is a description of a substance, and he defends this claim by invoking an "apprehension" of "real relation" in the self's activities. In short, a self is a substance because a substance is, by definition, an entity with the causal properties and mode of unity described above, and these are "apprehended" by the self in its activities.

It is this argument which must now be examined. It is convenient to schematize the argument in order to help focus attention on the role of Farrer's appeal to apprehension in defense of the claim that the self is a substance.

(1)   Anything is a substance, or is an instance
        of substantial connection, if the above descrip-
        tion of a substance is properly applicable
        to it.

(2)   X (= a segment of my behavior) is a deliber-
        ately performed action.

(3)   In choosing and enacting X I apprehend substan-
        tial connection. (My deliberate act brings
        about the next phase of myself in a way
        which is not analyzable in terms of regular
        phenomenal sequence and contiguity, but
        yet which can be explained only by saying,
        "I chose X", or "I did X deliberately".)

(4)   So X is an instance of substantial connection.

Some comments on this argument are in order. First we
can dispose of what might appear initially to be an objection
to the suggestion that these four statements adequately express
Farrer's argument that the self is a substance; it might seem
in virtue of (2), (3), and (4) that what these statements represent
is, at most, Farrer's argument for substantial connection in discrete
acts. But there is no difficulty here nor any misrepresentation
of Farrer's position; for the issue of substance is the issue of
real connection. Farrer's account of the unity of the self is no
different in principle from his account of real connection in the
single act of will; the question of the substantiality of the self
is focussed in the question of the substantial connection in the
single act (121, 229). Hence, although the four statements above
seem to refer only to the single act, this is no disadvantage since
they focus attention upon the issue which is fundamental for
Farrer, namely, whether or not there is among events that kind
of relation which Farrer calls "substantial". We can now proceed
to consider some points that are of greater significance.

In this argument, (2) neither entails nor is equivalent in
meaning to (4). Nevertheless, (2) is relevant to the acceptance
of (4) at least to the extent that it describes the range of human
behavior and experience in which substantial connection is most
clearly apprehended. On the basis of this fact it is possible to
make a short comment about (3), the appeal to apprehension.
Farrer insists that substantial connection is not apprehended without the mediation of reflection upon the active relations between
the self and other things (68, 222), or upon the nature of relations
other than substantial relation (80ff., 84f.), or upon sense experience (97), or upon a comparison of acts which are fully deliberate
with those which are less so, such as actions which spring from
desire (144f.), or upon the different aspects in which the self

can be said to be one self but which nevertheless fail to be identical with the substantial unity of the self (222ff., 229). In short, substantial connection is not apprehended "neat", so to speak. This consideration, in fact, does much to explain the structure of Farrer's argument for the substantiality of the self; for it is plain that we are expected by reflecting on our activity as Farrer does on his, to apprehend our substantiality (78). These facts strongly suggest that there is a very close connection--one is inclined to say, "an evidential connection"--between (2) and (4), and that an understanding of (3) will depend to a large extent on clarity about the relation between (2) and (4).

But why shouldn't we say that clarity about the relation between (2) and (4) depends upon clarity about (3)? The answer to this question must be made in terms of the strategy I am following in the attempt to give a clear account of 'apprehension'. The matter can be put as follows: If we already knew what apprehension is, then presumably we would also be able to say a great deal about the relation between (2) and (4). But we really do not know yet what apprehension is, but are trying to find whatever data might be available either in the text or in the structure of Farrer's argument which will shed light on the appeal to apprehension. And it seems that the relation between (2) and (4) might be an important clue, for Farrer does seem to regard the truth of (2) as relevant to our coming to know the truth of (4), and it is in exactly that context that the appeal to apprehension is made.

What conclusions can we draw from the preceding discussion which will contribute to a description of the logical issue or issues in relation to which 'apprehension' is introduced? First, to characterize something as a substance is to attribute to it a certain description. Second, the aptness or inaptness of applying this description to anything is not to be determined by reference to sensation either directly or by deductive or inductive inference from what can be known by sensation; nor is it to be determined by mediate or immediate inference from certain ordinary-language descriptions of human action. Third, Farrer's account of the will and the self shows, nevertheless, that it is by reflection on human action that we are allegedly aware of substantial connection; the account of the will and self is thus in some way relevant to the epistemic acceptability of the claim that the self is a substance.

Of these three conclusions the second and third are of greatest interest in relation to the present task of describing the logical problem which 'apprehension' is introduced to solve; for what these conclusions tell us is that Farrer's ordinary description of the will and the self supposedly help us to come to know that the self is a substance even though that description neither entails nor inductively supports the claim to know that the self is a substance. Clearly, if the descriptions of will and self did entail or inductively support the conclusion that the self is a substance, there would be no need to appeal to apprehension. To put the matter briefly, 'apprehension' is introduced in order to fill an epistemological gap between (2), 'X is a deliberately chosen act', and (4), 'X is an instance of substantial connection', a gap which consists in the fact that (2) does not entail or inductively support (4), and yet our knowledge that (4) is the case supposedly depends in some way upon our being aware of the kind of situations described by (2) or sentences like (2). What the appeal to apprehension must accomplish, then, is to enable us to overcome this gap; or to dispense with the metaphor, the task of 'apprehension' is to enable us to assert (4) on the basis of (2). This is not, of course, a completely satisfactory account of the role of 'apprehension' in the argument for the substantiality of the self; for it does not tell us how the appeal to apprehension can warrant us in asserting that the self is a substance, nor does it explain how an account of human action can be a basis for that claim. But it at least indicates the kind of problem for the resolution of which 'apprehension' is introduced, the epistemological context in which 'apprehension' is to function; and this is all we were seeking to determine at present. Further analysis of the task which the appeal to 'apprehension' must perform will be presented after I outline Farrer's argument that knowledge of God rests on an appreciation of the nature of finite being.

Structurally, this argument is exactly the same as the argument for the substantiality of the self; I will therefore treat it more briefly. The argument, again, involves three moves. The first consists essentially of an analysis of what Farrer calls the "cosmological idea", i.e., the theist's scheme of God and the creature in relation (16). Now how are we to understand this cosmological relation? First, the relation is conceived of as a relation between existing beings and not merely a relation within a set of linguistic terms. (17). Second, it is not any kind of relation between existing beings which is exemplified in observation, since it is simply not the case that God's activity is observable in any ordinary sense of 'observable'; hence, this relation is not analyzable in terms of observed regular sequence and contiguity. Third, this relation, if present at all, is present universally since every creature is related to God in exactly the same way in so far as it is a creature. Fourth, the cosmological relation involves a kind of dependence of finite beings upon infinite being such that the finites derive their existence from the infinite. Now as was pointed out above, Farrer conceives of theistic argument as an attempt to exhibit finite being as composed of various elements so disposed that relation to the creator is a necessary condition for the existence of finite being. In short, the theist is asking the question, 'What can be thought of as existing in its own right'? And he is insisting that a complete account of the conditions for the existence of finite beings must include reference to divine activity.

Farrer points out that this question is just what was being asked by philosophers who made distinctions among 'substance', 'attribute', and 'accident'; and consequently, he argues, whether the theist realizes it or not he is discussing issues which traditionally have been discussed in substance-language (17f.). The second move in the argument, then, is a metaphysical description of finite substance stressing a distinction between essence and existence (= modality and activity) in order to call attention as clearly as possible to the alleged existential insufficiency of finite being (265). Finally, Farrer argues, in view of the distinction between essence and existence in finite being, we "jump to the cosmological intuition", i.e., we apprehend God as the being in whom this distinction is transcended (262, 265).

Clearly, both in the argument for the substantiality of the self and in the argument for the existence of God, the same epistemological strategy is employed. In both arguments Farrer bases certain conclusions, namely, that the self is a substance and that God exists as the creator of finite being, on certain descriptions, respectively a description of the self as a rational agent engaged in voluntary activity, and a description of finite being, this description itself vindicated by the previous argument that the self is a substance. In both arguments, also, what the descriptions describe is that through which the conclusions are known; and the appeal to "apprehension" in both cases designates that evidential relation. This much seems clear on the basis of the analysis and argument I have presented thus far. What is not yet clear is precisely how the appeal to "apprehension" accomplishes the task Farrer sets for it. How it is that a description of the self as a rational agent engaged in voluntary activity, for example, can serve as the justification for the claim that the self is a substance? I shall now proceed to examine that issue.

If one were to be skeptical that the self is a substance, in Farrer's sense of the term, one way of presenting the reasons for one's skepticism would be to argue as follows: [1]

> (a) The only non-analytic propositions that can be believed with warrant are those that can be justified by reference to one's own experiences or which can be derived from propositions describing one's experience.

For the sake of clarity let us construe this premise in an empiricist manner; by 'experience' then, we will mean 'sense experience' although we do not need to presuppose a sense-datum analysis of the notion of sense experience. Let us go a little beyond

Hume, too, and agree that the notion of derivation of one proposition from another includes both demonstration and inductive reasoning. This premise, then, has to do with our sources of knowledge. It is the assertion that there are no sources of knowledge, that is, ways of showing that a proposition is worthy of belief, other than by reference to observation by the senses, or by derivation from propositions that can be known in that way. (I am ignoring memory; it is not relevant to what we are examining.)

A skeptic might then add a second premise, as follows:

(b)   That the self is a substance is not a proposition which is warrantable by reference to one's own experience, or by derivation from what can be known by reference to one's own experience. Therefore,

(c)   We do not know that the self is a substance.

Such a line of argument could be deployed against the considerations which Farrer offers in defence of the claim that the self is a substance. The skeptical argument, briefly, is that the epistemological gap between the proposition that the self is a substance, and the kind of data adduced by Farrer in his account of human action, cannot be overcome because propositions describing human action neither entail nor inductively support the proposition that the self is a substance, and neither is that proposition warranted by any of the accredited routes to knowledge. An examination of possible responses to such an argument might shed light on Farrer's attempt to defend the claim that the self is a substance by appeal to "apprehension".

Any deductive argument of the form (a.b.), therefore c, can be reversed by denying the conclusion and one of the premises. One reversal of the above argument, then, is as follows:

(not-c) We do know that the self is a substance.

(b)   That the self is a substance is not a proposition which is warrantable by reference to one's own experience, or by derivation from what can be known by reference to one's own experience. Therefore,

(not-a) It is not the case that the only non-analytic propositions that can be believed with warrant are those that can be justified by reference to one's own experiences or which can be derived from propositions describing one's experience.

Someone who argues in this way is claiming, essentially, that there is another source of knowledge in addition to sense perception and inference by which factual beliefs can be justified. Such a source of knowledge, by which we are alleged to gain knowledge of what cannot be known by sense perception, memory, self-awareness, or by inductive and deductive reasoning, has frequently been called "intuition". I shall use this term to signify the line of argument just described. The task of a philosopher, who can argue in this way, is that of making credible the suggestion that there is such a source of knowledge.

However, there is another possible reversal of the skeptical argument outlined above:

(not-c)   We do know that the self is a substance.

(a)   The only propositions that can be believed with warrant are those that can be justified by reference to one's own experience or which can be derived from propositions describing one's experience. Therefore,

(not-b)   That the self is a substance is a proposition which is warrantable by reference to one's own experience, or by derivation from what can be known thereby.

Unlike the intuitionist, someone who argues in this way is not advocating additions to the usually recognized set of accredited routes to knowledge. His task, then, is not to show that there is an unusual source of knowledge additional to those usually accepted, but to show how beliefs ruled out by the skeptical argument are warranted by appeal to the usually accepted sources of knowledge. I shall call this the criteriological approach, since it involves the attempt to specify epistemic criteria by reference to which we can understand how problematic beliefs of the sort in which Farrer is interested can be believed with warrant.

I have outlined two responses to an argument which would show that we cannot know that the self is a substance. Now Farrer's appeal to "apprehension" in defence of the claim that the self is a substance can be seen as a response to such a skeptical argument. Obviously, Farrer wants to deny the conclusion of that argument. Just as clearly, Farrer would reject epistemological commitments leading to the conclusion that we cannot know that the self is a substance. Furthermore, Farrer's claim that we apprehend the substantiality of the self is plainly an allegation that in spite of the skeptic's second premise (that neither experience and inference therefrom can tell us that the self is a substance), we are nevertheless entitled to hold that belief, because of "apprehension". But which of the two responses most closely approximates to Farrer's position?

It is not possible for me to argue here in detail that the intuitionist response is not what Farrer is offering. [2] Numerous texts conflict with an intuitionist interpretation of 'apprehension'; and texts which at first sight seem to support such an interpretation can be explained readily in other ways. Furthermore, the fact that Farrer writes a book containing much argument in support of his claim that the self is a substance seems to me to be a decisive methodological consideration against an intuitionist interpretation of 'apprehension'; for there would be no need of argument were apprehension a modality of perception, a "sixth" sense perhaps, by which we discern substantial connection in a way analogous to our awareness of color patches by visual perception. I shall proceed now to outline a criteriological interpretation of 'apprehension'.

III. 'Apprehension': A Criteriological Interpretation

It is important to be clear at the outset about the nature of the enquiry now to be undertaken. We are not asking, now, what considerations Farrer offers as evidence for the claim that God exists, or that the self is a substance. We have already taken note of the considerations which Farrer offers as being relevant to the epistemic acceptability of such claims. What we are now asking is, How can such considerations have the evidential role which Farrer attributes to them? For example, given Farrer's concept of substance as a unit of activity capable of a certain sort of independent operation, and an ordinary description of the self as a thing which deliberates upon and chooses between alternative courses of action, what authorizes us to assert the former on the basis of the latter? This is what we must now determine.

When a statement or hypothesis is proposed to us for belief, we typically assess or grade it. We express our assessment by terms such as 'credible', 'doubtful', 'incredible', 'certain', and so on. In short, we apply one of a large set of epistemic grading labels to express our estimate of the cognitive worth of a given hypothesis or statement.

Now what are the criteria on which we base such appraisals? As the history of philosophy shows clearly, there have been many answers to this question. For example, empiricist philosophers have frequently wanted to claim that no non-analytic proposition, including those that express ordinary perceptual judgments about the colors of physical objects is acceptable unless it is either a proposition describing a state of affairs about which one cannot be mistaken, or is probable in relation to such a proposition or to a set of such propositions; an example of an independently acceptable proposition would be, "I seem to see a blue patch now", whereas "The wall is blue" would be an example of a dependently acceptable proposition. It was thought that there must be some propositions that are independently acceptable in order to supply a "foundation" for the rational justification for propositions expressing our ordinary perceptual beliefs about physical objects. Since it was thought that one could not be mistaken about one's immediate perceptual states, propositions expressing what one is aware of when one is in such states were thought to be propositions of the required sort. What confers credibility on propositions of that sort is just the occurrence of the experiences which the propositions express. These occurrences could then be said to be states of the subject which whenever they occur are infallible marks of the worthiness for belief of propositions expressing those immediate states of awareness. A criterion of epistemic worth for basic propositions, that is, a condition which if satisfied confers rational acceptability upon such propositions, would on such an account be a state of the perceiving subject such that the subject could never be mistaken as to whether or not he is in that state, and such that whenever he is in that state propositions expressing that state of awareness are warranted for him. Some current treatments of theory of knowledge regard the attempt to describe criteria of epistemic worth in terms of awareness about which the subject cannot be mistaken as wrong. Nevertheless, the problem of the criterion has been conceived in this way; and it is helpful to have such a statement of it before us, for some of the things that Farrer says about 'apprehension' are readily intelligible in contrast with such a background, as will become apparent as we proceed. Empiricist epistemology of the sort described above, with its challenge to rational theology and to metaphysics, is one of the dominant features of the philosophical landscape within which Farrer's own argument in **Finite and Infinite** is set. As we shall see, Farrer's criterion of epistemic worth is in some ways considerably less stringent than the empiricist's.

I am using the expression 'criterion of epistemic worth' to signify a condition which if satisfied confers rational acceptability upon a proposition. I shall now argue that as Farrer uses the term in relation to the propositions that the self is a substance and that God exists, 'apprehension' signifies satisfaction of such a criterion. I shall argue further that this criterion is adequately expressed as follows:

> C = If S <u>takes it for granted</u> that p (under relevant standard conditions) then S is warranted in believing that p.

For our present purposes, 'p' ranges over the propositions that the self is a substance, and that God exists. I shall now refer to and comment upon some texts which lend support to this interpretation of 'apprehension'.

We recall that in Farrer's argument for the substantiality of the self the crucial issue was whether we could apprehend real relation. A relation which would merit being called "real relation" would be found in a sequence or collocation of events which is non-fortuitous and yet is not analyzable in terms of regular observable sequence or contiguity. Farrer then referred us to situations of deliberate choice between alternative courses of action as the prime context in which we apprehend real relation. The relation between one phase of the self and its succeeding phase, in such a situation, is non-fortuitous inasmuch as it is the outcome of rational choice, and it is not an instance of a general statement expressing an observed regular sequence (130). In so far as we engage in deliberate activity, then, we in fact presuppose that we are substantial units (109). That this is Farrer's view is evident in his account of how the conception of the world as a scheme of interacting substances can be the scheme of "common sense":

> If we treat the world, as the savage does however absurdly and superstitiously, as consisting of beings having several values and claims, and in our behaviour show this and have some terms to describe these differences, it is enough. There is no need to consider thinghood, nor, since we take our responsible freedom for granted, selfhood either. [3]

The point being made here, I suggest, is the naturalness, even the inevitability, of taking ourselves to be substances. What, then, justifies us in believing that we are substances? We can formulate Farrer's answer, I suggest, by saying that what justifies us in accepting the claim that we are substances is that we take it for granted--find it unavoidable, natural, inevitable to believe that--we are substances in the determinate conditions to which Farrer calls our attention, that is, in the situations of deliberation, decision, and carrying out of an intended course of action, and so on.

Again, closely similar considerations hold with respect to apprehension of divine activity. We can find in Farrer two very closely related epistemological commitments regarding this issue, commitments about what he clearly treats as ultimate lines of defence of the claim that God is known through finite being. The first is the notion that what convinces us of the reality of divine activity is the actual tendency of our thought when we reflect on the nature of our own existence. The second is the view that there is a spontaneity, a naturalness, or even an inevitability about our taking ourselves as finite beings. I shall deal with these in turn.

Farrer holds that when we reflect upon the kind of active existence which we exercise we quite naturally begin to deploy concepts which are of use to the rational theologian in his attempts to give logical content to the notion of absolute being. For example, when we compare some of our own acts with other acts of ours we sometimes recognize that some of them are more free, that is, more directed by rational considerations, than are others, and in the same way we come to know what it is to cope with the limitations under which we operate as rational agents (50f., 160-170, 292f., 295). What Farrer means can be illustrated as follows: We usually wish to base decisions only on sufficient data. Sometimes, however, we do not have sufficient data, whether through failure to put forth the effort to acquire it, or because it is practically impossible for us to acquire it, and so on. But we know what we would have to do to put ourselves in position to exercise a progressively more rational choice. In other words, while recognizing the limitations of knowledge under which we must make decisions we have some idea of a mode of rational will which is not subjected or not subjected as extensively as we are to such limitations, and we strive, "aspire", to attain a more satisfactory relation to the conditions under which we exercise will. Such an idea of rational will which is not subjected to human limitations is used by the rational theologian to fill out the concept of absolute being. But is it not an idea derived from theology:

> . . . however applicable to theology once it has been obtained, the 'idea' arises quite independently of any theology through the consideration of human activity as such. To think it fully, we need only the thought of its limitations and its scale, and an aspiration involving the bare notion of an indefinite upward extrapolation of the scale. [4]

Our ability to think about God at all depends on our ability to distinguish in ourselves levels of activity. Distinguishing one act from another in degree, that is rationality, of activity makes it possible for us to distinguish between activity as such (existence) and any mode of activity (essence). Again, this is a purely non-theological distinction (262, 267f.). But it lends itself to employment in rational theology because it makes it possible to raise the question, "Why is it so?" of anything in the world. Thus:

126

> . . . our own being presents us with the spectacle
> of a scale of degrees within itself, for freedom
> and knowledge 'aspire' to become more absolutely
> themselves and in so doing point to an archetype
> in which they are quit of their limitations. [5]

Now according to Farrer when one asks, "Why is it so?" when one is sufficiently impressed by the distinction between existence and essence, both in the kind of beings which one encounters in one's ordinary experience and in oneself, to regard it as a fact requiring explanation, one has already made a leap into rational theology and is betraying an "implicit" awareness of absolute being:

> . . . our actual implicit awareness of God's cre-
> ative action in the finite is made explicit by
> a train of reasoning which analyses the finite
> by an implicit comparison with God, condemns
> it as composite by the same implicit comparison,
> and judges the composite to be dependent by
> the implicit awareness that this compositeness
> is the effect of divine creation, placing a qualified
> and finitised image of the divine being outside
> God. [6]

It is in this way that Farrer explains our ability to ask of anything, "Why is it so?"

Now we need to distinguish two different issues that are involved in this explanation. First, there is Farrer's claim that a natural tendency of the mind leads us to the point of asking, "Why is it so?" Second, in asking that question we are manifesting our "implicit" awareness of God as absolute being. Farrer later rejected this second claim, and it is worth examining his argument on this point for it discloses an important epistemological commitment on his part.

Summarizing his argument in **Finite and Infinite** Farrer says:

> If 'it' puzzles us by being 'so' rather than
> otherwise, it is because we contrast it with an
> 'it' that should stand above and be exempt from
> such arbitrary determinations; that is, an active
> existence or existent activity which should be
> full, absolute or entire, having all the 'suchness'
> or modality that is worth having. [7]

He notes that he was aware at the time he wrote **Finite and Infinite** that ". . . it is not clear that we are under any obligation to think of the 'scale of being' as running up to a determinate maximum." [8] He states further that such a doctrine, stated abstractly, would not be convincing. What was his solution?

> I had to admit that the doctrine, thus abstract-
> ly stated, would never convince. But (I argued)
> nothing in so high and metaphysical a field of
> speculation ever will convince us, unless it is
> carried by an actual tendency, or dynamism,
> of our thought. [9]

Now what was wrong with this solution, in his opinion? It is important to note that what he later saw as a defect in his former argument was not the view that an actual tendency of the mind impels one to raise the question, "Why is it so?" but his claim that in coming to think of ourselves as metaphysically limited beings we are implicitly contrasting ourselves with absolute being. That claim, he later thought, could not be supported in the light of a careful examination of what we seem to be aware of when we find ourselves impressed by our metaphysical limitations, that is, when we ask of ourselves the question, "Why is it so?" Farrer argues, in criticizing his former argument in **Finite and Infinite**, that when we contemplate finite existence what we are implicitly aware of is, "A determining act; an act which (to escape an unending regress) must be purely originative, or sovereignly free." [10] Farrer goes on to assert that from the proposition that an effect is an act of sovereign freedom one cannot derive without further argument that the effect is due to an act of absolute being. He then goes on to state his new position on the question of what we are aware of when we ask, "Why is it so?"

> If we see something arbitrary, something
> betraying external appointment, about any active
> existence's taking on any one form or modality,
> why should not we be contrasting it with the
> case of an existence which should clothe itself
> (its action, that is) with no form but the form
> it freely chooses? [11]

The question Farrer asks here is purely rhetorical; it is not raised as a prelude to further inquiry, but as an indicator that an answer to the question of what convinces the theist of the reality of divine activity has been found, for what remains of his original position is that it is the tendency of the mind which leads us to the point of asking, "Why is it so?"

Now what is the epistemological importance of the claim that it is a natural tendency of the mind that leads us to the point of asking "Why is it so?" Farrer is telling us here that the case for theism rests on "an actual tendency, or dynamism, of our thought." Now this is not merely an observation about the psychology of theists. Farrer is expressing his own epistemological commitment here. He is, in effect, laying bare for us what in his judgment is the actual epistemological situation in which theists find themselves; reflecting on the structure of theistic belief Farrer has concluded that what the theist actually regards as determinative of his right to believe that God exists as creator of finite being is the sheer naturalness of the belief, or better, its seeming inevitability in the determinate circumstances in which the theist comes to entertain that belief.

It bears stressing that Farrer is not adducing a supposed God-ward orientation in human thinking as a fact about the world from which the existence of God can be deductively or inductively inferred; nor is he urging that the existence of God be postulated in order to account for belief in God. He is addressing himself to the question, 'What assures the theist of the reality of divine activity?' And his answer to this question is that the theist is assured simply by the fact of his coming to have that belief after careful consideration of the nature of his own existence and of the nature of the kind of beings of which he has ordinary empirical knowledge.

Farrer makes a closely similar point in another place. Asking whether we have any positive reason for believing that the cosmos is grounded in God he refers to:

> . . . the contingency of all things--they might be there, they might not be there, all might be otherwise, and we are impelled to see the Eternal and Necessary behind them. Yet the conclusion is not logically inevitable . . . why should we suppose them other than merely contingent? And yet the mind is impelled to the step. Short of supposing a universal deceiver let loose in the world--in which case goodbye to philosophy!-- why are we not to believe that this impulsion also is due to the divine 'word' through things? [12]

Here Farrer indicates quite clearly his commitment to the view that the supposed naturalness, or better, the inevitability of theistic belief had a criterial role in relation to the question, "What gives one the right to believe in God as creator of finite being?" It is only a very short step, a step which, I believe, involves merely a choice of terminology, from what Farrer says here to saying that Farrer is embracing the view that if one takes it for granted that God exists as creator of finite being, under the determinate circumstances in which theists come to that belief, then one is warranted in holding that belief.

I suggest that the line of argument which we have been considering in relation to our alleged knowledge of the reality of divine activity in finite being calls for construal in terms of the "taking for granted" criterion of epistemic worth. Farrer has stressed the supposed spontaneity of our taking ourselves to be creatures, the apparent inevitability of arriving at that belief in the determinate circumstances in which the theist arrives at it. His view is that when we carefully consider the nature of human existence, we simply do believe that God exists as creator of finite being; and what we believe after serious and careful consideration of all of the factors in the situations in which we come to entertain that belief, we have the right to believe.

I conclude that the evidence I have adduced adequately supports my claim that Farrer's justificatory appeals to 'apprehension' are very plausibly understood in terms of the notion of the satisfaction of a criterion which confers worthiness of belief upon a proposition; and that this criterion is satisfactorily described in terms of the notion of "taking it for granted that p".

NOTES

1. My strategy here is influenced by Roderick Chisholm's discussion of "the problem of the criterion" in his **Theory of Knowledge** (2nd ed.) ch. 7. (Prentice-Hall, 1977).

2. I argue the point with detailed analysis of texts from **FI** in my unpublished doctoral dissertation. "Austin Farrer's Notion of Apprehension: An Analysis and Appraisal of His Claim to Knowledge of Substance" (University of Toronto, 1974) 157-178.

3. Austin Farrer, **Finite and Infinite** (London: Dacre Press, 1943) 86.

4. Ibid., 51.

5. Ibid., 264.

6. Ibid., 265.

7. Farrer, **Faith and Speculation** (London: Adam & Charles Black, 1967) 116.

8. Ibid., 116.

9. Ibid.

10. Ibid., 117.

11. Ibid.

12. Farrer, "The Rational Grounds for Belief in God", in **Reflective Faith,** ed. Charles C. Conti (London, 1972) 21.

AUSTIN FARRER'S NOTION OF
"CONSCIENCE AS AN APPETITE FOR MORAL TRUTH":
ITS METAPHYSICAL FOUNDATION AND IMPORTANCE
TO CONTEMPORARY MORAL PHILOSOPHY

John Underwood Lewis

> The Christian is not just to do certain things: he is to be a certain kind of person.
>
> LADY HELEN OPPENHEIMER

> . . . morality is more genial and generous when we act as we ought because the effects will be happy than when we act as we must if we are not to incur the effects of breaking the rules.
>
> PROFESSOR THOMAS GILBY, O.P.

INTRODUCTION

There is, I think, one characteristic trait of mainstream modern and contemporary ethical theory that above all others distinguishes it from its classical and mediaeval counterparts. That trait is its formalism, its emphasis and oft-times exclusive concern with the formal character of ethical rules and the consequent disinterest in philosophizing about their contents. There are exceptions here, of course, even within the mainstream. G. J. Warnock's view in his **Contemporary Moral Philosophy** [1] that it is possible intelligently to elaborate the thesis that "morality has some at least roughly specifiable content" [2] is a case in point. He too, however, seems well aware that his is perhaps a minority view of what constitutes genuinely philosophical discourse about moral matters, for he finds it necessary to ask the following two questions: "Is it one's task to elucidate . . . the formal character of moral discourse, its general character as a system of 'prescriptions' or 'evaluations'? Or is one to attempt to elucidate the content of morals, to describe in outline and to make distinctions within the general range of phenomena to which moral concepts are applicable?" [3] Warnock's thesis is that it is both, but the fact that he found it necessary to ask these questions indicates that he sees that for better or for worse modern and contemporary philosophers have a radically different understanding of what it means to do moral philosophy than the Greek, Roman and mediaeval moralists did. The reason for this is because they have an understanding of the nature of the moral life that differs from their earlier counterparts.

If one accepts these propositions, H. A. Prichard's seminal article, "Does Moral Philosophy Rest on a Mistake?" can be read not only as an highly sophisticated and serious (and, I would say, seriously wrong) piece of moral philosophy, but also as a succinct summary of the historical development of moral philosophy in western civilization. I am thinking here of his claim that the "moral question" as he called it, namely, "Is there really a reason why I should act in the ways in which hitherto I have thought I ought to act?", has on the history of the subject been given basically two different kinds of answer. One is, because "doing so will be for our good . . . for our happiness;" the other is, "because something realized either in or by the action is good" or right. [4] The first answer is of course and most notably Aristotle's; the second is Kant's. Indeed it is Kant's above all, for he so unhinged moral rules specifying what is right from the goals of human living that the relation between them would necessarily be seen as merely contingent. This led him, as Alasdair MacIntyre has pointed out, "to enjoin us to seek not to be happy, but to be deserving of happiness." [5] Self-interest became selfishness, and lost its place in an authentic ethical life. And as I read the situation Kant created, its significance consists mainly in this, that the concept of virtue would increasingly be replaced by that of duty in moral living and in philosophizing about it, and that furthermore, given the reason the concept of virtue was displaced by duty, namely, again, that ends to be attained through human living were no longer thought of as norms for determining moral righteousness, the criteria for determining whether an act or intention was moral or immoral would have to be purely formal. The centrality of the concept of "the good" as "that which is fulfilling" thus came to be replaced by the concept of "right" as meaning "that which conforms to a rule;" and it took moral philosophers only a century to redefine the scope of their discipline to mesh with this transformed conception of the moral life.

Let me put this last point a little differently. So dominating has Kant's characterizing of morality become that now, in our own time, a person's moral life is thought to be restricted to his or her dealings with other persons (and by some, brute animals as well) [6] evaluated in terms of formal justice or fairness. Self-regarding acts and acts performed for self-regarding reasons, such as the desire for happiness, are thought to be amoral at best. They are referred to as "prudent" with "prudence" redefined to mean "expediency." In short, the content of morality of which Warnock wrote is no longer virtue but duty. The question is no longer "What would the just man do?" but "What does justice require?", and its answer is tested in formal terms, in terms of some basic formula such as its universalizability or its agreement with what rational men and women would do if by hypothesis they were living in the Rawlsian "original position."

Let me pause here briefly for an aside. I am not implying by what I have just written that Kant is the originating source of ethical formalism in western philosophy. He is not. The continental moral theologies of the 16th and 17th centuries, for example, were legalistic in a way that even Kant, for all his concern with duty, would have abhorred. That was, after all, the time when casuistry in ethics became so outrageously distorted; it was the time too when Jansenism was spawned, and it took no less than Saint Alphonsus Liguori (fl. 1748-1785), with his insistence upon the primacy of individual conscience over the claims of authority, to turn back its influence in both academic circles and in the hearts and minds of common layfolk.

To return now to my central point. The proposition that duties defined in terms of formal principles such as Kant's categorical imperative or Hare's notion of universalizability of Rawls' concept of fairness constitute both the core of moral living and the central subject of moral philosophizing is based on the assumption, tacit or explicit, that human beings are by nature wilful or wanton. [7] Recall that for Kant virtue "implies ability and readiness to <u>overcome</u> our inclination to evil on moral principles, . .. and that we possess virtues if, in the contest with immoral inclinations, our moral dispositions show themselves possessed of such strength that they always come out triumphant." [8] The significance of this statement can be seen by comparing it with Aquinas' definition of the concept of virtue, [9] taken from Saint Augustine. [10] "Virtue," he says, is the perfection "of being <u>inclined</u> to act in a certain way," namely so as to "make its possessor and his action good." [11] Not the overpowering of desire, but the desire for what is humanly fulfilling is for Aquinas, as it was for Aristotle, the aim of virtue. But for Kant, clearly, the central human task is perceived to be that of mastering or curbing one's natural bent, a task accomplished through subservience to laws, both moral and juridical.

In sum, Kant's understanding of human nature and moral responsibility stands in marked opposition not only to Aquinas' thought on those topics, but to the thinking of all those who with

Aristotle begin their philosophizing by noting that "every activity, artistic or scientific, in fact every deliberate action or pursuit, has for its object the attainment of some good." [12] Aristotle's overriding ethical concept is this notion of "the good," described as "that at which a thing for its own part seeks;" and his point in making that notion central is that what a person needs to know to attain moral perfection is not what rules to obey but what the good as such consists in, a good that "consists, on the one hand, in the attraction emanating, as it were, from the things that are good, and on the other, in our responsiveness and our willingness to consent" to it. [13] If I read him correctly, Dr. Farrer understood the moral life in this way too; and against the background of my introductory comments I'd like to elaborate that point.

AUSTIN FARRER ON
"CONSCIENCE AS THE APPETITE FOR MORAL TRUTH."

In 1936 Canon V. A. Demant wrote in **Christian Polity** [14] that the "characteristic Catholic outlook is always most deeply an outlook upon what things are, rather than upon what they do . . . Tell men only what they must do, what price they must pay for existing at all, and you will numb them into despair . . . But tell them what they are, of their dignity as made in the image of God . . . and you will help them to revive hope in this dispirited generation." [15]

I quote Canon Demant here for two reasons. First, his insistence upon grounding moral values on the metaphysics of human personality and, with philosophers such as Aristotle and Aquinas, refusing to think, as philosophers such as Prichard and more recently Alan Gewirth do, that men's moral lives are sui-generis or ideomatic, compartmentalized or walled off from the rest of human living, prefigures the line of thought that Dr. Farrer himself took.

Secondly, Canon Demant's reference to "this dispirited generation"--by which he meant the period of the 20s and 30s--is subsumed by him under the more general and insightful heading of "the spiritual heresy of our modern era;" [16] and in this too he prefigures Dr. Farrer who continually develops his moral philosophy against the background of what in **The Freedom of the Will** he calls the "positivist reduction." [17] Time and again Dr. Farrer undercuts the foundation of that reduction: "If the [rule] is laid down," he wrote in "A Moral Argument for the Existence of God," "that nothing is to be accepted for philosophical consideration but what is at least virtually contained in the flattest common sense and that the homme moyen sensuel is to be the measure of all things, the Christian argument has nothing to say." [18] That, again, was Canon Demant's position as well. His literary style was of course that of overstatement and challenging defiance, as was befitting a disciple of the Oxford Movement, but his point, like Dr. Farrer's, is sharply put: "When the men of the Enlightenment wanted to give man a status as the foundation of hope, it was a poor truncated man they tried to encourage--a being with no height and depth in him, turned loose to do lots of things and to be nothing in particular." [19]

This, then, is in general Austin Farrer's problem: to develop the outlines of a moral philosophy that would be compatible with the distinctive character of his own religious life and theological understanding of human personality, while at the same time enabling him to meet three criteria that history and his own Oxford life imposed upon him. The first was that his moral philosophy had to seem credible to humanists, who insist, and rightly, that "laws were made for man, not man for laws" [20] but who base that affirmation on the metaphysical assumption that human beings are not merely the most perfect of beings in the natural order [21] but, indeed, in the whole of reality. Secondly, he had to strive in the best tradition of Christian thinkers contemplatively to plumb the depths of Christian spirituality in an effort rationally to understand the profound significance of the fact that human beings are moral agents. Finally, he had to avoid at all costs the well-intentioned but fundamentally distorted ethical system-building of Kant, [22] his heirs and predecessors, including those in the 12th century who affirmed the thesis debated in their universities, but still on the agenda today, that human beings are by nature inclined to evil. [23] Indeed, as to the vitality of this view in our own time, I think it is true, as Henry Veatch wrote in a recent article in Ethics, that it is "currently fashionable" to picture "human beings as appetitive animals, bent in the pursuit and gratification of an indefinite variety of desires, impulses, inclinations, and what not, there being really only one major restriction . . . namely [that] in pursuing one's own goals, one should be careful, insofar as possible, not to interfere with the other person in the pursuit of his." [24]

The concept that Dr. Farrer employs in developing his moral philosophy is that of "conscience" defined as "an appetite for moral truth." I first ran across this notion in 1961 when I read his 1958 Michaelmas sermon preached at Pusey House, Oxford; [25] and it was only years later that I realized that his use of the concept there was a summary of its more fully developed treatment in chapters 13, 14 and 15 in **The Freedom of the Will.** It was put forth in "A Moral Argument for the Existence of God" too, of course, in the same year as he presented his Gifford Lectures.

Now as a strict, "essential" definition in terms of genus and difference, Dr. Farrer's understanding of conscience as "appetite for moral truth" presents certain logical and etymological problems; [26] as an insight into the nature of morality and into what it fundamentally means for one to be a human being, however, it cannot be improved upon. Let me address myself to these two points in turn.

(1) Conscience and the nature of morality.

Recall Prichard's proposition that the history of moral philosophy can be read as a continuing battle between what is sometimes called the ethics of virtue (e.g., Aristotle's **Nicomachean Ethics**) and the ethics of duty (Kant's **Groundwork of the Metaphysics of Morals**). It is a central aim of Dr. Farrer to champion at least some version of the former and to discredit the latter. "At bottom," he said at Pusey House, "conscience is not a set of precepts," [27] and this is all the more true to the extent to which they are articulated in abstraction from the demands and inclinations of human nature and from the circumstances and situations in which human beings with their habits and experiences, hopes and values find themselves. Writing in "A Moral Argument for the Existence of God" about the fact that people think that "drowning strangers are to be rescued, not laughed at" [28] he says that it falsifies the moral character of that situation to say that we decide that "the rescue as such is an obligatory performance [much] as we get the dog to regard it as due that he should fish out of the pond the stick we have thrown. What we come to a mind about is that our fellow-man is such that we should assist him in danger whether he happens to enjoy the advantage of our acquaintance or not. And so it is natural to say that we see something about him, namely that his humanity claims our succour." [29] Moral claims, Dr. Farrer wrote in **The Freedom of the Will**, "are shouted at me by the very existence of my neighbours . . . " [30]

If it be asked how this view of the foundation of moral judgment and action differs from Kant's, who after all did insist that one alternative formulation of the Categorical Imperative is "Always regard persons as ends, never as means," [31] the answer surely is that for Kant the reality that stakes out claims in our moral lives is the "Idea" of "Person," [32] whereas for Dr. Farrer it is, to stay with his own examples, Potiphar's wife who "makes passes at you," [33] John, "who though his death would darken my day, is no influence for good on my life," and Mary, "who though so dear, is so naughty." [34]

Thus he says,

> 'Rational agent' may be a true description
> of the proper object of regard, but it is not
> a complete description. I may say that it is with
> the insurance agent that I do business; it is irrele-
> vant that he is Mr. Jones and that he loves his
> children . . . It is not similarly the rational agent
> that I regard, but Tom, Dick, or Harry; and in
> regarding any one of them I abstract from nothing
> that makes the man. Beauty cannot move my
> senses, this lovely picture may. Rational agency
> cannot waken my regard, Henry may. [35]

The central point here is that Dr. Farrer is taking great pains to avoid developing any kind of ethical formalism--and this, of course, is why his work is so important to contemporary moral theory. He is refusing to think of judgments of conscience and ethical decision-making in terms of the legal model, something that comes through quite clearly in his Pusey House sermon where he describes and then dismisses the "dog and bone" picture of conscience according to which, when we "scratch about" for moral guidance, we uncover "the buried formula from the deep soil of our mind-- . . . the rule which bids us be chaste, or truthful, or whatever it happens to be." [36] Indeed, in **The Freedom of the Will,** Dr. Farrer devotes a whole section of the chapter on "Responsibility and Freedom" to this very topic, a section he entitled "Conscience de-legalized." [37] It will "always remain," he wrote there, "that the uncovenanted well-doing by which good men are good, is not a performance of duties," and this, because conscience is not the "interiorization of the [moral] law." On the contrary, he adds, "in her most developed, most sensitive activity, [conscience] leaves law clean behind." [38]

Given these statements it might seem that although Dr. Farrer is surely not a Kantian, he must certainly be a crypto-existentialist--or perhaps a situational ethician. He is neither; but to realize why, it is necessary to understand something of his philosophical and theological anthropology.

(2) Conscience and the human person.

In a monograph published eight years after Dr. Farrer's Gifford Lectures, Lady Helen Oppenheimer wrote a sentence that to my mind sums up Dr. Farrer's fundamental assumption about the moral life. "Christian morality," she wrote, " . . . is a response to a given situation, not a special set of values or . . . supernatural commandments." [39] That sentence summarized her sustained attempt to exorcize the view of many people, Christian and non-Christian alike, that God is "a Lawgiver, but . . . such an extra strict one that before Him one has only duties and no rights . . . " [40] "The claim of God is seen [by these people] as legal and external;" and it is "small wonder," she writes, "that when it ceases to be backed by legal and external sanctions it is thankfully allowed to lapse." [41] (Of course it is, one might add, because the surest way a person can find himself between a rock and a hard place is by thinking that the quest for moral excellence on the one hand and on the other the desire for personal fulfillment are somehow incompatible. As Dr Farrer's good priest-friend Eric Mascall said when discussing the proposal that we can "love God without regard for our eternal happiness," some things are psychologically impossible. [42] The attempt at an "entirely un-self-regarding devotion to the God who is supremely worthy of love" and the working belief that it is "sinful in wishing to achieve beatitude" [43] are surely high on the list.) Such assumptions seriously distort people's moral lives, and in what follows I should like to trace Dr. Farrer's reasons for thinking they do.

One way of getting at the core of Dr. Farrer's moral theory is through his metaphysics, more specifically through his rejection of Aristotle's insistence upon the reality of what Dr. Farrer refers to as "the timeless essence of man," [44] in relation to which the individual human person is seen as nothing more than an "accidental embodiment." [45] . . . That conception of the relation between any given individual man and the "essence of humanity" anchored Aristotle's entire ethics of virtue and gave him a basis for asserting that, ethically speaking, the good man is the one who lives a life of philosophical contemplation in accordance with moral and physical excellence, or "virtue." In Aristotle's view, in other words, individual men and women begin their lives as potentially perfect human beings whose central task was to become actually perfect--or as close to it as their abilities and social, political and physical environment allowed for. They were to do this by acquiring and exercizing the four "cardinal virtues" as they came to be known in early mediaeval times, of practical wisdom, justice, temperance and courage, as well as the "intellectual virtues" of science and contemplation. In such people the perfect "essence of man" was to find its only embodiment. And because it did not matter who embodied the "essence," the only relation between it and the individual person was, in Dr. Farrer's word, "accidental." It is not surprising, then, that he adversely criticized Aristotle for failing to make room in his moral philosophy for the fact that virtuous decisions must be "inventive." [46] "'Be human, my son,' was for the greeks the "supreme moral injunction," the Gifford Lecturer said; "'Be a Man with a large M.' What we call the pull of the ideal was simply the self-realization of the natural species man . . . For what are [men]" Aristotle maintained, "besides their human nature, struggling to be itself? Who could seriously respect in a man what was accidental to his being?" [47] If you'd have told Aristotle that you wanted to "do your own thing" or be "unique" or be an "individual" (which, incidentally, is the wrong use of that word in this context), he would have thought not so much that you had betrayed your moral sense as that you'd lost your mind.

And surely he is right, but only in a way. For we would want to affirm that, morally speaking, not just anything goes. Taking human nature rather than individual quirkiness seriously is the first step toward living a mature moral life. But when that nature is thought of as developing according to what Dr. Farrer calls "the timeless rule of [human] essence" [48] and makes no room for the fact that virtuous decisions can, must, be "as inventive as any," [49] then, we have come to think, the moral and metaphysical dignity of individual human persons is in fact not being taken seriously enough.

In exactly the same way, then, as the late Professor Gilson explained how Aristotle's "essentialism," with all its insight into the formal character of being itself failed to account satisfactorily for the metaphysical diversity amongst beings in the world, [50] so has Dr. Farrer made it clear why Aristotle's, and indeed anyone's moral philosophy is bound to be unconvincing if it develops from the idea that the formal nature of human personality, namely "rational animal" (or as with Kant, "rational being") is what attracts our respect and reverence. This is because, although Dr. Farrer didn't put it this way, the morally distinctive thing about human beings is not that they are rational, but that they are destined for heaven. True, like Dr. Farrer's definition of conscience as appetite, this way of defining the meaning of being human has its logical shortcomings; on the other hand it was good enough for St. Augustine who used it to stake off the City of God from the City of Man.

What I would like to do now is tie this way of understanding what it means to be a human person to Dr. Farrer's notion of conscience as appetite for moral truth. Along the way I'll continue my effort at exhibiting his affinity with classical and mediaeval moral theory.

In **The Freedom of the Will** Dr. Farrer writes that "Will, action, the creative moment in man, is the only object of consideration which opens a dimension of metaphysical depth, or promises to let through a single ray of uncreated light. Here alone we find a power of making anything to be or not to be, and it is this that raises all the questions of theistic philosophy." [51] Yes; St. Augustine had already affirmed this: "by will we sin," he wrote, "and by will we live aright." [52] But this living, although day-to-day stuff, is not merely that as, in Dr. Farrer's words, the "serious humanist, with the morals he learnt from long-haired novelists," thinks. [53] It is the living of a life that is being tugged at, enticed by--what? If you're a theologian it's God's love, if a philosopher it is, as Plato taught, the essence of Goodness itself.

Dr. Farrer "persuades" us of this, [54] "exhibits" it, as Rodger Forsman puts it in "The Role of 'Apprehension' in Austin Farrer's Epistemology of Theism," [55] in the following way. First of all, everyone who is in any way in sensitive touch with reality admits a duty to "cultivate regard for their neighbours." [56] These are persons who hear a voice deeper than social convention saying "'This is a serious matter' . . .'Frivolity would be a crime...'" [57] They are people who, for example, respect civil law and enforce it upon themselves "without any thought of danger from the police;" [58] they don't confuse morals with mores, and although they may think that "the appetite for moral truth, like other appetites, is just human nature" they have gotten at least this much straight: that if conscience is a built-in feature of human nature at least it's not their father or their old nurse. [59] These are people, finally, who perhaps can't answer Prichard's question, Why ought I to be moral? but who know they should be. And if they will persist in their moral seriousness, Dr. Farrer suggests, they will realize that their desire to take their fellows seriously can, ideally at least, have no limits--even though it will likely be limited in fact by the "frustration in [dealing with] the imperfections of men." [60]

At this point you have folk who perceive the necessity of acknowledging an "absolute claim and [who] spend themselves in answering it," [61] who dare without reservation to say "For better or worse" even without knowing what "for worse" means. They are those who--and here the metaphysics begins--affirm that there is a "true Mary" buried in an actual Mary who, as I earlier quoted Dr. Farrer as saying, "though so dear, is so naughty." [62] Is this "true Mary" a Platonic form to which the actual Mary is related as appearance is related to Reality, as an imperfect instantation is related to an eternal Form? Clearly not. For there is something about Mary herself, Dr. Farrer says, that, if we only look, establishes her claim to our moral reverence. It is "what a believer calls the divine image in us, and the unbeliever the human ideal." [63] And although he nowhere attempts to demonstrate that the unbeliever has not quite got it right, that what he calls an ideal is actually God's own knowledge of what Mary, and all of us, are to become, Dr. Farrer did say in his Pusey House sermon that if you tell me that "the true Mary, or the true John, is just an idea in my own head, [while] I cannot disprove you, neither can I believe you. I ought to be ready to die for the true Mary," but if that means "to die for my own notion of [her] destiny, it would be nothing but colossal arrogance... [The] very idea is preposterous; I cannot think of dying, except for something that [Mary] is; just as I cannot love anything, but what the person really is." [64] Lady Helen Oppenheimer makes much the same point. Christianity can "make sense of morality," she writes, not by showing that non-believers can't be genuinely good nor by explaining that because men absolutely need a moral focus in their lives that therefore God exists as the source of moral meaning and value. [65] It is just that without God "the things which engage one's personality, though still entirely valid in themselves, would be miscellaneous, unrelated . . ." [66]

The point then is this: persuasion rather than demonstration is the order of the day here because although a correct intellectual perception that a certain way of acting is good is required before a person can desire to act in that way, it is also true that he must desire to know what that way is if he is actually to know it. [67] People who take their moral lives seriously "obey dictates of conscience, not so much because they are dictates, but because they love these dictates," is the way Gerard Smith S.J. put it in **The Truth That Frees**; [68] they "are our allies, not because they have declared war along with us against . . . evil (although they have declared war), but because we have wished them to be our allies . . . " [69] As Dr. Farrer says, you "will not find God in the conscience, any more than you will in any other direction, unless you go all the way there is to go, and uncover the ultimate claims which, without destroying your soul, you cannot refuse. You see these claims to lie in the true being of mankind . . . " [70] It is, precisely through this "true being of mankind" that the good shows itself to us and is seen to be such by those who look, and who in looking, love. As Plato, Aristotle and mediaevals such as Aquinas repeated over and over again, it is "the nature of goodness that it appeals to us, . . . somehow calls us . . . invites us to go out to it. And it is the very nature of our will to be, within its depths, a willingness open and responsive to this appeal." [71] Thus as Margaret Yee pointed out in her paper, [72] the quest for truth is doomed to fail unless it springs from what she called "an integrity of mind." This is, I think, because that integrity is synonomous with intellectual humility, the willingness to see the realities imbedded in the situations one finds oneself in and the refusal to distort them. This, after all, was Aristotle's reason for saying that there is a reciprocity between prudence, or practical reason, on the one hand and the moral virtues of justice, temperance and courage on the other. For how can one be expected to see the good in another person, or really, the good which the other person is, if he is intent upon treating him unjustly?

Now when these philosophers talked about moral goodness, they were not referring simply to this good or that, but to the good as such. This is because men's responsiveness to goodness if not limited to responding to some particular, limited good but is an unlimited capacity for responding to as much good as comes one's way. The man in the parable who went after the pearl of great price makes the point; so does St. Augustine's prayerful statement, "My heart is restless 'till it rests in Thee." The philosopher says, somewhat less elegantly (for unlike saints, philosophers become tongue-tied in this realm of discourse) [73] that the heart is "restless and insatiable until it rests with the bonum subsistens . . . " [74] The pull of that good, the tugging by it of the human will, a good which for Dr. Farrer is God in his creatures, is the originating source and determinant of moral truth. It is our appetite for it that he calls "conscience."

CONCLUSION

There are two paradoxes in the moral order that a theology such as Dr. Farrer's has to make room for and which in fact only his sort of theologizing can make sense of. The first is that human beings, as such, are autonomous, self-governing even while at the same time subject to an objective order of spiritual and moral truth. But if one takes autonomy seriously and refuses to think of it as a "mere relative privilege, valid only in subordination to God," [75] how can this be? How can one be self-governing and yet subject to the objective demands of moral goodness?

The second paradox may be stated as follows. On the one hand our fellow human beings are, in themselves, truly objects of our reverence although, as Dr. Farrer puts it, "it is God's will for them, God's love for them," that is, God himself who is the One "conscience is up against." [76] Who is it, one is prompted to ask, God, or his creature, who commands our moral respect?

As to the first paradox, that human beings are at once morally autonomous and subject to objective moral truths not of their own invention, recall this fundamental theistic proposition: God is bonum subsistens. Now if he were to show himself to us as he is in himself, our only freedom would be that "perfect freedom" of necessarily choosing to enter into union with him. As it happens, of course, none except the mystic perceives him that way, and translated into the moral order, this means that although God is indeed the object of men's consciences, he is not necessarily seen to be such. [77] In other words, God presents himself in the moral order as one finite good among many and even then, only in the guise of his creatures. (This means, conversely, that our love of him is hidden in our love of any one of those creatures, [78] a point of central importance to the resolution of the second paradox.)

Now this situation we are in as moral agents makes it possible for us voluntarily or involuntarily not to have an eye on the proper good that can serve to inform those judgments. "It is tempting to suppose that in the bottom of their hearts all men are set on their true and everlasting good," Dr. Farrer says; [**79**] but "alas, the facts are otherwise." As Aquinas points out, for a person to desire or will something, all that is needed is that he apprehends it as good for him whether it actually be so or not. [**80**] And of course whether one does apprehend something as good is pretty much up to him. Therein lies the source, subjectively speaking, of his autonomy.

In sum, Dr. Farrer's way of resolving the paradox here is by saying that although objectively the truth in the moral order for which men have an appetite is found when they seek in themselves and in others what God is making them to be, nevertheless (questions about the theology of grace aside), God always leaves it up to the men themselves to decide whether they will seek that truth or not. (On the matter of grace I remind you of Charles Hefling's statement that "what God does in Christ is, first to provide human aspiration with its object, the will of God, in a human life; and second, to conform the efforts of finite aspiration to this object.") [**81**]

One final point. Aquinas wrote that an "appetite is nothing else than an inclination of a person desirous of a thing towards that thing [and that] every inclination is to something like and suitable to the thing inclined." [**82**] If, then, we sometimes point ourselves in the wrong direction, or have an appetite not for what is genuinely good but for what is only apparently so, the defect lies on our side. Our judgment and subsequent action will in that case be immoral, or at least wrong in some other way. And the way to keep from that, Dr. Farrer insists, is not by learning some moral rules that have a fixed content with a limited range of application (for that is the dark side of casuistry) but by freely adhering to a rule that is not "legally interpretable, even by the man himself." [**83**] This is the "rule of keeping one's eyes open for certain sorts of demands in certain situations." [**84**] In the classical tradition it was called "being virtuous" or more specifically "being prudent," for prudence in that tradition was defined as the ability joyfully and with ease to understand the reality of past and present situations and, in the light of that knowledge, to make judgments about what one ought to do in the immediate future. [**85**]

In sum, what prudence requires is determined objectively by the realities that coalesce into a specific moral situation; it is, however, up to the moral agent to align himself with the prudential judgment and act in its light. In this last lies his autonomy, the tremendous value of which is found not so much in the fact that it makes the moral life possible (although it does) as it does in making it possible, as Gabriel Marcel puts it, for a man to say that no "single answer from outside me will be able to satisfy me when it does not coincide with my own answer, when it is not in the last resort my answer." [86] Let me take these notions in hand and turn to the second paradox.

Here the situation may be described thus: we are to love our fellow human beings for their sakes and God, in them, for his, but not disjunctively, not in such a way that our beloved is at one moment some human person and at another the divine. It looks here as if someone will have to come in second best.

No attempt to resolve this paradox can even get launched unless it be granted that the moral agent who is serious about resolving it in his own life will allow his appetite for moral truth to carry him behind or beyond the good which other persons are in order to see what he'll find. This is because, Dr. Farrer says, what he will find is something more than mere humanity. It is certainly something more than, and quite different from, a "greatest good for the greatest number." It is, as Professor Gilby puts it, the "all-embracing and transcendent good, which is God." [87]

But one must be careful here. When one seeks to go beyond the good which his fellow man is to the Good which God is he must, if he is to do it right, not think of or use the man as a conduit. Rather it is in the man himself that, in one's daily life, God is found. "God the creator of the man is seen in the man," Dr. Farrer says, [88] and in saying it places himself firmly on the side of theological orthodoxy, according to which, persons are said to be like God as an image (similitudo imaginis) and not "like" him simply as one of his traces, or "foot prints." [89]

To think otherwise would indeed commit one to the notion that he has to pay heed to God one part of the time and to his fellows the other part. The better view is that in respecting the man for his own sake, one is reverencing God for his. It is better for the following reason: God loves the man for the man's own sake and we ought do no less. Indeed, the marvelous thing is that the more we do love the man for his own sake, the more, that is, we love the one God loves, the more like God we become. And because we were meant by God to be his images, the more like him we become, the more we become ourselves. As Charles Hefling said quoting Dr. Farrer: "The control of our Creator is not an alien control, preventing us from being ourselves; the more he directs us, the more we are what we have it in us to be." [90]

The reason all this is marvelous, then, is that becoming God-like, becoming images of him, is what he had in mind in the first place. He really got it right! one is tempted to tell him. In fact, one should; doing it is called praise. Austin Farrer devoted himself to it the first thing in the morning, every morning, at the altar. What should humble not only the "long haired humanist" but all of us is the knowledge that at this point the only two persons who fully understand the connexion between Dr. Farrer's altar and his study in the Warden's residence at Keble are Dr. Farrer and God. [91]

NOTES

1. G. J. Wornock, **Contemporary Moral Philosophy** (London: Macmillan, 1967).

2. Ibid., 57.

3. Ibid., 56.

4. H. A. Prichard, "Does Moral Philosophy Rest on a Mistake?" reprinted in Jones, Sontag, Bechner, Fogelin, **Approaches to Ethics** (Toronto: McGraw Hill, 1962, 1968) 470.

5. Alasdair MacIntyre, **A Short History of Ethics** (London: Macmillan, 1966) 267.

6. Joseph Pieper, **The Four Cardinal Virtues** (Indiana: Notre Dame Press, 1966) xii.

7. This is of course not an exclusively modern view of the moral status of the human person. The mediaevals, for example, debated the question, Whether man is by nature inclined to evil?

8. Immanuel Kant, "Duties of the Virtuous and the Vicious," **Lectures on Ethics,** translated by L. Infield (New York: Harper Torchbook, 1963) 244.

9. Thomas Aquinas, **On the Virtues in General,** J. P. Reid, trans., (Providence, R.I.: The Providence College Press, 1951) 9.

10. St. Augustine, **De Libero Arbitrio,** II, 19. Quoted by Aquinas, ibid., article 2.

11. Aquinas, ibid.

12. Aristotle, **Nicomachean Ethics,** J. A. K. Thomson, trans., (Harmondsworth, England: Penguin, 1953) I, i; 1094 al.

13. I. Th. Eschmann, "St. Thomas' Approach to Moral Philosophy," Proceedings, American Catholic Philosophical Association, Vol. 31 (1957) 30.

14. V. A. Damant, **Christian Polity** (London: Faber and Faber, 1936).

15. Ibid., 39.

16. Loc. cit.

17. Austin Farrer, **The Freedom of the Will** (New York: Charles Scribner's Sons, 1958) 306.

18. Austin Farrer, "A Moral Argument for the Existence of God," **Reflective Faith**, C. C. Conti, ed., (Grand Rapids, Michigan: Eerdmans, 1972) 129.

19. Demant, op. cit., 39.

20. Austin Farrer, "In the Conscience of Man," **God and the Universe** (London: Mobray, 1960) 33.

21. See Aquinas, **Summa Theologiae**, I, 29, 3c. " . . . Person signifies what is most perfect in all nature . . . Hence since everything that is perfect must be attributed to God . . . this name person is fittingly attibuted to God."

22. See Farrer, **Reflective Faith**, 128.

23. See, e.g., Bartholomew Medina (1520–80), **Expositio** [on Aquinas] **Summa Theologiae**, 1–2, Question 94, article 2 (Venice, 1590), translated by Frater Seraphinus.

24. Henry Veatch, "Is Kant the Gray Eminence of Contemporary Ethical Theory?" Ethics 90 (Jan., 1980) 218.

25. See note 20 above.

26. The difficulty is in thinking of conscience as an appetite, even "rational appetite," or will. The word itself, not found in Greek philosophy and containing no moral reference in Stoic writings, means "the witness of oneself within one's own mind, to know oneself." (= concientia = conscire). See Gilby, op. cit., 181. In spite of this etymology and the moral theory behind it, I shall argue that Dr. Farrer is thinking of conscience at a deeply metaphysical level, one at which the human intellect is seen to be appetitive.

27. Farrer, "In the Conscience of Man," 32.

28. Op. cit. 131f.

29. Op. cit., 132.

30. <u>Op</u>. <u>cit</u>., 276. Although Dr. Farrer adds, "facts do not shout," and with that his analysis of moral experience moves to a radically deeper level.

31. Immanuel Kant, **Groundwork of the Metaphysics of Morals,** translated by H. J. Paton under the title, **The Moral Law** (London: Hutchinson University Library, 1966) 90ff.

32. <u>Ibid</u>., 66–67, "The <u>object</u> of reverence is the moral <u>law</u> alone . . . all reverence for a person is properly only reverence for the law (of honesty and so on) of which that person gives us an example."

33. Farrer, "In the Conscience of Man," 32.

34. <u>Ibid</u>., 35.

35. Farrer, "A Moral Argument of the Existence of God," <u>op</u>. <u>cit</u>., 122.

36. Farrer, "In the Conscience of Man," <u>op</u>. <u>cit</u>. 30f.

37. Farrer, **The Freedom of the Will** 273ff.

38. <u>Ibid</u>., 277.

39. Helen Oppenheimer, **The Character of Christian Morality** (London: Faith Press, 1965) 74.

40. <u>Ibid</u>., 71.

41. <u>Ibid</u>., 58.

42. E. L. Mascall, **Grace and Glory** (New York: Morehouse Barlow, 1961) 65f.

43. <u>Ibid</u>., 53f.

44. Farrer, **The Freedom of the Will,** 308.

45. <u>Ibid</u>., 311.

46. <u>Ibid</u>., 277.

47. <u>Ibid</u>., 303.

48. <u>Ibid</u>., 308.

49. See note 46 above.

50. See e.g., Gilson, **God and Philosophy** (New Haven: Yale University Press, 1941) esp. 32-37.

51. Farrer, **The Freedom of the Will**, 302.

52. St. Augustine, **Retractiones**, Bk. I, ch. 9 in **Patrologia Latina**, vol. xxxii at 596.

53. Farrer, "In the Conscience of Man," op. cit., 32.

54. Not proves, but persuades, although the persuasion is "of a very special kind." "A Moral Argument for the Existence of God," op. cit., 129. See C. C. Hefling, "Origen Redivivus: Farrer's Scriptural Divinity," infra., 35-50.

55. R. Forsman, "The Role of 'Apprehension' in Austin Farrer's Epistemology of Theism," infra., 111-130.

56. Farrer, op. cit., 129.

57. Farrer, "In the Conscience of Man," op. cit., 32.

58. Farrer, **The Freedom of the Will**, 273.

59. Farrer, "In the Conscience of Man," op. cit., 32.

60. Farrer, "A Moral Argument for the Existence of God," op. cit., 129.

61. Ibid., 130.

62. Farrer, "In the Conscience of Man," op. cit., 35.

63. Farrer, **The Freedom of the Will**, 302.

64. Farrer, "In the Conscience of Man," op. cit., 35.

65. Oppenheimer, 74f.

66. Ibid., 75.

67. In the scholastic terminology of Aquinas, " . . . it is requisite for prudence, which is right reason about things to be done, that man be well disposed with regard to ends; and this depends on the rectitude of his appetite." **Summa Theologiae**, 1-2, 57, 4c.

68. Gerard Smith, S.J., **The Truth that Frees** (Milwaukee: Marquette University Press, 1956) 57.

69. Loc. cit.

70. Farrer, "In the Conscience of Man," op. cit., 36.

71. Eschmann, op. cit., 30.

72. M. Yee, "The Epistemological Significance of Farrer's Concept of Image in Revelation."

73. For why this is so, consider the following exchange in Aquinas, **Summa Theologiae**, I, 2, 2, objection 3: " . . . if the existence of God were demonstrated, this could only be from his effects. But his effects are not proportioned to him, since he is infinitude and his effects are finite, and between the finite and the infinite there is no proportion. Therefore, since a cause cannot be demonstrated by an effect not proportioned to it, it seems that the existence of God cannot be demonstrated."

Reply: "From effects not proportioned to the cause no perfect knowledge of that cause can be obtained. Yet from every effect the existence of the cause can be clearly demonstrated, and so we can demonstrate the existence of God from his effects; though from them we cannot know God perfectly as he is in his essence." (underlining mine).

74. Gilby in Aquinas, **Summa Theologiae**, Blackfriars edition, vol. 18, 132.

75. As Eschmann, e.g., refuses to· op. cit., 25.

76. Farrer, "In the Conscience of Man," op. cit., 36.

77. See e.g., Aquinas, **Summa Theologiae**, 1–2, 19, 6, ad. 2.

78. G. Smith, S.J., "Eternal Joy," A Trio of Talks (Milwaukee: Marquette University Press, 1971) 28ff.

79. Farrer, op. cit., 34.

80. See Aquinas, **Summa Theologiae** 1–2, 8, 1c.

81. Hefling, op. cit., 42.

82. Aquinas, **Summa Theologiae** 1–2, 8, 1c.

83. Farrer, **The Freedom of the Will**, 274.

84. Loc. cit.

85. It is a virtue that cannot be exercised unless the moral agent be courageous, just and temperate as well, but that is another topic.

86. G. Marcel, **Le mystere de l'être**, Part Two (Paris: Aubier, 1951).

87. Gilby, op. cit., 141.

88. Farrer, "A Moral Argument for the Existence of God," op. cit., 127 (italics mine).

89. See e.g., Aquinas, **Summa Theologiae** I, 33, 3; 39, 7; 93, 6. See Gilby, op. cit., 58 at note "g".

90. Hefling, op. cit. 45.

91. Aquinas, **Summa Theologiae** 1-2, 19, 10: "In the state of glory . . . all will see in each object of their love its proper place in God's willed order; and then their will will be conformed in everything to his not merely in the form of their willing, but also in the material it is about."

THREE NECESSARY CONDITIONS
FOR
THINKING THEISTICALLY

Jeffrey C. Eaton

Today, theology is understood to be not one, but many. That is to say, theology is methodologically plural, a state of affairs which many believe to be enriching to the theological enterprise. This pluralism is misunderstood if it suggests that the object of theological investigation(s) is plural. What the present pluralism in theology indicates, or should indicate, is that there are various ways of thinking about God. If an approach is sound, it should disclose something true about the object of investigation. The elusiveness of theology's object makes it unlikely, however, that any one approach, any one methodology will provide a comprehensive account of that object; hence, the benefit of theological pluralism for helping theology to come to grips with its object.

What follows is intended neither to praise nor to bury theological pluralism, but simply to offer a set of necessary conditions for identifying whether or not a species of theologizing is in fact theistic. If, I shall be arguing, theology is not minimally about the God of theism, it is difficult to say what, if anything, theology is about. Whether or not the propositions in which these conditions are set are true is a controversial matter which cannot be resolved by the mere application of propositional logic to them. They are contested affirmations which cannot be reduced to an analytic calculus. What should not be controversial, however is the necessity of these conditions for thinking theistically. It may well be that we can no longer believe the picture of God that follows from them, but without them, there is nothing to believe or disbelieve. Thus, what these conditions are intended to do is to sharpen the distinction between theistic theologizing and theologizing which is non-theistic, and thereby to help us make our way through the contemporary theological thicket.

I have found it useful in setting forth these conditions to make reference to theological positions which, in my view, offend against them. My purpose in so proceeding is to illustrate the force of the conditions and the consequences of their abandonment. The fact that the positions herein criticized are generally considered "liberal" is not intended as an endorsement of, shall we say, a more "evangelical" brand of theologizing. The "liberal" positions arose in response to the intractabilities of traditional-evangelical views, and I shall take the liberals' criticisms of those views as read. In any case, it is theological reasoning, not theological politics, that concerns me here.

A theological position which satisfies these conditions without retreating to pre-critical bastions has been argued persistently and elegantly by Austin Farrer, a thinker whose work figures far too little in contemporary theological debates. The conditions which I identify in the following pages are educed from Farrer's writings and introduced both as a resource for clarifying the theological enterprise and as encouragement to further consideration of Farrer's contribution to theological reflection.

The first condition for thinking theistically is stated in the following proposition: "God's actuality is prior to the world's actuality." That is to say, God has a life that is uniquely God's, apart from the lives of all creatures, a life to which the existence of the world is not essential. This, of course, is the founding proposition of creationist belief. God effects the world and acts in it, and does so from a position ontologically prior to, above and before, all worlds. Is there a theological position that does not assert this as a minimal condition for thinking about God? Indeed there is: process theology.

Taking as its starting point our experience as relational selves, as fields of becoming, process theology holds that God's perfection resides in both the absoluteness of God's existence, abstractly considered, and the absoluteness of God's relativity to all other beings, actually considered. It was, according to the process theologians, this latter pole of the divine life that was neglected--nay, denied--in theologies under the tutelage of Aristotle, and it is the rediscovery of this pole that process theologians argue is the advantage of doing theology under the categories of process. The notion of divine relativity is, they claim, the very thing that Christians wanted to assert of God all along; viz., that there is a real internal relatedness of world to God and God to world. God is not unmoved by creatures' troubles and joys, but rather is eminently involved in creatures' lives at every level. The classical absolutist attributes of deity--immutability, impassivity, aseity--must, therefore, be re-interpreted in terms of God's supreme relativity.

This absolute relativity would be inconceivable were it not for the fact that God is understood to be abstractly absolute. According to the process doctrine of dipolarity, the consequent actuality of God's perfect relativity is grounded in the antecedent abstraction of God's absoluteness. If God were not the principle of concretion antecedently, the perfection of God's consequent relativity would not be thinkable. Whitehead, the patriarch of process philosophy, states the case in these words: "The consequent nature of God is the fulfillment of his experience by his reception of the multiple freedom of actuality into the harmony of his own actualization. It is God as really actual completing the deficiency of his mere conceptual actuality." [1]

The application of the categories of process philosophy to Christian theology have had the beneficial effect of calling into question--on religious as well as on philosophical grounds--the outworn theological absolutism that had its roots in the thought of Aristotle and Plotinus. But need the retreat from theological absolutism go as far as the process theologians have suggested it must? I think not. It is quite possible to maintain, without incoherence, that God is concerned for and responsive to the lives of creatures, without contending, as the process theologians do, that God is necessarily so concerned. God's actuality is not merely consequent to world process, but is prior to that process as well: God has a life above all worlds, perfect in itself, out of which God creates whatever world there is.

Process theology claims, in the doctrine of dipolarity, that God is abstractly absolute; God's abstract perfection is the empty form by virtue of which the "creative advance into novelty" congeals into concrete creaturehood. This conceptual nature of God is presupposed as the basis of the world's actuality, but it is not itself actual; rather, it is the primordial potentiality of the world. But if God posssesses no actuality prior to the world, how differs God from the operation of nature, and if no actual difference is being asserted, where is the warrant to talk theology? If it be claimed that the abstract perfection of God signifies the directing intention of cosmic process, that God is the mentality of the world, operating in the world in a way analogous to the operation of the mentality of me, the question still remains whether God acts this part by nature, or whether God has, out of the prior actuality of a perfect life, freely initiated the process God is now guiding. In the language of process philosophy, what is the "whence" of the "creative advance into novelty"?

This is a question for which process metaphysics fails to provide a satisfactory answer, and this failure is understandable once we see the extent to which the process position is finally committed to what Austin Farrer has described as an uneasy compromise between positivism and metaphysics. The process theologians have acknowledged the indispensibility of metaphysics to the theological enterprise, but they have shown a reluctance to pursue their metaphysical speculation beyond the realm of finite happenings.

> The metaphysician in us pushes us so far as to insist that the "principle of concretion" is at root the operation of an actual mentality of some mysterious or cosmic sort. The positivist in us reminds us to keep talking about events in the world, and the way they go; if we must mention the divine mind, it must be as a purpose exhaustively displayed in finite occurrences. [2]

This compromise is impossible. If the actuality of God prior to the world is not maintained, the very idea of divine transcendence dissolves. So anxious have process theologians been to rescue God from the perversities of classical theological absolutism and introduce God into the stream of time, that they have in the effort slipped into a half-theology which gives up the assertion of God's uniqueness, vis-a-vis God's prior actuality. Thereby God is understood to be not the world's creator, but rather the mind of the organic process which the universe is presumed to be.

But the universe is not an organic process. It is rather a tissue of processes, each conditioning one another as fields of activity. What we call the universe is the diagram of these conditionings, generated by a mind which has the capacity to unite them in a single focus. That it is within the capacity of the divine mind to focalize the entire array of conditionings we call the universe does not entail that God is bound to the world, nor that God's action is simply identifiable with the action of organic process. "God is not an act of thought resulting from the world order; God is the act of thought from which whatever of world order there is results." [3] Nor does the capacity of God to enter the temporality of every creature obligate God to our temporal order. There is nothing to prevent God from coming to creatures, entering their temporality out of the divine life, which is itself time-transcendent and which is not dependent upon any specific order of temporality. Confining God to the temporal conditions that constrain finite creatures relegates God to the status of a mere constituent of the universe, and this is to give up the theistic hypothesis. Contemporary theology must, it is true, admit the inadequacy of traditional theological absolutism and be willing to re-think the doctrine of divine transcendence, but it need not and cannot abandon the assertion of the prior actuality of God in order to do so.

II

The second condition for thinking theistically may be
expressed in the proposition, "God is personal and cannot be conceived otherwise." The word "personal" is here being used analogically. God is not personal in the identical sense that you or I
are personal. God does not, like our friends, occupy a space somewhere beside us. Rather, God is, if we take our first proposition
seriously, at the very springing point of our being. But if we try
to conceive of the originating Cause of ourselves and all that
is in terms of physical (as opposed to personal) interaction, the
otherness of God evaporates into the operation of nature, and,
losing the otherness of God, we lose the motivation for thinking
theistically. And yet, does not the casting of God in a personal
image have the effect of confining the divine nature, making
the object of our "ultimate concern" somewhat less than ultimate?
Some have thought so and argued persuasively against that idola-
trous propensity. Tillich comes to mind.

Despite his use of personality language to refer to God
(Tillich consistently uses the masculine, third-person, singular
pronoun, "he" to discuss his ultimate concern), Tillich has urged
his readers to think of God as "the ground of being," as "being
itself," or as "the power of being," in the belief that reference
to God as a being signifies the reduction of God to finite categories,
draws God down to our own plane of existence by giving some
aspect of our finite world the devotion which only God can properly
command. Indeed, Tillich warns us that we verge on such idolatry
when we even think of God as existing, that this is a sign that
we have lapsed into thinking of God as a being, rather than as
the absolutely transcendent power of all being.

Tillich claims that when we speak of God as "being-itself"
we speak non-symbolically of God. This contention is essential
if his defense of the analogia entis is to succeed. Insofar as we
participate in being, we can work up concrete assertions about
God as the ontological ground in which we and all other finite
entities have our existences. According to Tillich, "The analogia
entis gives us our only justification of speaking at all about God.
It is based on the fact that God must be understood as being-
itself." [4]

There are, however, grave difficulties with this proposal.
The analogia entis has traditionally been offered as ontological
satisfaction of the question. "Why is it so?" when, in the contempla-

tion of a finite existent, the force of the question is felt. But what is felt in the contemplation of a finite effect is not the idea of sheer Being, but rather a determining act, which is absolutely free and originative. The proper analogy, the analogy which alone satisfies the cosmological question, "Why is it so?", is the analogia operantis, the infinite term of which is not the form of Being itself, but is instead an Unconditioned Will. Theism is in substance the assertion of the analogue of rational will as the determinator of all finite being, and to evade this assertion with talk of a "divine ground" is to empty out the very content of theism. Theism's object is that personal will which suffers no a priori determination.

In saying this I am not offering a direct description of deity. I am talking analogically, but the proposed analogy, I am claiming, is a proper one; i.e., though irreducibly analogical, "creative volition" expresses the character of the divine life and is the only justifiable basis for talk about God. The "power of being" can only be thought of as a sovereign Agent. That that Agent is the plenitude of being might well be the case, but that would have to be shown and not simply asserted. Tillich's formalist doctrine of God is a profound statement of the way of remotion, its benefit being that it reminds us of the impossibility of applying predicates univocally to deity, its liability being that it leaves us with nothing to say, in any proper sense, about God. In affirming God as personal, it is true, we run the risk of anthropomorphizing God, but we are warranted in taking the risk inasmuch as the fact of finite existents confronts us with a cosmological question which can only be answered by One "who is all he wills to be, and wills to be all he is." [5]

There is a further observation to be made on this matter. If God is not personal, that is, if God is not understood in terms of the character of creative volition, in what sense can it be said that the "ground of being" is ontologically distinct from the being God is said to ground? And why not, then, limit ourselves to talking naturalism in our efforts to deal with the practical anxieties of modern existence? The personality of God is the very character of divine transcendence, out of which God is free to participate in the lives of creatures. One can, it is true, speak only of divine personality in stretched analogical terms. But the personal analogy is appropriate and, indeed, necessary. Tillich says as much himself: "The symbol 'personal God' is absolutely fundamental because an existential relation is a person-to-person relation." [6] But if such a relation is possible, as the life of religious devotion maintains, the one with whom we are related must be genuinely other, genuinely individual, or else what sense is there in talking about a relatum? Tillich, it seems, is willing to admit the practical necessity of referring to God in personal terms, but he refuses to admit the ontological necessity of God's (personal) otherness. But if the practical necessity is not finally rooted in the ontological structure of the divine life, what motive is left for talking theology at all? It would seem that theological discourse, under such conditions, is no more than an arbitrary symbolization for the way reality is thought by us to go. Austin Farrer put the dilemma well when he said: "For we challenge anyone to tell us what middle position is there between a serious personalism in religion, and that pious atheism which has no other god than the backside of human nature." [7]

For theology to be worth doing, it must be about a God worth having, and without the assertion of God's personal otherness and the personal nature of the relation of ourselves to the divine life, we are left with nothing but a metaphorical trapping, having no more substance than the contextual support such a noble thought as "God" might give to our moral aspirations. But that, it seems to me, is something very much less than the Ultimate, and Tillich has done yeoman service in warning us about giving ourselves to a concern that is less than the genuinely ultimate.

III

The third condition for theism's thinkability is that, "There is a real relation between created spirits and actual Godhead," which is to say, there must be some empirical grounds for theistic assertion. Theology cannot evade the empirical demand which attaches to any assertion of a real subject. We know and explore our world by virtue of the contact we have with it; physical discoveries are the product of physical interference, and although the subject of theological investigation(s) is not physical, the knowing of God and the knowing of physical reality cannot be essentially different acts. It is theology's task to acknowledge the (supposed) reality of God and to draw out the implications of this knowledge.

At least one contemporary theologian thinks such an understanding of theology's task is misguided. In An Essay on Theological Method Gordon Kaufman contends that the concept of "God" is an imaginative construction, and hence that theology's proper calling is constructive, not descriptive. As such, theology is distinct from religion, the latter being fundamentally an act of "devotion to the symbols of the faith," the former being an effort to understand those symbols and to reconstruct them should they need it. A presupposition of Kaufman's work is that whatever may be the order of being (how things are in themselves), we must make our own way in the order of knowing (how we understand things to be). Consistent with this contention, he argues that our knowing act is conditioned by a host of factors and thus can never give unmediated access to the object known. What theology is properly about, therefore, is the distinctive terms and complexes in which this mediation takes place, especially the concept "God." It is a category mistake, according to Kaufman, to think of God as an object ontologically over and against ourselves. It is his view, following Kant, that the concept "God" functions as a regulative idea, the ultimate ordering principle of all of life and thought, that the real significance of theology is not to refer to an objective reality, wholly other than ourselves, but that theology is about the clarification, indeed, the construction of the idea of such a reality. Thus theology is not to wear itself out seeking an ever closer correspondence of its ideas to the objective reality, God, but rather should attempt to generate a coherent and useful model for understanding the world and projecting the fulfillment of humanity.

What is a fitting response to this proposal? First, we shall thank Professor Kaufman (and Kant) for reminding us of the folly of naive linguistic realism which proposes to find a simple and direct correspondence between our thought and the external world. And we shall admit that our knowledge emerges out of an interaction between ourselves and those forces and agencies which comprise our environment. But we shall also want to know whether in the end theology is about some real being whose existence makes an experienceable difference or not, a question which Kaufman thinks untoward. No matter how unruly the question, however, it must be asked, for what thought can we have about any reality about which we can do nothing but think? [8] As necessary as it is to establish the coherence of the concept "God," there must be something more we can do about God than this. There must be some real relation of finite to infinite activity that can be lived and which is not simply reducible to the sum of inter-finite exchanges. If, in short, there is no cosmological relation of finite and infinite agency to be explored, what warrant is there for theological construction? If the concept "God" is well-founded, if it truly points the way to the fulfillment of human existence, it does so because it most truly represents to creaturely imagination the reality of the one who alone is in a position to know what it is that constitutes the fulfillment of humankind. The concept's usefulness depends upon the accuracy of its representation of the cosmological relation, a real relation of finite and infinite correspondents.

In plumping for the necessity of such a relation as a condition for speaking meaningfully of God, I am not suggesting that a person so engaged has direct access to the working of Infinite Agency. To be sure, we see only in a glass darkly; our knowledge is analogical, but the analogies we employ must be rooted in some set of experiences, or else, how decide their propriety? Kaufman

is entirely correct when he says the criteria for theological construction are pragmatic, but the practical confirmation or disconfir-
mation of the construction arises out of one's interaction with
God. The reality of this relation is, of course, deniable. Unlike
the existence of other finite minds, which we come to know through
personal interaction and which cannot be denied without self-
stultification, the reality of God's living act is supernatural and
so, deniable by anyone who refuses to admit the ultimate explanation of the world to which practical theism gives substance. The
analogy of Unconditioned Will, which was introduced in the previous
section, is, for example, a construction of faith and speculation.
If the analogy is justifiable, it is so because it is empirically verifiable in the believer's experience of life-in-God. It is this experience
of and response to God's action that is the content of the cosmological relation. Theology is properly the effort to understand
and explicate this relation; theological construction, truly accomplished, is an ever-corrigible description of this relation of created
and uncreated act. The relation is mediated through inspired images,
and it is through these that knowledge of God is disclosed. These
images are not, however, simply the result of the free deployment
of theological imagination, but rather, they are a response to
the press of the inspiring will of God upon creaturely intellect
and action, a contact by which human intention is brought into
accord with divine intention.

There is certainly no pure datum of revelation (or of
anything else for that matter). That is an important moral of
Kaufman's essay. Divine revelation, and hence our knowledge
of God, emerges out of the interaction of minds, one human and
fallible, the other divine and perfect. Divine purpose is proved
in voluntary human action, but never proved so conclusively that
it could not be proved further. The experimental condition for
this proof is faith, a favorable subjective attitude toward the
evidence of God's living act. But Kaufman contends on methodological grounds that theological reflection must be pursued apart
from considerations of faith, a contention which betrays a vestigial
confidence in a pure datum theory of knowledge. For in maintaining
the separation of theology and faith, there is the implication
that we are more able to discover the psychological or epistemological origin of theological reflection prior to speech about God
than we are able to discover an unalloyed instance of supernatural
self-disclosure. In either case the attempt is to define the point
of punctuation between the finite and the infinite, but that is
quite impossible. If the point is identified in supposed instances
of divine revelation, we get Church dogmatics; if it is identified
in publicly available criteria, we end up with so-called secular
theology. Neither approach is adequate. The question of God is
not simply a practical matter of faith, nor is it purely a speculative
matter of reason. Both faith and speculation are required to support
the believer's assumption that religious existence is interaction

with God. If this interaction is anything more than a metaphor for the workings of nature, it should be possible to stipulate and satisfy <u>appropriate</u> empirical criteria for the verification of the interaction.

IV

These are, as I see it, the necessary conditions for thinking theistically. They are not proposed for the purpose of narrowing the range of theological investigation or to turn back the clock on the current pluralism in theology. They are, rather, intended as criteriological aid for those who are trying to find a sound theological position in the array of options served up in the present pluralist context.

The propositions which I have offered presuppose a further condition, implied, but heretofore not fully stipulated: i.e., the subject of theology must be a God that is worth having, or obversely, worth denying. This premise, never far below the surface in what has preceded, is crucial for assessing theological evidence. Customary rules of evidence will, by themselves, not conclude to God. It is the <u>value</u> of the (supposed) object of inquiry that evokes the voluntary response by which alone the evidence for God's existence becomes compelling. That is to say, God will have to be appreciated if God is to be acknowledged, and God is appreciable only insofar as one discovers a goodness in the Divine Will on which one may depend. If this dependency is not real, there is no subject for the theologian to study which could not be as well studied by the historian or the philosopher or the anthropologist or the philologist or the psychologist.

Austin Farrer believed this dependency was real and wrote as one for whom God and not merely the concept "God" made an experienceable difference. His work was an attempt to elucidate the assumptions of theistic belief and to show their reasonableness. When he set to answering the question, "Can reasonable minds still think theologically?" he was asking whether or not it is still possible to think meaningfully about divine transcendence, whether or not the necessary conditions for thinking <u>theistically</u> can be satisfied. It would be well if his conclusions on these matters were given greater consideration by theologians who today are searching for a position that is worth arguing.

NOTES

1. A. N. Whitehead, **Process and Reality** (New York: The Free Press, 1957) 411. A few pages earlier Whitehead says, "Viewed as primordial, he [God] is the unlimited conceptual realization of the absolute wealth of potentiality. In this aspect, he is not <u>before</u> all creation, but <u>with</u> all creation. But, as primordial, so far is he from 'eminent reality', that in this abstraction he is 'deficiently actual' and this in two ways. His feelings are only conceptual and so lack the fullness of actuality. Secondly, conceptual feelings, apart from complex integration with physical feelings, are devoid of consciousness in their subjective forms." (405) By "feelings" Whitehead means positive prehensions, or a subject's interaction with its entire environment, the means by which the qualities of one entity are transmitted to another entity.

2. Austin Farrer, "The Prior Actuality of God," **Reflective Faith** (Grand Rapids, Michigan: Eerdmanns, 1974) 187.

3. <u>Ibid.</u>, 188. Elsewhere Farrer says, "If there is a divine knower, he can know all there is to know about the many series of successions in the universe by enjoying individually the points of view proper to all phases of process. But he can do so only because he is not himself at any time." **Faith and Speculation** (New York: New York University Press, 1967) 165.

4. Paul Tillich, **Systematic Theology**, Vol. I (Chicago: University of Chicago Press, 1951) 240.

5. Farrer, **Faith and Speculation** <u>op</u>. <u>cit.</u>, 118.

6. Tillich, **Systematic Theology** Vol. I, <u>op</u>. <u>cit.</u>, 244.

7. Farrer, **Faith and Speculation,** <u>op</u>. <u>cit.</u>, 48.

8. <u>Ibid.</u>, 22.

THE EXPERIENTIAL VERIFICATION OF RELIGIOUS BELIEF IN THE THEOLOGY OF AUSTIN FARRER

Brian Hebblethwaite

Philosophical theologians have tended to play down the appeal to religious experience in the justification of Christian belief on the very good grounds that its inevitably private and inner nature prevents it from making any rational contribution towards the public verification of religion. It is commonly held that the argument between believer and unbeliever must remain firmly in the public arena if the convictions of either are to receive rational scrutiny, criticism or support. A great deal of Austin Farrer's work in philosophical theology does indeed remain in the sphere of public rational argument. His first major book, **Finite and Infinite,** constitutes an impressive argument for theism, yielding, in Farrer's own words, "the knowledge of existent perfection conceived through the analogy of spirit, and the knowledge that this Being is the creator of all finite existence." His Gifford Lectures, **The Freedom of the Will,** explore, again by sophisticated rational argument, the analogical base of this position, defending volition, activity and creativity against determinist attack. In **A Science of God?** we find the adumbration of an argument for design, based on careful examination of the public fact of the emergence, in the course of cosmic evolution, of a world of life and consciousness and rationality from the interaction of the basic constituents of nature. In the same work, in his writings on theodicy, and in **Faith and Speculation,** Farrer works out a persuasive account of the way in which divine providence "makes the creature make itself," and draws together the threads of evolution, history and individual life in ways that further God's purposes without faking or forcing the natural or human story. Again in his defence of Christian doctrine, in **Saving Belief** and in various occasional writings, Farrer proceeds by spelling out its inner rationality in such a way as to let its persuasive power commend itself publicly through exposition of the coherent and comprehensive sense it makes of our life in the world. This exposition takes place, of course, in the context of a tradition of belief

163

in revelation, whose rationality has been examined in the Bampton Lectures, **The Glass of Vision** and in a long contribution to **Faith and Logic** (edited by Basil Mitchell).

Admiration of this sustained rational defence of both natural and revealed theology may prevent our recognition of the crucial role played in Farrer's theology by the appeal to experience, notwithstanding its private, inner nature. Indeed it would scarcely be an exaggeration to say that the place of experiential verification in the justification of Christian belief provides the lynchpin of his whole position as a philosophical theologian. Thus, already in the Gifford Lectures, we find reference to the fact that "we embrace, co-operate with, or draw upon the divine will in doing what is right". And the more we are involved in this paradoxical relation between the creative and the creaturely wills, Farrer continues, the less imaginable we may find it to be, but what we lose in imaginative clarity is made up to us in actuality. "Just where we cease to <u>conceive</u> our dependence on God, we begin to <u>live</u> it" (my emphases). In **Saving Belief, A Science of God?** and **Faith and Speculation**, we find great stress placed on the fact that the only way of empirically verifying belief in God, belief in divine providence and belief in divine revelation is so to embrace the divine will that we find it in doing it. This is the only point at which, in the nature of the case, we directly encounter the object of theology; and it is this sinking of our will in the creative will of God that alone confirms the beliefs of the ordinary Christian and the philosophical theologian alike. Not surprisingly, this emphasis on experiential verification through the embracing of the divine will runs like a <u>Leitmotif</u> through Farrer's sermons as well.

The problem of the verification of religious and theological utterances was the chief problem in the philosophy of religion during the larger part of Farrer's writing life. The demands of the positivist criterion of verifiability, as expressed, for example, by Anthony Flew in the well-known debate on "Theology and Falsification" (reprinted in **New Essays in Philosophical Theology**, edited by Flew and MacIntyre) made it incumbent upon theologians to show what experienceable difference is made by God's alleged existence and activity. This empirical demand, as Farrer calls it, was normally thought of as a request for public verification; and one can understand the diffidence on the part of philosophers of religion about referring to inner, private, religious experience at this point. No one questions the fact that religious <u>belief</u> makes a difference to the believer in terms of his own inner experience, but the subjective nature of religious experience makes it difficult, if not impossible, to distinguish the effects of God's alleged activity from the effects of <u>belief</u> in God's activity. This was the problem which preoccupied philosophers of religion during the hey-day both of logical positivism and of philosophical analysis.

We see this in the work of Ian Ramsey and of the contributors to **Faith and Logic** as well as in the replies to Flew in the "Theology and Falsification" debate.

Farrer's response to the empirical demand is to be seen both in his rational defence of a theological framework in terms of which to construe the world religiously and in his insistence that, in the nature of the case, the appeal to inner verification cannot be excluded from the discussion. It has to be admitted, however, that, at first sight, it looks as if Farrer fails to meet the empirical demand in both these strands of his theology. The dilemma is this: on the one hand Farrer's rational theology involves the admission, indeed the insistence that "the hand of God is perfectly hidden" as "God makes the creature make itself" and that "the causal joint" between the Creator's action and that of the creature is absolutely inaccessible to us. The sceptical rejoinder is obvious. If the hand of God is perfectly hidden, how can it possibly make any experienceable difference? Thus Don Cupitt, who, in **Taking Leave of God**, appears to have succumbed without demur to positivist criticism of belief in an objective God, remarks: "it is said that 'God makes creatures make themselves', but this says no more than that creatures make themselves". [1] On the other hand, Farrer's insistence on appealing to the way in which we know the divine will only by embracing it seems to make no contribution to public verification whatsoever.

The first horn of this dilemma is easily resolved. We have simply to note the restricted scope of Farrer's insistence on the hiddenness of the hand of God. What is hidden, according to Farrer, are the divine first cause in itself and the mode of its operation. Its effects, however, are not hidden at all. God's revelation of himself, culminating in the life of Christ and what he achieves in and through the lives of the saints are observable effects of divine action in the world and the actual effect of embracing the divine will is to yield a saving knowledge of God that, for the believer, is certainly not hidden from him. Moreover, in the light of our knowledge of these effects of divine action, we are enabled to recognize in nature, in history and in individual lives the wider effects of God's creative and providential action. Indeed, if the arguments of **Finite and Infinite** and **A Science of God?** are right, we can, to some extent, discern the effects of divine action in the creation of a world of rational beings even prior to experiential verification.

This reply already indicates how the second horn of the apparent dilemma is to be dealt with. The reference to Christ and the saints shows that the experienceable effects of embracing the divine will are not, after all, purely private and internal. Although Farrer does insist on the essential role of the inner verification of Christian belief through actually willing the will of God oneself, he is perfectly well aware of the implausibility of pointing to one's own life as evidence of the reality of God; and so we find, at this juncture, attention being deftly shifted to the lives of other men and women, especially those of the saints, and supremely that of Christ himself.

I now wish to set out, in more detail, Farrer's treatment of the theme of the inner experiential verification of Christian belief. For, despite the references to Christ and the saints just mentioned, the brunt of Farrer's response to the empirical demand does consist in his spelling out the verificatory force of our actually coming to will and do the will of God. As I say, it is this that constitutes the lynchpin of his whole position.

Farrer has no time for appeal to the paranormal or the weird. Some empirically minded philosophers of religion have attempted to adduce as evidence the phenomena of parapsychology in order to meet the empirical demand. Already in the Bampton Lectures, Farrer was insisting that the obscure penumbra of our natural powers are not to be regarded as the main experienced point of contact with the supernatural. And in a splendid sermon on "The Witch of Endor" in **The End of Man** Farrer asks: "if God is a living will and a heart of love directly concerned for us, why look for him in the remote and dubious margins of our experience? . . . it is folly to look away from the point where God's will touches us in our present existence . . . The will of God is everywhere present; it is experienced by being obeyed."

The main places in Farrer's philosophical writings where he develops this theme are chapter six of **A Science of God?**, the chapter entitled "Experimental Proof", and chapters two, three and four of **Faith and Speculation,** the chapters entitled "The Empirical Demand", "Spiritual Science" and "Grace and Freewill". Indeed the whole of **Faith and Speculation** despite its importance for Farrer's rational theology and doctrine of providence, is constructed precisely as a response to the empirical demand.

In **A Science of God?**, summarizing the argument of the book so far, Farrer says, "The world order and human mentality suggest to us the hypothesis that wisdom made the world and supply us with the terms in which to formulate it", and then he goes on to ask how this hypothesis might be tested or proved. His answer is that, since God is not related to us as are the things that stand alongside us, but rather as the will which underlies our existence, gives rise to our action and directs our aim, we can have only experimental knowledge of that will by opening our will to it, and letting it take effect in us. God's work in us, as we embrace his will, has experimental value for us in that, in embracing it, we know it. Much more will be said in **Faith and Speculation** about the paradoxical fact that, as Farrer puts it here, the grip of God's purpose on the <u>voluntary</u> instrument is firmer than elsewhere because it offers more hold to him than brute things can do. Farrer also makes it clear, against Aquinas, that while it is perfectly true that it is more proper to speak of God's work on us rather than our work on God, nevertheless we do ourselves interact with the divine action in doing God's will. This prepares the way for the sharp contrast drawn in **Faith and Speculation** between scientific experiment where we work on brute nature and force it to yield experimental results, and spiritual science where in an utterly personal relation we allow ourselves to be worked on by divine grace in freely embracing the will of God.

The interest of the treatment of this theme in **Faith and Speculation** lies in the way in which Farrer subsumes both sides of this contrast--scientific experiment and spiritual science--under a broadly reformulated version of the empirical principle. It is this: "to know real beings we must exercise our actual relation with them." This principle is applied differently, of course, in respect of the different realities with which we have to do. In the nature of the case, our relation with God must be exercised as a personal relation, and as a deepening union of will. The only kind of verification of God's reality available to us in this present life is the knowledge of God we find through devoting ourselves to God's will. This is as "empirical" as the matter allows, although, in the light of our experience of grace, we recognize God's action at every level of our being, including that of the natural, physical world. Farrer notes that, since we cannot now experience the maintenance of this saving relation beyond death, the final verification of divine fidelity escapes us. To that extent he would agree with John Hick that reference to eschatological verification, though it may help to spell out the cognitive content of belief in terms of its implied expectations, has no bearing on the problem of verification <u>now.</u>

The exercising of the actual relation with God, which yields present experimental results, certainly includes prayer and worship, but is chiefly a matter of action. Contemplation is not enough; for the contemplation of God is dependent upon God's action in us and that action is the action of a holy will which must take effect in our action according to the will of God. Moreover, for Farrer, the experienced blessedness and enrichment of a life lived in accordance with the will of God "can at best be confirmatory evidence of a relationship which must be its own proof". This is quoted from **A Science of God?**, where Farrer is arguing that what has evidential value for us is the lived relation itself of willing the will of God.

These themes naturally find expression in many of Farrer's sermons. To give but two examples: from a sermon entitled,

"Supporting Hands" in **The End of Man:** "the evidence of faith is the evidence of Almighty Power to break and heal the will. And if we want to put it to the test, this is required of us: not to run away from God, but to face him . . . ", and from a sermon entitled "How Can we be Sure of God?" in **A Celebration of Faith:** "there is only one point at which we can possibly touch the nerve of God's creative action or experience creation taking place, and that is in our own life. The believer draws his active Christian existence out of the wellspring of divine creation; he prays prayers which become the very act of God's will in his will . . . "

There are two aspects of Farrer's treatment of the experiential verification of religious belief that I should like to single out for special comment. The first is Farrer's insistence that, while our willing of God's will alone has experimental value for us in verifying Christian belief, the activity of so willing the will of God cannot be embarked upon as an experiment. We cannot pray to see if prayer works; for that would not be a genuine prayer **(A Science of God?).** It is not appropriate to recommend religious exercises in the expectation of attracting grace, according to some "laws" of spiritual being. We exercise our relation with God as a personal relation **(Faith and Speculation).** "The first point about believing is that if you make yourself do it, you aren't believing, you are only pretending" (from a sermon entitled "What is Faith in God?" in **A Celebration of Faith).** "We cannot play at seeing things divinely; we have to live as we see, for we shall only see according as we live" (from a sermon entitled "Finding God" in **The Brink of Mystery).** I imagine that these points were made with the work of H. H. Price in mind. Price, in many ways a classical empiricist philosopher, made some interesting suggestions about the experiential verification of religious belief, both in a contribution to **Faith and the Philosophers** [2] entitled "Religious Experience and its Problems", and in the last chapter of his Gifford Lectures, **Belief,** [3] the chapter entitled "Religious Belief and Empiricist Philosophy". Price suggested that human beings may possess latent capacities for spiritual perception which may be activated by the meditative entertaining of, or dwelling upon, religious hypotheses. What first begins as a tentative entertainment of a hypothesis, by sustained dwelling on what it might be like if that hypothesis were true, may uncover spiritual capacities in us, and we may, perhaps to our surprise, find ourselves believing. As Price puts it, " 'Try it and see for yourself' is one way of formulating the empiricist principle". Farrer, I imagine, would not have been too happy with this proposal. For one thing it represents spiritual perception too much in terms of contemplation rather than of action, and in recommending spiritual exercises as an experiment it removes the condition of actually embracing the will of God in a real personal relation which alone, according to Farrer, has experimental value for us. On the other hand, it might be thought that there is more to be said for Price's view than for Farrer's, if we are talking about how an unbeliever might become a believer; for does not Farrer's view involve the "catch 22" situation of supposing that only the believer can "verify" religious belief. Price at least suggests a possible mode of transition from unbelief to belief. Of course we may actually be in a "catch 22" situation here, and Farrer may be right to refuse to let experiential verification carry the weight of the transition to belief. After all, unlike Price, Farrer sets discussion of experiential verification in the much wider context both of rational theology and of appeal to the public facts of Christ and the saints. For Farrer experiential verification does not have to do all the work, as it does for Price.

But before we accept this sharp dichotomy between Price and Farrer, we must consider a passage from chapter one of **Saving Belief** which has not yet been mentioned. There, in a discussion of "Faith and Evidence", Farrer says that the suggestion that there is a God contains built-in attitudes. "To think of a possible God is to experiment in having God. The heart goes out even to a possible God. To have faith is to let this attitude have its way and subdue its rivals." This looks very much like Price's view of experimenting with theistic hypotheses. But not quite so; and the way in which Farrer goes on to qualify these remarks shows that he is not really recommending that kind of experimentation. It becomes clear that what Farrer is really talking about here is the achievement of favorable conditions for the appreciation of the reasons for belief. As far as experimenting in "having God" is concerned, Farrer insists that "the possible God must be my God to each of us, not just a hypothesis"--otherwise one is not 'experimenting' in the faith-attitude itself. So I think that the contrast between Farrer and Price remains. For Farrer, we are in a "catch 22" situation regarding the experiential verification of religious belief--which is why, notwithstanding the crucial role of experiential verification, the weight of justification must, for Farrer, remain with the public arguments of rational theology and the public evidence of the lives of Christ and the saints.

I am not altogether convinced that Farrer is right against Price here. While his insistence on man under grace as existing in a real personal relation with God can hardly be gainsayed from the standpoint of Christian belief, Farrer himself acknowledges that God is also present to us at every level of our being, not only the personal. May not these more subliminal aspects of the spiritual dimension also manifest themselves in experience, as not only Price, but representatives of the Indian religions often claim? Farrer has little to say about other religions--and for that matter Price gives them little attention too--but there may be some scope here for supplementing Farrer's internal personalist account of religious experience with some more directly experimental recommendations for the opening up of the spiritual dimension.

The other aspect of experiential verification to be singled out for comment, however, does concern the very special role that our own voluntary embracing of the divine will plays within the broader creature/Creator relation generally. In one of his contributions to **Faith and Logic,** Farrer insists that, while, for belief, God is universal cause and his action cannot be excluded from anything, nevertheless there remains a difference between those things <u>into</u> which we have to read divine activity and those things <u>off</u> which we simply do read it--here the case under consideration is that of duty. In **A Science of God?,** in a passage from which I have already quoted, he says that "the creature that can conspicuously enter into God's creative thoughts is not <u>less</u> subject to the divine will. The grip of God's purpose on the voluntary instrument will be firmer because it offers more hold to him than brute things do". This is illustrated both by the saint whose action is supremely God's handiwork and by the association of our wills with God's working in them. As Farrer put the matter in a paper entitled "Grace and the Human Will" in **Reflective Faith,** "the way to experience grace will be to exercise our highest powers in the freest and most truly personal way; for by so doing we shall touch the point of transition in the hierarchy of being, where the divine action actively comes through into the creature". "God's grace may also be discerned in externalities, but primarily in the act by which a man comes to adhere to the prior will of God for him . . . " Farrer's insistence that the paradoxical relation between grace and freewill constitutes the paradigmatic case of the relation between primary and secondary causality and the key to our appreciation of God's special providence and action is well brought out in a sermon entitled "Grace and Resurrection" in **A Celebration of Faith.** Here he insists that what is most freely our own is most truly God's. Men can make dolls and machines. God alone can create creators and create through their hands. We see this supremely in Christ, but he is the pattern for us all. "The man who receives the grace of God says: Now I am really myself. The more it's God's, the more it's I, and the more it's I, the more it's God. That is the life of religion: everyone who has tested it knows it to be true." This emphasis on the special evidential value of the free embracing of God's will enables Farrer to make discriminations regarding God's providential activity within the universal Creator/creature relation which are not available to theologians who work with a more uniform notion of God's primary causality. Thus Herbert McCabe, in three recent articles on God in <u>New Blackfriars</u> (October and November 1980 and January 1981) is so persuaded of the dangers of anthropomorphism in attributing some effects more than others to the divine will that he refuses to appeal to God to explain why the universe is this way rather than that at all. We can only appeal to God as the prior cause of everything. McCabe's refusal to make further discriminations regarding divine action over and above this basic Creator/creature relation is most sharply seen in his treatment of freedom and moral evil. For McCabe, the traditional "free-will" defence in theodicy is out of the question because in no sense can my freedom be regarded as making me independent of God's creative activity. My free act is wholly God's act too. Indeed God himself creates my free act in so far as it is good. For, on this basis, the wrong acts of creatures are pure negations, proceeding solely from creaturely perversion, and it is wholly incomprehensible why God permits them. Farrer's treatment of freedom and theodicy is much more plausible than this. Certainly for Farrer, as for McCabe, the creative will of God underlies my being and activity in the basic sense of sustaining my creaturely existence. But God gives me the gift of freedom, and I may act well or badly, in accordance with or against his will. To that extent I am given a relative independence over against my Creator. But if I embrace God's will I find him acting in and through me by his grace in a manner over and above the basic Creator/creature relation. By opening my will to God's will I become the vehicle of God's special activity in providence and grace. Thus Farrer is able to do much more justice than McCabe to the particularity of God's action within the general framework of his creating and sustaining act, as well as to utilize the resources of these discriminations for theodicy, without denying the prior actuality and activity of God in the whole Creator/creature relation. I do not see how Christian faith can seriously be expected to survive without the possibility of such discriminations.

A similar insistence on the discriminations which Christian experience of grace requires us to make in speaking of divine action may be urged against the theology of Maurice Wiles. Although we do not have access to the different modalities of divine action as they are in themselves, our recognition of the special effects of divine grace in a life opened up to the divine will, enables us to posit special divine action in such a case over and above the universal presence, purpose and will of God, which the believer may claim to discern. For the experienced effect of grace in the free embracing of the divine will is indicative of a personal relation which cannot possibly be construed in a one-sided way alone. For Wiles, special activity can only be ascribed to the creaturely side of the relation. But Farrer's insistence that my free embracing of the divine will gives more scope to God's action in grace and thus enables God to do more than he can do in and through a recalcitrant will or in and through sub-human energies is much more faithful to the religious realities of the situation. For the believer experiences his relation to God as a particular personal relation in which the special activity as well as the universal purpose of God is to be discerned. Encouraged by this recognition of special divine activity in his own case, the believer is the readier to interpret other features of the world as providential. This is true, as we saw from **A Science of God?**, of the emergence of consciousness and mind in the course of evolution. It is especially true of the history of Israel culminating in the Incarnation and bearing fruit in the lives of the saints and of Christian men and women down the ages.

If we have concentrated in this paper so far on our own case, it is because, for Farrer, our own embracing of the divine will does constitute the main experimental evidence for Christian belief. It does so, because only at this point is divine activity experienced directly. Nevertheless, Farrer is perfectly well aware that one's own embracing of the divine will is likely to be fitful, weak and wavering and in need of the support that comes from the example of Christ and the saints. Moreover, reference to Christ and the saints provides a more public court of appeal than does reference to one's own inner experience. It is to this more public argument that I now wish to turn.

In a paper, entitled "On Verifying the Divine Providence", in **Reflective Faith,** although the main weight of the argument is still placed on one's own spiritual life, there is also reference to further factors, such as the persuasive power both of divine revelation and of the example of others as contributing to the plausibility of belief. Let us first consider the example of others. In **A Science of God?** Farrer points out that, unlike scientific experiments, spiritual experiments are unique and particular. They leave their deposit in spiritual writings, and each man's power to embrace the divine will is nourished by what apostles and saints have said and done. This introduces what Farrer calls the element of experience by proxy into the topic of experiential verification. Its importance has already been indicated by the preacher's diffidence about appealing to his own case and his own consciousness of the poverty of his own success in willing the will of God. The sermons are full of appeals to other men and women of faith, and especially to the saints. Thus in "Grace and Resurrection" from which I have already quoted, Farrer says "if we begin to doubt the evidence of divine grace our humdrum lives afford, then we look to the shining examples of heroic saints and beyond them to Jesus Christ himself". In another sermon from **A Celebration of Faith**--"Double Thinking"--Farrer remarks that the saints confute the logicians, not by logic, but by sanctity. They do not prove the real connection between religious symbols and everyday realities by logical demonstration but by life. With a reference to the slogan "solvitur ambulando" as the way to deal with Zeno's paradox of motion, Farrer suggests the paradox of religion as "solvitur immolando". The same idea finds expression in a sermon entitled "Physical Faith" in **The End of Man:** "It was not every part of Christ's body that equally convinced St. Thomas, it was the parts that carried the prints of the crucifixion. And it is not every part of Christ's body now that convinces us; it is the crucified parts--the saints who are marked with the signs of Christ's sacrifice."

This public evidence reaches its climax in Christ himself, who, as man, trod the path of experiential verification himself, and whose perfect embracing of the Father's will constitutes its supreme example. "Jesus Christ experimented with creation when he threw himself and all the world's hopes into nothingness by the death on the cross". That is from "The Painter's Colours" in **A Celebration of Faith.** The difference between this and the wrong, self-defeating sense of putting God to the test, is brought out in one of the Bible sermons in **The Brink of Mystery,** where Farrer, with reference to the temptations in the wilderness, asks if there was a testing-time when Jesus went into the gulf head-long and proved God to be his Father, being caught and upheld by the everlasting arms? He answers: "It was no test artificially contrived, no trap for the providence of God, when faithfulness to his calling brought Jesus to his death."

We are speaking now of the revelation of God in human history, in the incarnation of his Son. As Farrer puts it in **A Science of God?,** when noting that he has only dealt there with an aspect of Christian belief: "To realise a union with our Creator we need not scale heaven or strip the veil from ultimate mystery; for God descends into his creature and acts humanly in mankind." Such acting humanly involves just such an "experimentation with creation" as we have seen referred to in the sermons, but of course it also raises questions of verification in its own right. What is the evidence for construing Christ as God? According to the sermon, "Christ is God" in **Said or Sung,** the evidence is twofold--part, the (public) force of the thing itself and part experiential: "the evidence for this was that a life had come into the world which gave back to God the picture of his own face and the love of his own heart. And the second evidence was the power of it. By union with this life, men received a share in something not human at all, an eternal, divine sonship". And what was said above about the saints--the element of experience by proxy--applies not only in respect of belief in God, but of belief in Christ as the incarnate Son of God as well. Nor should we expect to be able to hold apart the question of verifying belief in God from that of verifying belief in Christ. For if verifying belief in God is a matter of embracing the will of God, that will, so Christians hold, is revealed, as nowhere else, in the story of Christ.

This matter of revelation was treated at length by Farrer in the second of his contributions to **Faith and Logic,** as well as in his Bampton Lectures. In the former essay he points out how, for Christian faith, the one God has given himself a personal history in relation to us. "Human history, which considered in itself has no theme, no centre and no goal, receives from the Incarnation an orientation." "God deals with each of us by extending to us the action of Christ; we know him by our dealings with him." Interestingly enough, this is one of the few places at which

Farrer makes an explicit reply to Flew's "falsification" challenge. We cannot, he says, proceed to deduce a priori, as Flew does, the way in which divine goodness would have to work. It is no use projecting our own ideas on to God and speculating how we would have acted in creating, say, a hedonic paradise. We must rather look to the self-revealing action of God in which God himself justifies his claim to almighty goodness. "We cannot fit our human similitudes on God, but God can and does take the human similitudes on himself and in that form deal humanly with mankind." The manner of God's dealing humanly with mankind is spelled out, again with explicit reference to Flew, in a sermon entitled "Emptying out the Sense", in **A Celebration of Faith:** "God fulfils his promises by crucifying their literal sense, in order to fulfil them by resurrection." In other words, the goodness of God is discerned in the story of our redemption and the promise of resurrection. Similarly, in the aforementioned paper on "God and Verification", Farrer again explicitly rejects Flew's selection of innocent suffering as evidence sufficient to falsify belief in divine goodness. Rather the relevant locus of verification is the spiritual life, in which the saving promises of God are experienced, albeit partially and in unexpected ways.

It is important to realize that divine revelation must itself be subject to both outer and inner testing. In the "Revelation" essay in **Faith and Logic** we find appeal to both public criteria-- historical evidence, intrinsic power, and the sense which this revelation makes of everything else--and private experiential verification--the mind of Christ being extended to the disciple and to the believer by the operation within them of a divine presence. Summing up, Farrer lists four points at which the believer finds himself confronted by the divine: the Incarnation itself, the apostolic witness, living Christians, and the believer's own heart.

It should not be thought that, for Farrer, religious experience is self-authenticating. It may be that, once we have in fact embraced the will of God, there can be no questioning of the saving knowledge of God that such an actual spiritual relation yields. But whether we have in fact embraced the will of God cannot be settled simply by appeal to religious experience. Farrer does not treat religious experience as an infallibly guaranteed mode of verification. We have seen how important experiential verification is for his whole position, but we must now realize that religious experience itself must be subject to critical scrutiny. This aspect of Farrer's treatment of experiential verification comes out most clearly when he is dealing with inspiration--the category most naturally used by the religious mind in speaking of divine action in revelation and in the appropriation of revelation. Here, as elsewhere, for Farrer, there is no guarantee of getting things right. He explicitly rejects all "pure datum" theories of revelation and inspiration. Divine saving activity takes place and is discerned in and through fallible human response. And there are criteria of discernment: for, as Farrer says in the sermon "Inspiration", in **The End of Man**, we should always suspect claims to inspiration which bypass reasoned argument. God has more reasons, not less, for what he wills and does. In the "Revelation" essay, Farrer mentions a number of tests: efficacy, scrutiny of effects, mutual support, rationality, applicability to fact. Once again, we realize that alleged experiential verification cannot stand by itself in the justification of religious belief. Not only must it be related to the rational theology and to experience by proxy--the lives of the saints--it must itself be subject to rational criticism by oneself and by other Christian minds.

It must be admitted that Farrer's treatment of revelation and inspiration contains one element where he is perhaps the least convincing in all his writings on philosophical theology. Through out the Bampton Lectures and in the brilliant reply to his critics, "Inspiration, Poetical and Divine" in **Interpretation and Belief**, Farrer endeavors to make a case for treating the inspiration of the Biblical writers as a special case--an extension of the revelatory events to which they are a response, a form of inspiration to be differentiated from all other inspiration, divine or otherwise. The great biblical images are themselves, Farrer suggests, the God-given vehicles of revelation, both in the mind of Christ himself and in the minds of prophets and apostles. Certainly we may agree that there is a difference between the objective control exercised by the revelatory and saving events of Christ's life, death and resurrection and that exercised by the natural and human worlds generally--though poetic response to these may surely be claimed as a vehicle of divine "inspiration" as well. But I do not see that there is a difference in principle between the divine inspiration by which the biblical writers appropriated and internalized the revelatory event of Christ and that by which all other believers embraced and embrace that concrete form of the divine will and action.

In conclusion, however, it is the virtues of Farrer's treatment of experiential verification that I wish to stress. One of those virtues is the way in which he endeavors to relate and keep together all the evidence for belief, holding the rational, the public and the inner elements in proper balance. As he says in **Faith and Speculation,** it is important to get the relation between saving faith and philosophical reflection right. In a sermon already mentioned, "How Can we be Sure of God?", Farrer says, "I will tell you how to disbelieve in God. Split the evidence up and keep it apart. Keep the mystery of the world's origin carefully separate from your experience of God and then you can say that the cosmic facts are dumb . . . Keep the believer's experience of God by itself, and away from the general mystery of nature; then you can say that it's so peculiar, so odd a little fact in this vast, indifferent universe, that to attach universal importance to it is too absurd . . . Now I will tell you how to believe . . . " And he speaks at one and the same time of rational belief and of Christ and of the saints and of our own poor lives. "Poor they are and too thin to bear the weight of the evidence: but then they do not stand alone. We see clearly enough that what we have an inkling of, the saints apprehend and Christ simply achieves. Ah, but is not this whole phenomenon of life invaded by the divine a mere freak in the vast material solid of the universe? Nonsense, the universe isn't solid at all . . . it is, as a totality, unexplained, and subject to the appointment of creative will in all its infinite detail." Thus Farrer links together our own experience, experience by proxy--that of the saints--God's revelation of himself in Christ, and the object of rational theology, namely, the creative will of God in the whole natural world. Similarly in the first of his essays in **Faith and Logic**, Farrer observed that there is no need to choose between an evidence by impact and an evidence lying in the way things are. "The impact is through the way things are . . . " and "we try to explain how our view of the way things are is illuminated by our acknowledgement of the divine impact."

One of the defects of Price's account of religious experience was that it had to do too much work by itself, as well as tending perhaps to falsify the actual nature of spirituality. Farrer's reliance on genuine spirituality is very great in his overall apologetic, but it is not detached from the rational considerations and indeed is itself to be subjected to rational scrutiny. Moreover at the point where our own experience seems implausibly to have to carry too much weight, attention is shifted to the public evidence of the saints and of Christ himself. Thus the rational arguments, the appeal to Christ and the saints and the appeal to our own experience are held in creative tension. The dialectic between our own experience, experience by proxy and rationally justified interpretation is maintained throughout Farrer's apologetic. I called the moment of experiential verification the lynchpin of Farrer's defence of Christian theism. Clearly, without that lynchpin the whole structure cannot stand, but equally the lynchpin is no use by itself. The great merit of Farrer's apologetic lies in the way in which experiential verification and rational theology are held together.

NOTES

1. D. Cupitt, **Taking Leave of God** (London: S.C.M., 1981) 6.

2. J. Hick, ed., **Faith and the Philosophers** (London: Macmillan, 1964).

3. H. H. Price, **Belief** (London: Allen & Unwin, 1960).

TWO APPROACHES TO THE PHILOSOPHY OF RELIGION

Basil Mitchell

When Austin Farrer lent me the MS of **Faith and Speculation** and asked me for my criticisms, I am ashamed to say that I returned it to him without comment. I cannot remember what excuse I made, but in retrospect I think I can detect the reason why I was so very unhelpful. The book failed to satisfy my expectations of it and I was, at the time, too preoccupied with other matters to try seriously to come to terms with it. I had expected an improved version of the sort of rational theology that Farrer had first developed in **Finite and Infinite** and revised and corrected in various of his occasional writings. Instead, in the opening chapter of this new book, he appeared to deny the need for precisely the kind of justification of religious belief that I had been looking for. It is true that he insisted (**FS** 13) that "the philosopher who attempts the question from the angle we have suggested will be excused none of the topics belonging to traditional discussion", but he largely nullified this insistence, or so it seemed, by contending that "no progress is possible so long as it is supposed that faith is or contains an elementary, or an implicit, or any other sort of philosophy, which believers are bound to defend, since upon it their confidence reposes" (**FS** 14). Farrer, it seemed, had become a sort of fideist, content to rest the truth of Christianity upon the believer's sense of being nourished by the tradition in which he has been raised. At the time I found myself in complete agreement with the protestations of the philosopher in the little dialogues with the believer which occur throughout the chapter.

There are, as Farrer in that chapter recognizes, two dominant approaches to the philosophy of religion. According to the first of these, which I shall call "rationalist", it is incumbent upon the philosopher to determine, so far as he can, whether there is reason to believe in God. He must consider whether the concept of God is coherent, and, if it is, he must distinguish and assess the various reasons for belief in God, examining the force of each and the contribution each makes to the overall case for

177

theism. He must also examine argument against belief in God. And finally he must decide whether, on balance, the case for God's existence is strong enough to warrant its acceptance. A good recent example of this sort of approach is to be found in Richard Swinburne's two books, **The Coherence of Theism** and **The Existence of God.**

The alternative approach defines itself in the first instance by an outright rejection of the first, which it accuses of entirely misrepresenting the believer's spiritual and intellectual development. No one actually acquires his religious beliefs, in the manner proposed, by a dispassionate review of the arguments for and against the existence of God. The believer is, as a rule, brought up to believe in God and he accepts this, as he accepts so much else, from his home and the culture in which he is nurtured. Nor is it reasonable to require of him that on reaching maturity, he give up his belief or place it, as it were, in parenthesis in the manner of Descartes, in order to undertake the sort of inquiry that the first approach recommends. If, to use Farrer's expression, it goes on "nourishing" him, he has the best of reasons for continuing to adhere to it. This approach is argued for in Nicholas Wolterstorff's **Reason Within the Bounds of Religion** and in many of the writings of Alvin Plantinga.

The case for this latter approach seems to me now much stronger than it did when I first read **Faith and Speculation,** but I am as reluctant as I ever was to give up the first approach entirely. So I want to make at least a preliminary attempt to reconcile them.

At first sight reconciliation does not appear too difficult, for Swinburne and Wolterstorff are, surely, concentrating on different things. Swinburne is interested in theism as a system of beliefs-- what Plantinga calls a "noetic structure"--in abstraction from what any given individual in his particular situation ought to believe. His is a philosophical investigation and it does not follow from it that we all ought to be philosophers and base our fundamental convictions upon philosophical reasoning. Nor, even, does it follow that, if we are philosophers, we ought to attempt to re-build our entire noetic structure de novo before we are entitled to rely upon it in the living of our lives. Questions about the rational justification of a religious (or any other) system of belief are to be distinguished from questions about the ethics of belief.

Let us pursue this line of thought for a while. Let us accept, for the time being, Swinburne's account of the philosophical case for theism. Let us agree that it is an inductive case which derives its strength from its ability to explain, better than any of its rivals can, the existence and orderliness of the universe, together with such particular features of it as the development of conscious beings and the occurrence of "revelatory" events. Can we, while accepting this account, do justice to Wolterstorff's description of the way in which religious belief is characteristically maintained and defended? I suggest that, up to a point at least, we can. The noetic structure in question is subtle and highly complex, beyond the capacity of any individual fully to test or even comprehend; and so, of course, are its rivals. It would be absurd, therefore, for anyone, however intelligent and well-informed, to adopt a policy of believing only what he himself was able independently to explain and defend. This would be the case, even if the noetic structure in question was of academic interest only, but in fact it is not. It has inescapable implications for the way he should live and the sort of man he should try to become. He cannot wait until he has worked it all out for himself, even if he were in principle able to do so. Human beings are not like Athena, sprung fully grown from the head of Zeus. They achieve maturity slowly, and what they believe and what they are depends largely upon their parents and the other innumerable influences upon them, over which they have little or no control. As Farrer says, "How did religion get into our heads? It was taught to us, was it not?" (FS 3).

What has just been said will be true, of course, of any individual, no matter what the noetic structure into which he has been initiated. And at this point it looks as if the rationalist's concession has to stop. For noetic structures differ, more or less radically, and the rival systems cannot all be true. But the individual, surely, has an overriding duty, (and indeed interest), to seek the truth; and this must mean that, as soon as he becomes aware of the existence of alternatives, he has to try to make a rational choice between them. Hence--so we must suppose the rationalist to be arguing--at some stage he must be prepared to raise the question to what extent the system into which he has been inducted can be rationally defended. Of course, it is entirely reasonable for many people, perhaps for the great majority, to decide this question, not by engaging in philosophical enquiry, but by relying on authority of a formal or informal kind; but, somewhere along the line, there must be those who do engage in such enquiry, and they, if they are theists, will have to fall back on the kind of rational justification that Swinburne has provided. No doubt the fact that they themselves, and innumerable others, have been "nourished" by the system will be far from irrelevant to this justification--it will itself be an important ingredient in the overall case--but it will not be enough; for the followers of rival systems will presumably claim to have been nourished by them too.

Will the overtures so far made by the rationalist be enough to satisfy a fideist like Wolterstorff? I fancy not; for his complaint against the rationalist is not only that he gives an unrealistic account of the way people develop and maintain their religious and other convictions: it is the rationalist's <u>epistemology</u> that he wishes to find fault with. The proposed rational justification of theism cannot, in his view, succeed, <u>as</u> a rational justification. It is conceived in a manner that is wholly mistaken. This is because a rationalist like Swinburne is committed to the thesis that it is unreasonable to believe in God unless the hypothesis that there is a God (and "hypothesis" is here the right word) is supported by evidence in the form of facts that are less open to question than is the theistic hypothesis itself. These facts are either brute facts themselves or require in their turn the support of other facts, until a layer of basic facts is reached which require no support, because they are inherently incorrigible or self-authenticating. And Wolterstorff has no difficulty in showing how problematic is this conception of basic incorrigible data.

So the fideist directs our attention back to his original account of the process by which the individual is inducted into a noetic structure, and insists that, in it, he was not just describing what actually happens; he was commending that process as a rational procedure--indeed as the only rational procedure open to us. And against this, like Farrer's philosopher in those brief dialogues in chapter one of **Faith and Speculation**, one feels bound to protest. How can it be a rational procedure, if there is no provision for rational criticism of the noetic structure (whatever it happens to be) that the individual has inherited and finds himself "nourished" by? The fideist answers that he has said nothing that rules out rational criticism. His opponent has simply made the elementary mistake--so common in philosophy--of identifying "rational criticism" as such with his own conception of what "rational criticism" must be, i.e. solely in terms of a "foundationalist" model. But <u>of course</u> he himself recognizes that the individual has a duty to seek "consistency, wholeness and integrity" in his body of beliefs and commitments; and, so long as he does this, he achieves all the rationality that is either desirable or possible.

Our two opponents have now moved some little way towards one another but a sizable gap still remains. Is it any good trying to narrow it further?

We can get some encouragement, I think, from a somewhat surprising fact. At a crucial stage in his argument Swinburne himself moves away from his official inductivism in a direction which brings him closer to Farrer and even to Wolterstorff. In his chapter on religious experience he does not argue, as one would expect him to do, that the phenomena of religious experience represent data which are more convincingly explained by the theistic hypothesis than by any other on offer. Instead he introduces a Principle of Credulity in virtue of which (in the absence of special considerations) if it seems (epistemically) to a subject

that x is present, then probably x is present: what seems to someone to be the case on the basis of perception is likely to be the
case.

What is significant about Swinburne's use of this principle
is the very wide scope he gives it. If its scope were to be limited
to sense-perception as ordinarily understood, or even if it were
extended somewhat so as to cover numinous or mystical experiences,
it would be compatible with a modified form of "foundationalism".
The foundations of knowledge would still consist in perceptions,
but it would no longer be claimed that these were incorrigible;
only that there is always a presumption in favor of statements
made on the basis of them. But Swinburne resolutely refuses to
limit the scope of his principle in any such way. He insists, for
example, that, if it seems to an observer, on the basis of perception,
that there is a Russian ship in his field of vision, then it is likely
that there is a Russian ship there. And he is willing to apply it
to perceptions that are theory-laden, such as claims to observe
elliptical galaxies or blue-dwarf stars.

The significance of this for our present discussion can
be seen from a quotation:

> For many people life is one vast religious
> experience. Many people view almost all
> the events of their life not merely under
> their ordinary descriptions but as God's handi-
> work. For many people, that is, very many
> of the public phenomena of life are viewed
> religiously and so constitute religious experi-
> ences [of the first type] . . . that God is
> at work is no inference for these men, but
> what seems (epistemically) to be happening. [1]

And, by the Principle of Credulity, since it seems to them
that God is at work in all the events of their lives, it is probable
(unless the claim can be successfully challenged) that he is. Experiencing the world as God's handiwork is one way, at least, in which
someone may be "nourished", in Farrer's sense. And so we can
take Swinburne to be saying that such people are being "nourished"
in something of the way Farrer describes; and Swinburne is maintaining that it is reasonable for them to continue in their faith
for so long as they are being "nourished" by it.

Thus Swinburne seems to be adopting precisely the position
which we initially dubbed fideistic and which we contrasted with
the rationalist approach of which he appeared to be a leading
exponent. But, as we saw, what he says about the principle of
credulity is subject to an important qualification, and we need
to ask what difference that makes and whether Wolterstorff would

accept it. For, Swinburne says, it remains reasonable to go on believing that the world is sustained by God, on the ground that it seems to one that it is, only for so long as the claim is not successfully challenged. What form would a challenge have to take to be successful?

Swinburne mentions a number of possible challenges to a perceptual claim, but only two of them are relevant to the religious case:

(1) There may be background evidence that what was claimed to be perceived was not in fact present.

(2) There may be evidence that, whether or not it was there, it was not, probably, a cause of its seeming that . . . etc.; e.g. there may be evidence that something else was probably the cause of the experience.

However, given God's omnipotence, the only way of showing that God was not present would be to prove or render it highly probable that he does not exist. Failing that, only the second form of challenge remains. That is to say, one would have to show that the experience is capable of an alternative explanation which is more convincing than the ostensible theistic one. However Swinburne argues that this also can be done only by showing that God does not exist, for, no matter what other cause is posited for the experience, it always remains possible that God brought that cause into operation. So the second challenge collapses into the first and the sole way of showing that God is not responsible for the putative experience of God is to show that there is no God.

It seems to follow, therefore, in spite of initial appearance to the contrary, that Swinburne agrees with Wolterstorff, that the individual who seems to experience in his life the sustaining power of God has reason to go on believing that there is a God unless his theistic "noetic structure" can be shown to be logically incoherent.

Now it may be objected that Wolterstorff is talking about a system of beliefs, which the individual has been brought up in, while Swinburne's discussion is about perception. The vast majority of believers in God would not claim that sort of lifelong experience of his sustaining activity which provides the basis for Swinburne's argument, so the argument will not work in their case. However the force of this objection is greatly diminished when allowance is made for testimony. For, complementing the Principle of Credulity there is, according to Swinburne, a further Principle of Testimony, viz. that (in the absence of special considerations) the experiences of others are probably as they report them. In so far as believers rely on the testimony of others who

<u>have</u> enjoyed this type of religious experience, they too have reason to go on believing.

It seems, then, on this showing that the theist is in a very strong position. He is entitled to remain a theist for so long as his theism is not shown to be logically incoherent. Not only is he not required to prove, or even render it probable, that there is a God; he need not take account of merely probable arguments against theism.

But this is not, of course, Swinburne's final conclusion. He does not conclude that theism is in this virtually unassailable position, but rather that there is a cumulative argument in its favor (to which the argument from religious experience makes a crucial contribution) in virtue of which it is more probable than not that there is a God.

We are not concerned here with the interpretation of Swinburne's book for its own sake (though it fully deserves it) but for the light it throws on our central problem. From this point of view what is interesting about it is the way in which (to an extent he seems not to realize) it exemplifies both the positions which are under discussion. He does not actually, so far as I can see, reconcile them, but the fact that he does give expression to both of them reinforces one's suspicion that there must be some way of reconciling them.

As things stand, at this stage in the argument, the fideist position commands the field. Theism does not need any inductive justification; and any justification of that sort that might be offered is infected with the taint of foundationalism.

But <u>is</u> the fideist position quite as unassailable as it at present seems to be? In seeking to answer that question the first thing to note, I suggest, is that there is an ambiguity in the concept of "noetic structure" as I have been using it. I have talked rather loosely of the individual's noetic structure and of theism as a noetic structure; from which it would seem to follow that, if someone is a theist, theism is his noetic structure. The demand for consistency in his noetic structure, which everyone in the debate regards as legitimate, is naturally taken to require consistency in theism, and that in turn is taken to mean consistency in the idea of God. But no theist is <u>just</u> a theist. Along with belief in God any theist subscribes to innumerable beliefs which are not specifically theistic, derived from commonsense, history, science and his personal experience of life. And in addition to such beliefs there are doubtless innumerable others which he ought to accept, even if at present he does not. His noetic structure must at least include the former set and ought not, it would seem, to leave the latter out of account.

Wolterstorff is fully aware of this and some of his most interesting discussion concerns the various strategies open to a Christian when confronted with theories which are not specifically Christian. (Note that Wolterstorff is concerned with Christianity rather than just with theism. This affects the discussion only to the extent that the Christian starts with a greater burden of commitment than the theist). Wolterstorff clearly would not be satisfied with a purely defensive strategy in which the Christian deliberately confined his noetic structure within a narrow perimeter of beliefs readily conformable to Christian faith, and simply did not attend to any claims which fell outside it. The Christian, he insists, must, when incompatibilities appear, revise his system of belief so as to eliminate them. Failure to do so renders him irrational.

The strategies Worterstorff considers are these:

(1) The Christian may revise his current conception of what constitutes Christian doctrine in order to accommodate what he takes to be historical or scientific truths.

(2) He may accept these truths and seek to place them in a larger Christian context.

Both these strategies are "conformist" in that they presuppose that, in case of conflict between religious and scientific or historical claims it is the former that must give way. But this conformism cannot, he maintains, be accepted as an overriding principle. Hence a third strategy is possible.

(3) He may modify scientific or historical claims so that they become consistent with his Christian commitment.

We can recognize at once that these are the strategies that are open to the Christian thinker. Some doubt may at first be entertained about the legitimacy of (3), but we need to remember that science is not a single homogeneous structure. In most branches of science--especially in the biological and social sciences--controversy is endemic, and in case of conflict between scientific theories it may be reasonable to prefer one theory to another on general metaphysical grounds, to reject Skinner's behaviorism, for example, on the ground that it is incompatible with the emphasis on human freedom and responsibility which is shared by Christians and humanists.

But what processes of reasoning do these strategies involve? Their object is to achieve a coherent noetic structure which takes proper account of all the relevant considerations. The impression has been created by Wolterstorff's attack on foundationalism that consistency is the sole test, for to consider how well supported a position is would seem to commit one to foundationalism. But the requirement of consistency alone will not enable one to determine in a particular case <u>which</u> of the three strategies ought to be adopted. Consider, for example, someone who has been brought up as an extreme fundamentalist and derives from the Bible the doctrine that each species was produced by a separate act of divine creation. When confronted by the scientific evidence for natural selection he has three options:

(1) He may accept this evidence and revise his belief about the origin of species; at the same time modifying his principles of Biblical interpretation.

(2) He may "explain away" the evidence, precisely because, if accepted, it would require him to give up beliefs which he regards as authentically Christian.

Of these two strategies both would achieve consistency in his total body of beliefs, but Wolterstorff's whole discussion presupposes that this is not enough. Two other considerations are involved. The first is that, in deciding how to treat the scientific theory which conflicts with his fundamentalism he has to take into account how well supported the theory is, i.e., how sound the evidence is on which it is based and how fully integrated it is into the relevant corpus of scientific knowledge. In this case he will find the theory so well supported as to be commonly accepted fact. (By contrast Skinner's psychological theories are highly controversial.)

The second is that, in deciding whether and, if so, how far to modify his existing system of belief, he has to be guided by some such considerations as simplicity, explanatory power, comprehensiveness, coherence, etc. It may well not be the most reasonable policy to achieve bare consistency by making the minimum amendments to his existing set of beliefs, e.g., by conceding that the Bible makes some factual errors, although predominantly inerrant. Hence the <u>third</u> option:

(3) He may radically revise his principles of biblical interpretation. This would reduce the risk of similar clashes in the future, and, arguably, make for a more plausible doctrine of the inspiration of scripture.

The problem which this discussion sets the fideist is now apparent. It begins to look as if, in order to carry out his own programme, he has to engage in precisely the sort of reasoning which he is committed to rejecting as foundationalist. Wolterstorff sees the problem but does not tackle it:

We have not at all discussed the norma-
tive issue of whether, given one's beliefs
at a certain time, there are some theories
that one is warranted in accepting or in
not accepting. Many have concluded from
the collapse of foundationalism that there
are no such warranted actions--that "anything
goes". I disagree. Throughout this discussion
I have presupposed that there are some theories
that one is warranted in accepting or not
accepting. I have repeatedly spoken of what
the scholar <u>ought</u> to do. But to argue the
case here would be well beyond my scope.
Let me simply say that, given the collapse
of foundationalism, the issue will have to
be formulated, as I have formulated it above:
<u>Given such and such a body of beliefs,</u> is
the scholar warranted in accepting or warranted in not accepting theory T. Warrant
will have to be relative to a body of beliefs.
It cannot be relative to a body of certi-
tudes. [2]

It is time to review the argument up to this point. We
started with two approaches to the philosophy of religion which
appeared to be incompatible. One was rationalist and maintained
that theism required to be justified, and was in fact justified,
on the basis that it provided a simpler and more coherent explanation of the facts than any system could do. The other was fideist
and maintained that no such justification was either necessary
or possible. The believer may reasonably continue to believe so
long as he finds himself nourished by the system of belief which
he currently holds. We found that, under examination, both positions
needed to be modified, in each case in a direction that brings
it closer to the other. The rationalist must admit that, because
of the complexity of the issues and the limitations of any individual
believer, it is not reasonable for anyone, in seeking a faith to
live by, to attempt to start from scratch and construct an entire
theistic metaphysic for himself on the lines suggested. In practice
every believer must take over most of what he believes from
others, and he is entitled to go on believing it until he finds sufficient reason for doing otherwise. Similarly the fideist must concede
that the believer should be prepared to modify his initial position
to take account of theories that are inconsistent with it, if those
theories are well supported. But if to modify, why not in certain
circumstances to abandon? For might not the facts and well-
supported theories that his current "noetic structure" cannot accommodate combine to support a rival world-view which has a
better claim to take care of all the facts, including those he
himself has all the time relied on? In the case of the fundamental-

ist it might turn out that his conception of God and of God's relationship with the world was inconsistent with virtually the whole of modern science; and there is no shortage of naturalistic world-views which purport to provide explanations, claiming the authority of science, of the fact that men have the sort of religious experiences and beliefs they do, so that even very much more subtle and reflective forms of theism are not beyond critical challenge. So it is no longer the case that the theist is entitled to maintain his position so long only as it is not shown to be logically incoherent; for he might have reason to abandon it, if a rival world-view could be shown to be very much better supported.

But, if this much is admitted, the concession that the fideist has to make is a considerable one. The distance between himself and the rationalist has been reduced, certainly, but the fideist has had to shift his position most. Will he be content to accept reconciliation on these terms?

Not entirely. For right from the start he has maintained that the rationalist is committed to foundationalism, and that foundationalism is indefensible. So, let us return to Swinburne and ask if his approach is inescapably foundationalist. If it is, it is odd, to say the least, that he nowhere defends or even formulates his foundationalist convictions. It is true that he mentions certain facts which, he argues, can be explained more convincingly by theism than by rival systems. He does not discuss the nature of their status as facts: he seems content to regard it as entirely non-controversial. The facts to which he appeals are such as the following:

> That there is a universe.
>
> That the universe exemplifies order.
>
> That men worship God, have moral knowledge, possess free-will.
>
> That there are felt desires, associated with pleasure and pain.

and so on.

That men have moral knowledge and exercise free will he recognizes to be open to dispute, and would elsewhere be prepared to defend as true, but, as for the rest, he does not expect them to be challenged. Does it follow that he regards them as incorrigible in some strict sense as the foundationalist is said to do with his basic facts? It is not clear that he does; and, as we have already noted, there is a presumption to the contrary in his treatment of the Principle of Credulity. If incorrigible statements are to be found anywhere one would expect to find them among statements made on the basis of perception, more especially sense-perception. Yet Swinburne goes no further than to grant statements based on sense-perception the benefits afforded by his Principle of Credulity.

So it seems that our gap has narrowed even further. Swinburne is not a foundationalist as Wolterstorff understands that term, i.e., he does not hold out for basic incorrigible data; and Wolterstorff agrees that some defensible notion of support is needed, if the theories to be taken seriously in assessing the adequacy of one's noetic structure, are to be well-supported ones, as presumably they must be. Both positions need, and neither is able adequately to articulate, such a notion of support.

At this point it is tempting to leave the matter. If philosophers of religion, starting from different initial positions, find themselves able to reach agreement on the basis of a shared assumption which is, in any case, plainly demanded by common-sense, should they be worried by the fact that specialists in epistemology find it problematic? Leave them to it and they will sort it out in time (one can almost hear Farrer saying this).

Nevertheless, if only to do justice to Farrer, it is worth pursuing the question a little further. Farrer writes, "If all thinking based on uncriticized assumptions is groundless, then all thinking is groundless" (**FS** 12). Any passage of thinking will have to be conducted against a background of assumptions that are not, for the time being, criticized. This does not mean that they are uncriticizable; and, if they are criticized, it will be necessary to defend, modify or abandon them. But this exercise, too, will involve assumptions not at the time under challenge. We cannot saw off the branch we are sitting on, but we can move to another branch and then saw off the first one—though not, of course, now the new one. However, criticizing assumptions is not the same as simply rejecting them. Criticism must be reasoned criticism to deserve the name. It is not enough to imitate the young child's incessant "why" in an entirely routine fashion. And if an assumption is being criticized, it will be for some such reason as that it is (when more closely examined) logically incoherent or not adequately supported, either because the evidence appealed to in its favor does not support it at all, or gives better support to an alternative hypothesis, or because the evidence itself is open to challenge.

But, if sense is to be made of this entire process, there must be the possibility of an appeal to experience, and experience must not have a "nose of wax" which can be made to take the imprint, with equal readiness, of any of the rival theories between which it has to help us adjudicate. And in statements based on experience we should look, not for incorrigibility, but for a more or less strong presumption of truth such as is provided by Swinburne's Principle of Credulity.

This discussion has been excessively abstract and, in the space that remains, I want to bring it back to the substantial question which engaged Farrer in **Faith and Speculation.**

It seems to me that when he talks of the believer's being "nourished" by the faith in which he has been reared, Farrer is not thinking just of his having a set of beliefs which have been found to work, nor even of his "experiencing the world" in a certain way, but of his being aware, in however fragmentary and incomplete a fashion, of a kind of interaction with the divine, of which the appropriate analogy is our familiar intercourse with one another: "There is, then," he writes, "no thought of God without analogy; but there is in the believer's eyes a dealing with God which is no mere interpretation of nature through a strained analogical scheme, but an enjoyment of 'life in God', which is to him self-authenticating" (**FS** 129). One is reminded of Traherne's remark about a saintly friend who "was as familiar with the ways of God in all ages as with his walk and table".

But the question is, does this settle the matter, in such a way as to rule out the possibility, even in principle, that some alternative, atheistic view of the world might in the end be true? Is the believer's experience in that sense self-authenticating? Even if we accept, as I would do, Farrer's view that to deny the existence of our neighbor's is self-frustrating, whereas to deny the existence of God is not, there remains even in that case room for considerable dispute. It is easy to assume that, when we have pointed out the self-frustrating character of denying other minds, we have ipso facto relieved ourselves of all controversies of a metaphysical kind about the nature of human personality. But this is far from being the case. That there are minds is, perhaps, now beyond dispute, but what it is to be a mind remains highly controversial. I mentioned earlier Skinner and **Beyond Freedom and Dignity.** Confronted by that book and its crude stimulus-response theory of human relationships, I am inclined to take my stand with Shakespeare and exclaim:

> Let me not to the marriage of true
> minds Admit impediment. Love is not love
> which alters when it alteration finds . . .

Skinner's is a particularly extreme and, I should say, fairly obviously unsatisfactory example, but there are other accounts of human nature on offer, more plausible than his, but no less inconsistent with the understanding of man which Christian humanism has so long accepted. That they are true I do not believe, and the chief reason why I do not believe it is that they cannot, so far

190

as I can see, make sense of the mutual trust and love that we
all enjoy with our family and friends. I take this to be a powerful
reason but not one that is in logic entirely unassailable. To go
back to the somewhat cold-blooded language I was using earlier,
I believe myself to have good reason for retaining this part of
my noetic structure, though I do not think that that commits
me to refusing to admit that I could conceivably be wrong. I
want to remain a theoretical rationalist, but a practicing fideist.
I should like to think that this was Farrer's standpoint too and,
I wonder, would it be too strained an interpretation of Shakespeare
to claim to find the same dual loyalty in him:

> If this be error and upon me proved,
> I never writ, nor no man ever loved.

NOTES

1. R. Swinburne, **The Existence of God** (Oxford: Clarendon, 1979) 252-3.

2. N. Wolterstorff, **Reason Within the Bounds of Religion** (Grand Rapids,
Michigan: Eerdmans, 1976) 98.

A CHRONOLOGICAL LIST OF
AUSTIN M. FARRER'S PUBLISHED WRITINGS
1933-1981

Compiled by Charles Conti

Additions to the list compiled in **Reflective Faith** (S.P.C.K., 1968) are marked with an asterisk*.

1933

"A Return to New Testament Christological Categories," Theology 26, 304-318.

* Review of **Life of Jesus** by M. Goguel in Theology 26, 229-230.

1935

* Review of **Polarity** by E. Przywara in Theology 31, 361-363.

1936

Review of **The Doctrine of the Word of God** and **God in Action** by K. Barth in Theology 32-33, 370-373 (the former is Vol. 1, part 1 of the 2nd edn. of **Prolegomena to Church Dogmatics**).

* Review of **God Transcendent** by K. Heim in Church Quarterly Review 122, 334-337.

1937

"Eucharist and Church in the New Testament," **The Parish Communion** ed. A. G. Hebert (London: S.P.C.K.) 75-94.

Review of **Der christliche Glaube und die altheidnische Welt** (2 Vols.) by K. Prümm in Journal of Theological Studies 38, 95-97.

Review of **Religion and Reality: An Essay in the Christian Co-ordination of Contraries** by M. Chaning-Pearce in Church Quarterly Review 123-124, 328-330.

1938

"The Christian Doctrine of Man," **The Christian Understanding of Man** ed. T. E. Jessop, II, Oxford Conf. Series (London: Allen & Unwin) 181-213; reprinted in **Interpretation and Belief** 69-94.

Review of **Die Kirche und die Schöpfung** by E. Gerstenmaier in Church Quarterly Review 125-126, 345-346.

1939

*" 'Fact' and 'Significance' in the Gospels," Theology 39, 371-372.

" 'The Blood is the Life' and the Blood of Christ in the New Testament," Oxford Society of Historical Theology 1933-42/43, 60-67; abstract of a paper read 23 February 1939 on Eucharistic theology.

"The Theology of Morals," Theology 38, 332-341; reprinted in **Interpretation and Belief** 176-185.

Review of **Philosophie de la Religion** by P. Ortegat in Journal of Theological Studies 40, 100-101.

* Review of **A Companion to the Summa: II, The Pursuit of Happiness** by W. Farrell O.P. in Theology 38, 153-154.

* Review of **Thomas Aquinas: Selected Writings** ed. M. C. D'Arcy S.J. in Theology 39, 319-320.

1940

* Review of **Ideals of Religion** by A. C. Bradley in Theology 40, 461-463.

Review of **The Problem of the Future Life** by C. J. Shebbeare in Journal of Theological Studies 41, 343-344.

* Review of **St. Paul and the Church of the Gentiles** by R. Knox in Church Quarterly Review 129, 339-341.

1941

Review of **The Nature of the World, An Essay in Phenomenalist Metaphysics** by W. T. Stace in Journal of Theological Studies 42, 108-110.

Review of **The Realm of Spirit** by G. Santayana in <u>Theology</u> 42, 123-125.

* Review of **Language and Reality** by W. M. Urban in <u>Church Quarterly Review</u> 131, 277-280.

1942

* Review of **St. Paul's Epistle to the Ephesians** by F. C. Synge in <u>Theology</u> 44, 62-63.

Review of **The Philosophy of David Hume** by N. Kemp Smith in <u>Journal of Theological Studies</u> 43, 229-232.

Review of **The Revelation of St. John** by M. Kiddle, (assisted by M. K. Ross) in <u>Journal of Theological Studies</u> 43, 227-229.

1943

Finite and Infinite (Westminster: Dacre) 2nd edn. 1959 with revised Preface; also published by Macmillan and Humanities, 1966.

"How was Jesus Divine?" <u>Socratic Digest</u> I, 24-25.

1944

"Can we know that God Exists?" editor's summary of a discussion by the Revd. A. M. Farrer and Mr. MacNabb, <u>Socratic Digest</u> 2, 12-13.

1945

"Can Myth be Fact?" <u>Socratic Digest</u> 3, 36-44; reprinted in **Interpretation and Belief** 165-175.

1946

"The Ministry in the New Testament," **The Apostolic Ministry** ed. K. E. Kirk, republished 1957 with new "Foreword" by Farrer (London: Hodder & Stoughton) 113-182.

"Epigrams," <u>Theology</u> 49, 238 (two poems).

Review of **Christ in the Gospels** by A. E. J. Rawlinson in <u>Journal of Theological Studies</u> 47, 77-78.

Review of **Religious Experience** by C. C. J. Webb in <u>Theology</u> 49, 23.

1947

Catholicity: A study in the conflict of Christian traditions in the West (Westminster: Dacre) a report presented to the Archbishop of Canterbury by a committee of Anglicans of which Farrer was a member.

"The Extension of St. Thomas's Doctrine of Analogy to Modern Philosophical Problems," Downside Review 65, 21–32, reprinted as "Knowledge by Analogy" in **Reflective Faith** 69–81.

"On Credulity," Illuminatio I No. 3, 3–9; reprinted in **Interpretation and Belief** 1–6.

"Thought as the Basis of History," The Listener 37 (20 March) 424–425, a broadcast talk on R. G. Collingwood.

"Does God Exist?" Socratic Digest 4, 27–34; reprinted in **Reflective Faith** 39–47.

* Reviews of **The Authority of The Biblical Revelation** by H. Cunliffe-Jones; and **The Old Testament in the New Testament** by R. V. G. Tasker in Theology 50, 351–352.

1948

The Glass of Vision (Westminster: Dacre) Bampton Lectures.

1949

A Rebirth of Images: the Making of St. John's Apocalypse (Westminster: Dacre). Also by Beacon Press, 1963 with a new Preface by K. Burke; rebound in hard cover by Smith, 1964.

* Review of **The Glory of God and the Transfiguration of Christ** by A. M. Ramsey in Christendom Dec., 134–135.

1950

Review of **Abelard's Christian Theology** by J. Ramsay McCallum in Journal of Theological Studies NS I, 221.

1951

"A Midwinter Dream," University: A Journal of Enquiry I, 86–90; reprinted as "A Theologian's Point of View," The Socratic 5 (1952) 35–38; abridged version reprinted as "Theology and Philosophy" in **Reflective Faith** 1–4.

A Study in Mark (Westminster: Dacre).

"Editor's Introduction," **Theodicy: Essays on the Goodness of God, the Freedom of Man, and the Origin of Evil** by G. W. Leibniz, ed. A. M. Farrer, tr. E. M. Huggard (London: Routledge & Kegan Paul) 7-47; excerpt reprinted as "The Physical Theology of Leibniz" in **Reflective Faith** 91-113.

"Messianic Prophecy," Theology 54, 335-342; a sermon preached at Oxford, Hilary Term, 1951; reprinted in **Interpretation and Belief** 23-31.

1952

The Crown of the Year: weekly Paragraphs for the Holy Sacrament (Westminster: Dacre). Also Morehouse-Barlow, 1953.

"A Liturgical Theory about St. Mark's Gospel," a review of **The Primitive Christian Calendar** I, Introduction and text by P. Carrington, Archbishop of Quebec, Church Quarterly Review 153, 501-508.

Review of **Holy Communion and Holy Spirit** by J. E. L. Oulton in Theology 55, 107-108.

Review of **The Originality of St. Matthew** by B. C. Butler in Journal of Theological Studies NS 3, 102-106.

1953

"An English Appreciation," **Kerygma and Myth: A Theological Debate** ed. H. W. Bartsch; tr. R. H. Fuller (London: S.P.C.K.) 212-223, pbk. 1972.

"Loaves and Thousands," Journal of Theological Studies NS 4, 1-14.

"The Trinity in Whom We Live," Theology 56, 322-327, originally a broadcast talk, "Meditation for Trinity Sunday," 8 June 1952; reprinted in **Lord I Believe** as Chapter 2.

1954

St. Matthew and St. Mark Edward Cadbury Lectures, 1953-1954 (Westminster: Dacre) 2nd edn., 1966; also by Macmillan.

* Review of **The Birth of Christianity** by M. Goguel in Theology 57, 466-467.

1955

"Absolute," **Twentieth Century Encyclopedia of Religious Knowledge** ed. L. A. Loetscher, I, (Grand Rapids, Michigan: Baker Book House) 3.

"Analogy," ibid., 38-40; reprinted as "The Concept of Analogy," in **Reflective Faith** 64-68.

"Being," **ibid.**, 120-121.

"On Dispensing with Q," **Studies in the Gospels** ed. D. E. Nineham (Oxford: Blackwell) 55-88.

"The Queen of Sciences," **Twentieth Century** 157, 489-494.

1956

"An Examination of Mark 13:10," a reply to G. D. Kilpatrick, Journal of Theological Studies NS 7, 75-79.

" 'The Dies Irae': A New Translation," Theology 59, 155-157, published separately in card-form by S.P.C.K., No. 3218, 1957.

"How do we know we have found Him?" **Christ and the Christian** (London: Mowbrays) 21-27; a sermon in a course of sermons on "Evangelism in the Church" preached in the chapel of Pusey House, Oxford; reprinted in **Said or Sung** as "Assurance" 83-88.

"Important Hypotheses Reconsidered. VIII. Typology," Expository Times 67, 228-231.

A Short Bible ed. with general introduction (London: Fontana) 5-15, published in the U.S. as **Core of the Bible** Harper, 1957.

1957

"The Everyday Use of the Bible," **The Bible and the Christian** (London: Mowbrays) 55-60; a sermon in a course of sermons preached in the chapel of Pusey House; reprinted in **Said or Sung** as "The Doctor of Divinity," 147-152.

(new) "Foreword," **The Apostolic Ministry** (republished from 1946) v-xviii.

The New Testament ed. with a general introduction and note to each book (London: Collins) 7-19.

"Revelation," **Faith and Logic** ed. B. G. Mitchell (London: Allen & Unwin) 84-107.

"A Starting Point for the Philosophical Examination of Theological Belief," **Faith and Logic** ed. B. G. Mitchell (London: Allen & Unwin) 9-30; reprinted as "A Moral Argument for the Existence of God" in **Reflective Faith** 114-133.

1958

The Freedom of the Will Gifford Lectures for 1957 (London: Adam & Charles Black) 2nd edn.--Scribners, N. Y., 1960; London, 1963--includes a "Summary of the Argument" 316-320; also published by Macmillan and Humanities.

Lord I Believe: Suggestions for turning the Creed into Prayer (London: Faith) 2nd edn., revised and enlarged, reissued by S.P.C.K. in pbk. 1962; also Seabury, 1962; Morehouse-Barlow, 1959.

1959

Introduction to **The Easter Enigma: An Essay on the Resurrection with Special Reference to the Data of Psychical Research** by M. C. Perry (London: Faber & Faber) 11-16.

"On Looking Below the Surface," Oxford Society of Historical Theology 1959-1960, 3-18; a Presidential Address, 22 October 1959, replying to Miss Helen Gardner's Riddell Lectures in **The Business of Criticism** O.U.P. 1959; reprinted in **Interpretation and Belief** 54-65.

"Predestination," **Christianity According to St. Paul** (London: Mowbrays) 37-44; a sermon in a course of sermons preached in the chapel of Pusey House, Oxford; reprinted in **The Brink of Mystery** 96-101.

1960

"In the Conscience of Man," **God and the Universe** (London: Mowbrays) 30-37; a sermon in a course of sermons on "Signs of God" preached in the chapel of Pusey House, Oxford; reprinted in **The Brink of Mystery** 119-125.

Said or Sung: an arrangement of homily and verse (London: Faith) published in the U.S. as **A Faith of Our Own** with Preface by C. S. Lewis, World Publishing Company, 1960.

1961

"The Gate of Heaven," a pamphlet-sermon preached at the patronal festival of St. Edward's House, Westminster; reprinted in **The Brink of Mystery** 48-52.

Love Almighty and Ills Unlimited containing the Nathaniel Taylor Lectures for 1961 (Garden City, New York: Doubleday). Published in England by Collins, 1962; Fontana, 1966.

"Messianic Prophecy and Preparation for Christ," **The Communication of the Gospel in New Testament Times** Theological Collections, 2 (London: S.P.C.K.) 1-9; originally a sermon at Oxford, 1958.

1962

"Continence," **Lenten Counsellors:** A Catena of Lent Sermons (London: Mowbrays) 83-90 published in the U.S. by Morehouse-Barlow as **These Forty Days:** Lenten Counsels by Twenty-one Anglicans; reprinted in **The Brink of Mystery** 128-133.

"The Descent into Hell and the Ascent into Life," **The Gospel of the Resurrection** (London: Mowbrays) 13-18; a sermon in a course of sermons preached in the chapel of Pusey House, Oxford; reprinted as "Gates to the City" in **A Celebration of Faith** (London: Hodder & Stoughton) 95-99.

* Review of **The Apocalypse of John** by C. C. Torrey in Church Quarterly Review 163, 255-256.

1963

Bible Sermons by C. F. Evans and A. M. Farrer (London: Mowbrays) 32-57; a course of sermons preached in the chapel of Pusey House, Oxford, to which each contributed four sermons; reprinted in **The Brink of Mystery** 22-40.

"Inspiration: Poetical and Divine," **Promise and Fulfilment** ed. F. F. Bruce (Edinburgh: T. & T. Clark) 91-105; reprinted in **Interpretation and Belief** 39-53.

"Mary, Scripture and Tradition," **The Blessed Virgin Mary: Essays by Anglican Writers** eds. E. L. Mascall and H. S. Box (London: Darton, Longman & Todd) 27-52; reprinted in **Interpretation and Belief** 101-125.

"Objections to Christianity," Theology 66, 317-318 (poems).

An untitled sermon on Psalm 116:12, 13 at St. Margaret's, East Grinstead, on St. Margaret's Day, 1962, St Margaret's Half-Yearly Chronicle 16, 2-6; reprinted in **The Brink of Mystery** 65-69.

1964

"The Datum in Divine Revelation," Oxford Society of Historical Theology 1964-1966, 10-11; abstract of a paper read on 19 November 1964; related to Chapter 6, **Faith and Speculation.**

Matriculation Sermon in the Chapel of the Good Shepherd, Friday, 30 October at Evensong, The Bulletin (of the General Theological Seminary, New York) 15-17.

* "Old Age: Why do we have to bear it?" North End Review The Parish Paper of St. Mark, St. Nicholas and St. Francis, Portsmouth, Hampshire, July 1964.

The Revelation of St. John the Divine: Commentary on the English Text (Oxford: Clarendon).

Saving Belief (London: Hodder & Stoughton) pbk. 1967; also by Morehouse–Barlow, 1965.

* Review of **Introduction to Thomas Aquinas** by J. Pieper in <u>Journal of Theological Studies</u> NS 15, 202.

Review of **Models and Mystery** by I. T. Ramsey in <u>Journal of Theological Studies</u> NS 15, 489–490.

* Review of **The Ship and Related Symbols in the New Testament** by E. Hilgert in <u>Journal of Theological Studies</u> NS 15, 152–153.

1965

The Triple Victory Christ's temptations according to St. Matthew (London: Faith). Pbk. by Morehouse–Barlow.

1966

"The Christian Apologist," **Light on C. S. Lewis,** ed. J. Gibb (New York: Harcourt, Brace & World) 23–43.

Reply to "Review Discussion of 'A Science of God?' " by Dorothy Emmet, Ted Bastin, Margaret Masterman, <u>Theoria to Theory</u> 1, 55–75.

A Science of God? (London: Bles) (published in the U.S. as **God is not Dead** Morehouse–Barlow, 1966).

Review of **Philosophie du fait chrétien** by H. Van Luijk in <u>Journal of Theological Studies</u> NS 17, 553.

Review of **St. Anselm's Proslogion** by M. J. Charlesworth in <u>Journal of Theological Studies</u> NS 17, 502.

* Review of **The Temptations and the Passion: The Marcan Soteriology** by E. Best in <u>Theology</u> 69, 123–124.

1967

Faith and Speculation containing the Deems Lectures for 1964 (London: Adam & Charles Black) hard and pbk.; also by New York University Press.

1968

"The Eucharist in I Corinthians," **Eucharistic Theology Then and Now** Theological Collections, 9 (London: S.P.C.K.) 15–33.

"Infallibility and Historical Revelation," **Infallibility in the Church: An Anglican–Catholic Dialogue** (London: Darton, Longman & Todd) 9–23; reprinted in **Interpretation and Belief** 151–164.

Review of **The Bounds of Sense: An Essay on Kant's Critique of Pure Reason** by P. F. Strawson in Journal of Theological Studies NS 19, 420–421.

* "The Lord's Prayer," **Modern Liturgical Texts** V (London: S.P.C.K.) 1–3.

1969

Review of **The Cambridge History of Latin, Greek and Early Mediaeval Philosophy** ed. A. H. Armstrong in Religious Studies 4, 287–288.

1970

A Celebration of Faith ed. L. Houlden (London: Hodder & Stoughton). Pbk. 1972.

1972

* **Reflective Faith** ed. C. Conti (London: S.P.C.K.). Pbk, (Grand Rapids, Michigan: Wm. B. Eerdmans) 1974.

1973

"Free Will in Theology," **Dictionary of the History of Ideas** (New York: Scribner's); reprinted in **Interpretation and Belief** 186–201.

* **The End of Man** ed. C. Conti (London: S.P.C.K.). Pbk. in the U.S. (Grand Rapids, Michigan: Wm. B. Eerdmans) 1974.

1976

* **The Brink of Mystery** ed. C. Conti (London: S.P.C.K.).

* **Interpretation and Belief** ed. C. Conti (London: S.P.C.K.).

1979

* **Finite and Infinite** reissued in pbk. in the U.S. by Seabury Press.

BOOKS AND ARTICLES ON FARRER

P. Curtis, "The Rational Theology of Dr. Farrer" Theology 73 (1970) 249-256.

"The Biblical Work of Dr. Farrer," Theology 73 (1970) 292-301.

J. C. Eaton, **The Logic of Theism** (Lanham, USA: The University Press of America, 1981).

D. Emmet et al., "Review Discussion of Dr. Austin Farrer's 'A Science of God?' " Theoria to Theory 1 (1966) 55-75.

H. Gardner. **The Business of Criticism,** (Oxford: Clarendon, 1959).

J. Glasse, "Doing Theology Metaphysically: Austin Farrer," Harvard Theological Review 59 (1966) 319-350.

M. Goulder, "Farrer on Q," Theology 83 (1980) 190-195.

B. Hebblethwaite, "Austin Farrer's Concept of Divine Providence," Theology 73 (1970) 541-551.

"On Understanding What One Believes," New Fire (No vol.) No. 7 (1971) 11-15.

"The Doctrine of The Incarnation in the Thought of Austin Farrer," New Fire 4: No. 33 (1977) 460-468.

"Providence and Divine Action," Religious Studies 14 (1978) 223-236.

C. Hefling, **Jacob's Ladder: Theology and Spirituality in the Thought of Austin Farrer** (Cambridge, Massachusetts: Cowley, 1979).

"Farrer, Austin M." in G. Wakefield ed., **A Dictionary of Christian Spirituality** (London: S.C.M.) forthcoming.

E. Henderson, "Knowing the World: The Process View of Austin Farrer," Philosophy Today 12 (1968) 204-214.

"An Appreciation of Austin Farrer," Interface: A Journal of Opinion 1 (1978) 46-56.

F. Kermode, **The Genesis of Secrecy: On the Interpretation of Narrative** (Cambridge, Massachusetts: Harvard University Press, 1979) 49-73.

E. Mascall, **Existence and Analogy** (London: Darton, Longman & Todd, 1949) 158–175.

F. M. McLain, "Austin Farrer's Revision of the Cosmological Argument," The Downside Review 88 (1970) 270–279.

B. Mitchell, "Austin Farrer" in P. Wignall ed., **The Anglican Spirit** (Cuddesdon: Ripon College, 1982) 41–44.

W. Proudfoot, **God and the Self: Three Types of Philosophy of Religion** (Lewisburg: Bucknell U.P./Associated University Presses, 1976).

N. Smart, "Revelation and Reasons," Scottish Journal of Theology 11 (1958) 352–361.

J. T. Stahl, "Austin Farrer on C. S. Lewis as 'The Christian Apologist'," Christian Scholar's Review 4 (1975) 231–237.

M. Wiles, "Farrer's Concept of Double Agency," Theology 84 (1981) 243–249; response by D. Galilee and B. Hebblethwaite and counter-response by M. Wiles, "Farrer's Concept of Double Agency: A Reply" and "Continuing the Discussion," Theology 85 (1982) 7–13.

M. P. Wilson, "Austin Farrer and the Paradox of Christology," Scottish Journal of Theology 35 (1982) 145–163.

THESES: Ph.D./D.Phil./B.D./Th.D.

C. C. Conti, "Descriptive Metaphysics: An Examination of Austin Farrer's Use of Cosmological Inference," Oxford 1973.

J. F. Day, "Austin Farrer's Doctrine of Analogy: A Study in the Metaphysics of Theism," Yale 1959.

R. Forsman, "Austin Farrer's Notion of Apprehension: An Analysis and Appraisal of his claim to Knowledge of Substance," Toronto 1974.

J. H. Glasse, "Creation and Creativity: An Essay in Philosophical Theology," Yale 1961.

R. L. Hart, "The Role of the Imagination in Man's Knowledge of God," Yale 1959.

C. Hefling, "Scripture and Metaphysics: The Unity of Austin Farrer's Christian Theism," Harvard 1981.

E. Henderson, "Two Metaphysical Theories of the Self: C. A. Campbell and Austin Farrer," Tulane 1967.

N. Schedler, "Methodology in the Metaphysics of Theism: A Philosophical Analysis of the Method of Austin Farrer and Ian Ramsey," Princeton 1967.

M. M. Yee, "A Critical Examination of the Theology of Austin Farrer with special reference to **The Glass of Vision**," Sydney 1976.

NEW AND FORTHCOMING PUBLICATIONS

Clouded Witness: Initiation in the Church of England in The Mid-Victorian Period, 1850-1875. By Peter J. Jagger. 1982.

Karl Barth's Theology of Culture: The Freedom of Culture for the Praise of God. By Robert J. Palma. Preface by H. Martin Rumscheidt.

Spirit within Structure: Essays in honor of George Johnston on his Seventieth Birthday. Edited by E. J. Furcha.

The Mystical Sources of the German Romantic Philosophy. By Ernst Benz. Translated by Blair Reynolds and Eunice M. Paul.

The Church in History: Essays honoring the Sixty-fifth Birthday of Robert S. Paul. Edited by Horton Davies.

Social Concerns in Calvin's Geneva, 1535-1564. By William C. Innes.

The Christology of Karl Barth and its Political Implications. By Robert E. Hood.

Freedom or Order? The Eucharistic Liturgy in English Congregationalism, 1645-1974. By Bryan D. Spinks. Preface by Geoffrey C. Cuming.

The Defense of the Reformed Faith. By Ulrich Zwingli. Translated by E. J. Furcha.

In Search of True Religion: Reformation, Pastoral and Eucharistic Writings. By Ulrich Zwingli. Translated by Wayne Pipkin.

The Emergence of Contemporary Judaism. Vol. 3: **Reformation, Renaissance, and the Dawn of Contemporary Judaism.** By Phillip Sigal.

The Emergence of Contemporary Judaism. Vol. 4: **Judaism in Tension, 1750 to the Present.** By Phillip Sigal.

The Quest of Unity in the Thought of John Calvin, Moïse Amyraut and Isaac D'Huiseau. By Richard Stauffer.